THE PRODUCTIVITY CHALLENGE

Also by Michael LeBoeuf

WORKING SMART
IMAGINEERING

THE PRODUCTIVITY CHALLENGE
How to Make It Work for America and You

Michael LeBoeuf

McGRAW-HILL BOOK COMPANY

New York · St. Louis · San Francisco · Toronto
Hamburg · Mexico

TO NANCY

Because the English language lacks a generic
singular pronoun that indicates both *he* and *she*,
it has been customary to use the masculine
pronoun to refer to either sex. In this book
I often use masculine pronouns for the sake
of readability and succinctness. All the
material here applies equally to both men and women.

1 2 3 4 5 6 7 8 9   FGR FGR   8 7 6 5 4 3 2

ISBN 0-07-036970-4

LIBRARY OF CONGRESS CATALOGING IN PUBLICATION DATA

LeBoeuf, Michael.
The productivity challenge.
Includes index.
1. Industrial productivity.   I. Title.
HD56.L42 1982   658.3′14   82-9897
ISBN 0-07-036970-4   AACR2

Book design by Roberta Rezk

ACKNOWLEDGMENTS

When I mentioned to a friend that I was writing a book on how to improve productivity he shook his head and said I was tackling an impossible task. Indeed, it has been a tough job, but it was made much easier by the terrific people who provided me with information, encouragement, and support.

Peggy Tsukahira provided invaluable assistance in the initial stages by helping focus and organize my basic strategy for the book. Her ideas were crucial in getting the project started.

In gathering research, several people were extremely helpful. Hisashi Kawakatsu of Tokyo Broadcasting System provided excellent research and insights about Japanese productivity. Fred Eickelberg allowed me to attend a *Business Week* conference on productivity problems and solutions. Telephone calls to Norman Bodek of the newsletter *Productivity* and to Carol Ann Meares of the Productivity Information Center resulted in a wealth of concepts, case histories, and research findings which were most helpful. And I also want to acknowledge the assistance received from the research publications of the Work in America Institute and the American Productivity Center.

In preparing the final manuscript, Kathy Ackermann did her always excellent typing job and Lou Ashworth added her editorial expertise to make this a better and more readable book.

Finally, I have to acknowledge my cheering section, who kept me going under the pressures of tight deadlines and information overload. Maurice Villeré, Artie Pine, and Richard Pine were always there when I needed them. And Nancy Hudson demonstrated enormous patience and poise by putting up with me as I scratched my way from the first page of the first draft to the last page of the final copy.

To all of you, I am forever grateful.

M.L.

CONTENTS

INTRODUCTION

"Unless we solve the problems of productivity, our children will be the first generation in the history of the United States to live worse than their parents."
—Lloyd Dobyns

W hy are you working harder and living poorer? Why have you been priced out of the housing market? And why is it you can't afford a new car every three years or send your children to college like your parents did for you? The ultimate answer to these and similar questions can be summed up in two words: *stagnating productivity*.

America's greatest economic crisis since the Great Depression is staring us squarely in the face—and time is running out. Changing world conditions coupled with numerous blunders by government and private industry have resulted in an America that is losing its ability to get things done. Productivity, the measure of how efficiently goods and services are produced, has been stagnating since 1967 and since 1979 productivity has actually decreased. Improving productivity is going to be America's Number 1 economic problem until at least the end of this century. As former Undersecretary of the Treasury Charles E. Walker put it: "If we don't get increased productivity in this country, we might as well put up a sign saying 'Going out of business.' Our economic survival is at stake."

1

This book is about productivity and its relationship to you. Part I looks at productivity problems from a broad perspective and answers questions such as:

1. What is productivity and why has it declined?
2. What role has government played in contributing to our productivity ills?
3. Why is Japan so productive and what lessons can we learn from them?

In Part II the focus narrows to look at productivity problems from an organizational perspective. Major topics covered are:

4. What's wrong with American management and how can we make it more effective?
5. Why are there so many turned-off workers and how do you turn them on to work?
6. How can the workplace be improved to make it more productive and satisfying for everyone?
7. What are quality circles and what basic tools do they use to improve productivity?
8. How can we increase productivity and our standard of living in the face of an aging population?
9. What can be done to reduce the tons of paperwork and red tape that keep all of us from getting things done?

In Part III the focus narrows even more and presents specific, action-ready techniques that you can use to improve your own productivity. It answers questions such as:

10. How do you set and measure personal productivity goals?
11. How do you get more done in less time?
12. How can you use your own creative ability to increase productivity?
13. How can you be more productive without becoming a burned-out workaholic?

14. What can you do to help yourself and America get back on the road to prosperity?

I think of this book as four books in one. First, it's a current events book that examines one of our greatest contemporary problems. Second, it's a management book that provides plenty of ideas for improving organizations. Third, it's a text suitable for productivity training programs and as a supplement for college courses. But, most importantly, it's a self-help book that contains hundreds of ideas you can use to work smarter and make America a better place for everyone.

For a decade millions of us have been working hard and doing a slow burn as we watch our standard of living slip through our fingers like grains of sand. And, true to our nature, Americans are searching for one or two simple causes and a couple of quick fixes for our productivity ills. Yet this very approach to solving the problem involves the same type of near-sighted, short-range thinking that's contributed to the problem. Forget about the fads, quick fixes, and hopes for an overnight economic recovery. It just isn't going to happen. Declining productivity is a long-term problem that's going to require long-range thinking and some fundamental changes on the part of management, labor, government, and everyone.

Fortunately, Americans are becoming very productivity-conscious—the first step on a long road back to economic recovery. In my work as a professor, lecturer, and consultant I've found students, executives, and everyone eager to learn more about falling productivity and how we can turn it around.

I know we can beat this thing. Make no mistake about it: We have some serious internal problems and face very stiff competition from abroad. But as soon as we get everyone pulling in harness, look out world, here we come! It is toward that goal and with great hope that this book is written.

1

The Big Picture

CHAPTER 1

THE PRODUCTIVITY PUZZLE

*"Something important has happened to productivity.
I don't know what it is . . . . but it is very bad."*
—Edward F. Denison

You may think productivity is an abstract concept that economists debate or that your boss worries about. Think again! Productivity growth is the key that opens the door to the good life. Productivity gains make shorter work hours, longer vacations, better homes, higher education, and early retirement all possible. And there's another thing that productivity makes possible—fatter paychecks. In fact, if productivity gains from 1968 to 1980 had been as high as for the previous ten years, the average U.S. household would have enjoyed almost $4000 more income in 1980. Starting to get the picture? Indeed, productivity is everybody's business.

For years we have been blaming our economic problems on inflation. Inflation is a symptom of the problem—but it's not the problem. The problem is that the rate of productivity growth has been falling in the U.S. for the past sixteen years. From 1947 to 1967 private sector productivity rose at a very healthy average annual rate of 3.2 percent. From 1967 through 1978 the average annual gain slowed to a snail's pace of 1.6 percent. But in 1979,

1980, and 1981 productivity actually declined. In fact, U.S. productivity growth has been poorer in recent years than any other major industrial nation, including Great Britain. It is true that the U.S. still leads the world in total output. However, if recent trends continue, by the end of this decade the U.S. will be in fifth place, behind France, West Germany, Japan, and Canada.

THE SHRINKING AMERICAN PIE

For the time being, the golden age of the American dream is over. The U.S. standard of living is shrinking and this certainly comes as no surprise to you. When the standard of living is measured in per capita income, the U.S. ranks fifth, behind Switzerland, Denmark, West Germany, and Sweden. From 1973 to 1980 real wages (measured in 1967 dollars) for private economy production and nonsupervisory workers fell from $109 to $95 per week. Wages for supervisory employees have done little better. Statistics on real disposable personal income per person look equally bleak. From 1967 to 1973 disposable income jumped 17.5 percent; over the next six years the gain slowed to 5.5 percent, and in 1979 the numbers started turning negative. The optimistic promise of living better has been shattered.

The implications of a shrinking American pie are ominous. As economic growth slows consumers spend less, business profits turn into losses, and massive unemployment becomes common. As the pie shrinks further, social and political tensions will escalate as ethnic groups, the poor, the elderly, and middle-American wage-earners scramble to maintain an eroding standard of living. One thing is certain. We have to turn this thing around before it gets totally out of hand. No, the sky isn't falling, but there are some serious holes in the ceiling—and it's thundering on the horizon.

WHAT IS PRODUCTIVITY?

Productivity is *doing more with less*, and this definition applies to individuals, groups, companies, industries, and nations. When productivity is improving the value of the economy's (or individual's) output is going up faster than the costs of the resources. Increasing the volume of a product or service doesn't necessarily mean productivity is increasing. It only means that production has increased. Productivity in the broadest sense is concerned with the overall effectiveness and efficiency of getting things done. It means making more from what you have and working smarter rather than harder. The ultimate goal of productivity is to make the best possible use of all resources to achieve a desired result. Output per manhour is the most common way we measure productivity.

Another way to express the same definition of productivity is as a ratio of all desired outputs (goods and services) to all the inputs used to create the goods and services. Such inputs may be labor, capital, tools, raw materials, and energy. Stated in a semimathematical form the ratio would look like this:

$$\text{Productivity} = \frac{\text{Outputs}}{\text{Inputs}}$$

$$= \frac{\text{Goods and/or Services}}{\text{Labor} + \text{Energy} + \text{Capital} + \text{Tools} + \text{Materials}}$$

Thus, when productivity is increasing, the value of the output is rising faster than the costs of production. In other words, society or the company or the individual is doing more with less.

One popular way to explain how productivity factors interrelate is to consider the case of Mom's apple pie. The labor component is Mom. We can improve her efficiency by sending her to cooking school, where she can learn better recipes and skills for baking more pies in less time. Or we might wish to upgrade productivity by getting better apples, which would produce a higher-quality pie and reduce the time Mom spends cutting out brown spots. Another way to increase productivity would be to invest capital in getting Mom a faster, more energy-efficient oven or a food processor. Finally, we could redesign Mom's kitchen for greater efficiency. New systems would cut preparation time and enable Mom to produce more pies in the same time or the same number of pies in less time. All of these factors will improve Mom's productivity, and she now has the option of doing several things with her productivity bonus. For example, she may choose to produce the same number of pies in less time and enjoy her increased productivity in the form of leisure time. Or she may wish to make more pies in the same amount of time and treat herself to a mink coat at Christmas. (Some pies, huh?) Or she may opt to reinvest the rewards of productivity into even better ways of producing more pies in less time and with less resources, energy, and so on. As long as productivity keeps improving, Mom is on her way to an ever-increasing standard of living. But lately it seems that Mom is working harder to produce a smaller pie.

In the U.S. today, you and I are Mom. We are working harder, living poorer, and feeling angry, frustrated, and confused. As a nation we seem to be losing our ability to get things done. What's the problem? How did we get into this mess?

CHOOSE YOUR FAVORITE SCAPEGOAT

There are many theories about the productivity crisis. Here is one viewpoint from an anonymous but overworked armchair economist:

> The population of the United States is 225 million but there are 63 million retired, leaving 162 million to do the work. Those too young to work total 86 million, leaving 76 million to do the work. Then there are 36 million employed by the federal government and that leaves 40 million to do the work. The number in the armed forces is 13 million, which leaves 27 million to do the work. Deduct 25,765,000, the number employed by state and local government and the 520,000 in hospitals and the like and you have 715,000 left to do the work. But of these 462,000 are bums and vagrants who won't work. So that leaves 253,000. Now it may interest you to know that there are 252,998 in jail, so that leaves two people to carry the load. That's you and I, and I'm taking a week's

vacation effective tomorrow. So carry on. you will be absolutely
terrific!!

When it comes to productivity, almost everyone has a pet
scapegoat. The government blames OPEC, businessmen blame
the government, labor leaders blame foreign competition, and
everybody blames inflation. One tongue-in-cheek analyst even
blames the sexual revolution, claiming that in prerevolutionary
days unhappily married people escaped their domestic woes by
working longer hours and thus increased national productivity.

One widely believed theory criticizes American workers as
being lazy. "People just don't want to work hard any more" is the
common cry. Or as one frustrated supervisor put it, "The only
thing fireproof around here are the employees."

While it is true that we do have a large number of dissatisfied workers, attitutde surveys strongly suggest that the
American work ethic is alive and well. For example, one survey
of workers' attitudes conducted by the Gallup Organization,
Inc., and the U.S. Chamber of Commerce yielded the following
results:

- Eighty-eight percent of the workers interviewed believe
  it's important to do your best at your job.
- Eighty-four percent say that they would work harder and
  do a better job if able to participate in making decisions
  affecting their jobs.
- Eighty percent realize that improvements in productivity
  can reduce inflation.
- Sixty-seven percent say that how hard they work and how
  well they do their jobs makes a big difference in the success of their companies.
- Sixty-two percent spend some time or a lot of time thinking about ways to improve the performance of their companies.
- Sixty-five percent say it's very likely or somewhat likely
  that any good ideas they have will be adopted.

In another poll, reported by United Press International, 80 percent of all Americans surveyed believed that declining productivity was a serious problem and 67 percent said they would be willing to sacrifice in order to increase productivity. Results of these and similar surveys suggest anything but an indifferent and lazy workforce. Either the work ethic is thriving or Americans are having fun fooling the pollsters.

Even more important, however, is the fact that the work-ethic issue is a red herring. In the final analysis a willingness to work overtime or give up coffee breaks will not solve our productivity problems. Working harder isn't the answer.

THE MAIN PIECES OF THE PUZZLE

Actually, the productivity problem is really a lot of problems rolled into one. I think of it as a puzzle with many interlocking pieces that create a total picture of sagging economic growth. The complexity of the problem is such that simple, quick-fix, one-shot solutions just aren't going to work. Economist Lester Thurow summed up the nature of the problem best when he said "It's akin to death by a thousand cuts. And if you have a thousand cuts the only cure is a thousand Band-aids."

The following are twelve of the major pieces of the productivity puzzle. This collection of pieces isn't meant to convey a detailed picture of our economic woes but rather to provide a broad overview. As you read the next several pages, stop and think about the ways each piece of the puzzle affects your life. Some of these you are painfully aware of. Others are more subtle. Also, notice how many of these problems feed and grow off of each other.

Piece 1—A Lack of National Commitment

Any good coach will tell you that when a team gets to be Number 1 the real enemy is complacency and a false sense of security. For years the U.S. was first in practically every economic category and at one time owned over 50 percent of the world's wealth. It's easy to see how somewhere along the way we became blinded by our own affluence and started to take it for granted.

During the 1960s and 1970s the U.S. made national commitments to such things as fighting a war in Southeast Asia, increasing medical care for all citizens, expanding job opportunities for minorities, increasing aid to the poor and elderly, protecting consumers, and environmental improvements. Yet there was little, if any, commitment made to increase the economic base from which all of these programs would be ultimately financed. We behaved as if American industry were an invincible giant that would take care of itself under any and all circumstances. Today we are paying the price for our naivete.

The old cliché "You don't get something for nothing" applies very well to productivity. And one sure way to lose productivity growth (or anything else) is to not have a commitment to it. How many of us ever consider how our jobs affect U.S. productivity? Or our industries' productivity? Or our companies' productivity? Yet each of these ultimately impacts on the other.

Simply put, all of us are going to have to become very productivity-conscious about *our* jobs if we are going to turn this crisis around. Leaders in government and industry are going to have to set the pace by raising the productivity consciousness of all Americans and making productivity improvement a top priority item. Everyone is going to have to realize that the good life isn't a gift from heaven. No house builds itself, no product sells itself, and no governmental program pays for itself. The sooner all of us commit ourselves to economic growth, the better off all of us will be.

Piece 2—The Lack of Incentives to Improve Productivity

It's great to talk about the virtues and necessities of a national commitment to productivity. But until everyone has an incentive to improve his* productivity, it isn't likely to happen.

---

* Remember the note on the copyright page: Because the English language lacks a generic singular pronoun that indicates both *he* and *she*, it has been customary to use the masculine pronoun to refer to either sex. In this book, I often use masculine pronouns for the sake of readability and succinctness. All the material here applies equally to both men and women.

For example, let's compare the incentive systems of Japanese and American factory workers. The Japanese worker has a lifetime-guaranteed job and gets a bonus based on corporate productivity and profitability. A new labor-saving device is no threat to his job security. It can only raise his bonus, so he is eager to learn how to adopt methods of new technology. It's in his best and direct interests to find better ways to do more with less.

Unfortunately, the typical American worker has no such incentives. His compensation isn't tied directly to productivity and he has no guarantee of lifetime job security. Any new labor-saving device is likely to knock him or one of his colleagues out of a job. Therefore technical changes are resisted and God forbid that he think up a new labor-saving way to do the job. That could be economic suicide! His incentives are to produce the minimum amount necessary to keep his job, think up restrictive work rules, and resist technical change. And who can blame him? He would be a fool to do otherwise.

Worker attitude surveys reveal that today's employees are more involved with their jobs than ever. However, involvement in a job and a commitment to doing the job are not the same things.

A recent Harris poll revealed that two out of three American workers would like to have their salaries directly related to their productivity. The implication of such a finding is that two out of three Americans are confident that they can find better ways to do their jobs if they are allowed to share the benefits. If we are serious about improving productivity we would do well to remember the words of Douglas McGregor: "Commitment is a function of the rewards associated with their achievement." Working smarter is going to have to be a good deal for everybody if it's going to be a good deal for anybody.

Piece 3—Aging Plant and Equipment

One key to productivity growth is capital formation. When businesses have access to capital they are able to invest in new and better ways to increase productivity such as buying new and better equipment. Much of this capital is borrowed from banks and savings institutions.

Unfortunately, the ravages of inflation coupled with our tax system have discouraged and eroded savings. During years of double-digit inflation banks were allowed to pay depositors meager interest on savings. Worse yet, the meager interest earned on savings was taxed—which penalized savings even more. The phrase "saving is suicide" became a cliché as many of us withdrew our hard-earned dollars from banks and invested in gold, real estate, collectibles, and other nonproducing investments. Today, Americans save about 5 percent of their disposable income: less than half the savings rate of any other industrial power. The Japanese save 20 percent of their disposable income and the West Germans save 14 percent.

Less savings means less capital for businesses to borrow, which in turn means less investment in updating and retooling methods to increase productivity. Consequently, many of our plants and manufacturing processes are woefully inefficient when compared to our foreign competitors. For example, Japanese assembly lines are much more automated than their American counterparts. The average age of American plant and equipment is about twenty years, which is twice as old as Japan's. Many U.S. steel mills still use turn-of-the-century techniques for producing steel while the Japanese retool every ten years. David Roderick, Chairman of U.S. Steel, summed it up when he said "You can't win a race if the opponent's in a Mercedes SL and you put your guy in a model T Ford."

During the seventies the U.S. spent the lowest percentage of total output on investment of the major free-world industrial powers. The figures on P. 16 speak for themselves.

If we are going to improve our productivity and standard of living we are going to have to start consuming less and saving more. And we will do this only when it's worthwhile to do so. Governmental policies that will reward rather than penalize savers are going to have to be created. Otherwise the capital that is

Nation	Spending for Plant and Equipment As a Percentage of Total Output
Japan	16.1
France	13.7
Canada	13.6
Great Britain	12.8
West Germany	12.4
United States	10.2

crucial to retooling and investing just won't be available. Trying to increase productivity without capital formation is like trying to make chicken salad without the chicken.

Piece 4—Foreign Competition

The international performance of U.S. industry in the past two decades was pathetic. In 1960, America produced over a fourth of the world's manufacturing exports. America's share of world exports shrank by 16 percent in the sixties and another 23 percent in the seventies. The decline of market share in the seventies alone cost us at least 2 million industrial jobs and $125 billion in lost production.

Meanwhile, as U.S. industry lost ground abroad imports began to account for a higher percentage of all goods purchased at home. For example, foreign cars (a negligible part of the American auto market in 1960) jumped to 28 percent by 1980. In 1960, about 95 percent of U.S.-purchased consumer electronics (radios, televisions, etc.) were made in the U.S. By 1979 imports had captured more than half the U.S. market. In fact, importers have increased their U.S. market share almost 350 percent since 1960.

The net result is that the U.S. trade deficit is rising and wealth is being drained out of the country. In 1970 the U.S. had a trade surplus of $2.6 billion, but in 1981 the balance of trade was in the red by some $39.7 billion. As the late Senator Everett

Dirksen remarked, "A billion dollars here, a billion there. Sooner or later it adds up to real money."

The sheer size of our domestic market has kept some of us from realizing that we have very strong international competitors. And this isn't a bad situation. The increased prosperity of Japan, West Germany, France, Sweden, and other countries means increased potential for U.S. exports if we are smart enough to take advantage of it. Our corporations and government must make a greater commitment to developing and expanding American markets abroad. For example, we have a competitive edge in areas such as high-technology items and marketing expertise that could be readily packaged and sold to other nations. One thing is certain. If we want to increase the American pie, we're going to have to pick a few foreign apples.

Piece 5—Skyrocketing Energy Prices

In any inflationary situation there are winners and losers. Generally speaking, the winners are the ones who charge higher prices and the losers are the ones who pay them. As energy prices soared, America was the loser and Arab sheiks were the clear winners.

When you stop to think about it, the energy crisis has really bled us. Look at it this way. In the seventies the U.S. spent hundreds of billions of dollars on imported oil. This means that hundreds of billions of dollars of U.S. wealth were given to foreign nations in exchange for a product. And what did we do with the product? We quickly burned it. Then we lined up at the pumps and waited for hours to buy more. In 1973 the U.S. had to produce one bushel of wheat to get one barrel of imported oil. Today we give up seven bushels of wheat for that same barrel of oil. To put it bluntly, we were had!

We seemed finally to learn our lessons about energy in 1979; U.S. energy consumption is slowing. The obvious long-range solution to this problem is to make America energy-independent. Compared to our industrial competitors, we are an energy-rich nation. Although we have less than 5 percent of the world's oil reserves we have plenty of natural gas and 23 percent of the world's coal. Additionally, we have the technology and research potential to develop alternate sources of energy such as nuclear power, solar energy, and synthetic fuels. The problem is that it takes years to develop and convert to new energy sources and our economy is currently set up to be highly dependent on liquid fuels. Our only short-range solution is conservation.

Piece 6—The Research and Development Slump

The history of America's productivity is tied directly to innovation and technology. New ideas have led to new and better ways to get things done. For example, in 1700 it took 186 men working a ten-hour day to harvest and thresh 60 acres of wheat. By 1910, the same job could be done by seven people. Today it takes only one person. In this century alone U.S. technology has given us the computer, television, the airplane, and numerous tools to increase productivity.

Unfortunately, there are signs that the U.S. is losing its ability to think up new ideas and turn them into successful products and services. Perhaps the most worrisome sign is that industry spent a lower percentage of total output on research and development each year from 1968 to 1979. At the same time, foreign competitors invested larger percentages of their total output on basic research. Worse yet, about 45 percent of U.S. basic research is for defense purposes, while nations such as Japan and West Germany allocate none of their research budgets to defense.

Another troublesome statistic is that the number of patents filed by U.S. inventors declined from 76,000 in 1970 to 64,000 in 1975. In 1966, the U.S. granted 13 percent of all patents to foreign nations, but by 1975 that figure had risen to 28 percent.

We simply aren't turning out scientists and technicians at the rates we once did. From 1954 to 1969 the annual growth rate of scientific and technical personnel was 5.9 percent. By 1979 the rate had slipped to only 2.8 percent. Today Japan is producing new engineers at more than twice the U.S. rate.

On the positive side, the U.S. is still the world's leader in almost every category of technology. Furthermore, industry is becoming very much aware of the crucial relationship between research, innovation, and productivity. One survey by *Business Week* revealed that major companies invested a greater percentage of their revenues in research and development in 1980 and 81 than in 1979, which is a very positive sign. The only problem is that there is a serious time lag between basic research and innovations that increase productivity. For the next several years we will probably feel the impact of the decreased research emphasis of the 1970s.

Piece 7—The Changing Composition of the Workforce

Part of our slowdown in productivity is due to the changing nature of the American workforce. More specifically, there have been three basic changes.

First, there has been a slowdown in movement from the farms to the factories. From 1948 to 1966, large numbers of workers moved from farms to factories, which greatly improved their output per manhour. The result was an increase in national productivity. However, since 1966 the shift has slowed. Today less than 5 percent of our labor force works on the land and we no longer enjoy productivity gains as a result of persons migrating from farms to factories.

Second, during the same period large numbers of inexperienced workers entered the labor force. The number of new workers soared as more women became employed and the post–World War II baby boom came of age. The new workers decreased productivity in two ways. First, they were less productive because of their inexperience. But, more important, the number of new workers grew at a faster rate than the economy's ability to create new capital. Therefore, instead of replacing human effort with other forms of labor, the reverse occurred and productivity was lowered. At the same time many experienced and productive workers were lured into early retirement with lucrative pension plans.

Finally, our economy seems to be changing the nature of its output from manufacturing to information. Americans used to spend about seventy of every hundred hours producing tangible products, but today's workforce devote only about forty hours to manufacturing. The other sixty hours go to shuffling papers, filling out forms, processing payrolls, writing reports, and making copies for everyone. Statisticians haven't come up with a uniform way to measure the output of clerks, lawyers, managers, financial analysts, and other service-oriented occupations. Intel's Andrew Grove summed up the problem this way: "We don't really know what clerks, financial people or managers do—how well they do it against some standard or in comparison with their peers. And if we can't measure it, how can we hope to make it more productive?"

Fortunately, a large part of the changing composition problem is behind us. Most of the influx of new workers has been absorbed into the labor force and their productivity will increase with experience and time. Another positive factor is that today's workforce (believe it or not) is more skilled than twenty years ago. In 1959, 30 percent of the workforce had eight or fewer years of schooling and less than 10 percent had four or more years of college. Today, only 9 percent of the workforce has eight or fewer years of schooling and nearly 18 percent has four or more years of college.

Another extremely important trend is that we are making steady progress in harnessing the talents of our single largest pool of human resources—women. Today's American woman is better educated and has more doors open to her than at any time in the history of civilization. Only recently have large numbers of women entered the labor force, but they are moving up steadily and performing well in their new roles. This can only be good for future productivity.

Piece 8—The Decline of Public Education

If America is losing its ability to get things done, it's only appropriate to look at the place where people first learn how to get things done. And that place is school. While it may be true that our workforce is more skilled than ever, there is also evidence that the overall efficiency and effectiveness of public education has been declining. High school achievement test scores are continuing to drop and semiliteracy is rampant among high school graduates. In 1978 Mobile, Alabama, required all high school seniors to take competency tests in basic educated skills. Fifty-three percent flunked! What's the problem? There are several.

First there is the problem of teacher competence. While most of our nation's 2.2 million teachers are conscientious, well-trained, and dedicated, the unfortunate fact is that many can't teach basic skills because they simply don't have them. In Chicago a third grade teacher wrote "Put the following words in alfabetical order" on the blackboard. In Oregon, a kindergarten teacher was found to be functionally illiterate. It was later revealed that she had been awarded As and Bs at Portland State University. In Mobile a fifth grader brought home the following note from his teacher: "Scott is dropping in his studies he acts as if he don't care. Scott want pass in his assignment at all, he had a poem and he fell tu do it." A friend of mine called his son's teacher inquiring how his son was doing in math. The teacher replied "It look to me like he gonna pull a D." These incidents would be funny if they were isolated and rare. But they aren't!

A second problem is that educators abandoned the basics in favor of faddish new learning theories in the sixties and seventies. Without thorough testing, educators jumped on bandwagons such as the "new math" and the "open classroom." All of which resulted in poor elementary math skills and noisy classes. Teachers were taught that if children felt good about themselves they would achieve, when the reality is that it is achievement that makes children feel good about themselves.

A third problem is that teachers, like many of us, are being hindered by mountains of paperwork and administrative hassle. In the past two decades, massive amounts of money were poured into public education. But most of this money was used to create a mammoth bureaucracy that insists teachers spend their precious time (which should be devoted to teaching, grading, and preparing for class) filling out forms, filing reports, and attending useless conferences.

Many of our most competent and dedicated teachers are becoming frustrated or burned-out and are leaving for greener pastures. And who can blame them? Salaries are low and violence rising: in 1979 one teacher out of twenty reported being attacked by students.

To make public education more effective, our teachers must be skilled in the basics and given the time and support to teach them. Teachers need to be tested for basic skills *before* they are hired. Current teachers who aren't competent to teach basic skills should be trained in these skills or, if they cannot or will not accept this training, be dismissed. We must also realize that meetings, forms, boards, regulations, and reports don't educate children. Teachers do. And they must be given the freedom from red tape to pursue this most basic and crucial job. Thomas Jefferson said it best: "If a nation expects to be ignorant and free, in a state of civilization, it expects what never was and never will be."

Piece 9—Burdensome Bureaucracies

In the words of systems expert Sid Taylor, "Red tape makes red ink." We live in an age of complex, rigid organizational structures surrounded by rules, policies, procedures, regulations, meetings, paper-shuffling, and computers—all of which are managed by too many chiefs. The result is that much of our productivity is being strangled by red tape. Today's organizations are much like prehistoric dinosaurs. They are huge and powerful but cumbersome, inflexible, and ill equipped to adapt and prosper in a changing world. And a changing world it is.

When the subject of counterproductive bureaucracy is raised, most of us think of the government. An Arthur Andersen & Co. study on government regulatory impact stated "The Lord's Prayer contains 56 words, Lincoln's Gettysburg Address

268, and the Declaration of Independence 1322 words. But a government regulation on the sale of cabbage requires 26,911 words!" Estimates are that each dollar Congress appropriates for regulation costs private industry an additional twenty. On that basis, private industry estimates that its yearly cost of complying with government regulation exceeds $100 billion—$100 billion that isn't being used for capital improvements to raise productivity.

Today some 35,000 attorneys devote their lives to government regulation. Japan has one attorney for every 10,000 people. The U.S. has 20. In fact, there are more attorneys practicing in the District of Columbia than in all of Japan.

In addition to massive amounts of regulation, the private sector also pays huge sums to finance government social programs and a huge defense budget. A recent study of major industrial countries showed that the two free-world nations which in the last twenty years spent the greatest percentage of their total output on defense—the U.S. and the United Kingdom— also had the slowest rate of productivity growth. The study also revealed that the two nations with the highest rate of productivity growth—Japan and Denmark—spent the lowest percentage on defense.

But government is only part of the problem. Large corporations create their own red tape, much of it counterproductive. Layer upon layer of middle management has created a huge, costly bureaucratic burden of meetings, memos, computer printouts, and mindless activities. At Ford Motor Company there are eleven levels of management between the factory worker and the chairman. Toyota has six levels. Japanese foremen report directly to plant managers while American foremen must struggle through three extra layers of management. This is one reason the Japanese can produce, ship, and sell a car in the U.S. for $1800 less than it costs U.S. makers to produce and sell a comparable model. Sears, Roebuck & Co.'s addition of highly paid executives to its corporate headquarters (rather than its stores) has turned the company into one of the nation's highest-cost retailers. America's skyscrapers are filled with people meeting, dictating, checking, reviewing, and shuffling papers. In Japan there are three accountants for every 10,000 people. In the U.S. there are 40!

We can no longer afford the luxury of massive governmental growth and complicated, cumbersome organizational structures. Simplicity in business and government is needed more than ever. We are going to have to review every government regulation, all jobs in organizations, every inch of red tape, and ask ourselves "Do we really need this?" If the answer is no, the solution is obvious.

Piece 10—Inept Management

For years American executives were admired worldwide as the best, brightest, and most capable in the world. Yet the past two decades of managerial performance have been anything but spectacular. The sad fact is that many of our nation's productivity problems have been caused by the way we train our managers, the pressures put on them, and their resulting behavior. There are several major problems, which I will only mention briefly here; the details and causes are in Chapter 4. Specifically, six major roadblocks are hurting today's managers:

1. **The short-run hurdle.** The pressure on today's executive is to look good today so he can keep his job and collect a bonus based on short-term results. Long-range consequences of management decisions are given little or no priority. This is often true even in the top echelons of management, where long-range planning is a primary responsibility. Making the bottom line look good today is the name of the game, and it is frequently done at the expense of reducing capital investment, research, and other necessary long-range projects. Pressures from Wall Street demand that companies produce steady increases in profits. Therefore, even though top managers frequently talk about the importance of the long run, it's short-run performance that takes priority.

2. **The bureaucracy hurdle.** Layer upon layer of middle management added to organizations has widened the communi-

cations gap between people at the top and the bottom. The result is that top management is frequently divorced from reality and unaware of what's going on at lower levels.

3. **The depersonalization hurdle.** Managers are forced to spend their time attending meetings, reading and writing reports, and tending to computer printouts and mounds of paperwork. After all this activity, little time is left for managing the company's greatest resource—people. Management has become depersonalized and the hands-on executive who knows and interacts with people at all levels of the company is mostly a thing of the past. The result is that employees feel alienated, ignored, and unappreciated and productivity suffers.

4. **The indecision hurdle.** Retired General Motors Chairman Thomas Murphy remarked "The seventies were all but a disaster. We seem to have spent most of our time not making decisions." Murphy was speaking of the failure of the auto industry to adapt after the 1973 Arab oil embargo, but such a statement is widely applicable to today's manager. The bold risk-takers and decision-makers of the Rockefeller, Ford, and Carnegie style have given way to a new breed known as the professional manager. While highly trained, the new breed is characterized by play-it-safe, look-good-today, and don't-rock-the-boat attitudes. Innovative mavericks who buck the system rarely, if ever, get to the top.

5. **The logic hurdle.** Today's professional managers are highly trained as logicians but almost totally untrained as visionaries. Business schools for the past twenty years have emphasized rational, scientific decision-making using computer-oriented decision models. Yet management is and always will be much more an art than a science. Training in creative problem-solving and human skills has been deemphasized. The result is that many managers make decisions exclusively by the numbers without paying attention to other important factors such as hunch or gut-level feeling. Only the left side of the brain—or a computer—is engaged in making decisions. And these logical decisions usually are based on short-term payoffs. As Robert Hayes of the Harvard Business School remarked, "You don't

have much of the spirit any more of the manager who simply looks at something and says: 'Dammit, this is a good product. Let's make it even though the payoff isn't apparent yet.'"

6. **The specialization hurdle.** Today's corporate managers climb the ladder of success by gaining a reputation for solving specialized problems. They may be super marketers, slick lawyers, or financial wizards, but rarely are they well trained in the art of putting the pieces of an organization together and making it function as a cohesive team. Overspecialized managers and departments create organizational empires where overall company goals are sacrificed in the name of departmental success.

Good managers are made, not born. To increase long-term productivity we must change the way we train, evaluate, and reward our managers. Management training needs to place less emphasis on cognitive techniques such as reading and implementing computerized mathematical decision models. A good manager has to be a creative visionary, a sound decision-maker, and—most important—a team-builder who knows how to motivate and lead individuals. These are skills that can be taught and improved with practice. Evaluation must take a longer-range focus and managers will have to be rewarded on their contribution to both the long haul and the short run. Every organization needs outstanding leaders to bring out the best in people. To quote a popular proverb, "It's hard to soar like an eagle when you work for a turkey."

Piece 11—Labor-Management Conflicts

Management and labor are traditional adversaries in America. Not only is this unfortunate and unnecessary, but we can no longer afford such a wasteful relationship. The answer to our productivity problems won't be found in fighting for a bigger piece of a shrinking pie but rather in working together to get everyone a piece of a much bigger pie.

Strikes, lawsuits, grievances, injunctions, and restrictive work rules are all counterproductive. Precious time and energy that could be devoted to making all of us richer and happier is diverted into needless game playing where everyone ultimately loses. Simply put, management and labor are going to have to get together, work as a team, and put differences aside. To insure cooperation, several changes will be necessary.

First, everyone involved in improving productivity must clearly understand how he will share in the benefits. Incentives will have to be created for managers, workers, and everyone else involved.

Second, management must begin to make better use of the intelligence, creativity, and know-how of the rank-and-file employee. The people closest to the job usually have the best ideas on how to do the job. As Michael Sonduck of Digital Equipment Corporation has remarked, "One of the most dehumanizing assumptions about work is that workers work and managers think. When we give shop-floor workers control over their work, they are enormously thoughtful."

Third, workers must be given job security and assured that a new and better production process (such as automation) will not threaten their incomes or jobs. Rather, they should be encouraged to participate in these changes and allowed to share in the profits.

Finally, both workers and management need to commit themselves to finding ways to improve the quality of the work environment. Productivity improvement programs that only stress productivity quickly lose worker support. But a total program of work improvement that provides incentives and makes work more enjoyable keeps everyone interested and enthusiastic.

Piece 12—Counterproductive Values

I saved this piece of the puzzle for last because in some way all of the other eleven pieces are caused by it. The beliefs, values, and assumptions we hold most dear determine our behavior, and it's our behavior as a nation that determines how productive we are. While the work ethic may be thriving, other values that are hurting our ability to get things done have evolved. As I see it, there are four basic values hindering our achievement.

First, we have embraced the "now!" value. As a nation we have become impatient seekers of instant need gratification. Oren Arnold noted that the prayer of the modern American is "Dear God, I pray for patience. And I want it *right* now!" Look around you and you'll see fast food restaurants, twenty-four-hour shopping, round-the-clock entertainment, and institutions promising to satisfy your every need—now! "Tomorrow be damned! I want mine now!" is a common societal value. Yet productivity improvement demands sacrificing somewhat in the present for future rewards. Time, effort, and earnings have to be invested in research, new plants, and equipment rather than just looking good today and enjoying the moment. Our economy grew steadily when a common social value was to sacrifice and invest today's efforts with the promise of a better tomorrow. In the past twenty years that value has faded.

Second, we have become a nation of risk-avoiders plagued by indecisiveness. More and more of us have opted for careers in "secure" bureaucracies. The entrepreneurial spirit and decisive bold risk-taking that was so characteristic of American economic growth has given way to a new ethic where decisions are delegated, cogitated, and ruminated but seldom activated. "I said maybe and that's final" best describes our seeming inability to make commitments to a course of action. And commitment is crucial to increasing productivity.

Another value hurting us is the complexity ethic. Just as a fish is surrounded by water, our very lives are drenched with complexity. Complex regulations govern our businesses and complicated organizational structures are the rule in industry. Complicated laws determine how much tax you pay while complex networks of computers gather, retrieve, and spit out reams of data. Experts propound complex theories on everything from relativity to why people fall in love. Somewhere along the way we began to believe that the value of an idea, product, or service was directly proportional to its complexity. And the unfortunate result has been an abundance of overly complicated, trivial, and meaningless activities.

Finally, our busy urban culture has embraced the depersonalization ethic. Time and again it's been shown that something as simple as caring about another person can make a huge difference in how productive and successful that person becomes. The sincere concern of a teacher, boss, relative, friend, or colleague can be a tremendous motivating force because the caring and support of other people is important to us all. Yet many of our relationships, particularly at work, have become transient and impersonal.

The idea of spending a lifetime working for one company has become practically nonexistent. People are hired, fired, transferred, and shuffled from job to job with too little concern for their personal feelings. Computer printouts and stereotyped rating scales are used to evaluate a person's job performance— all in the name of profits and objectivity. Have we gone too far? Have we become so busy tending to activities that we have forgotten that individual human beings with needs and feelings are the source of all productivity? It may sound strange, but if we want to increase productivity we are simply going to have to start caring more about people as individuals and considering their needs. Productivity will start to increase when people start to care more about people—and about getting things done.

PUTTING THE PIECES TOGETHER

There are no single causes or simple solutions to our productivity problems. However, out of all the causes, facts, and figures two clear pictures emerge. One is that due to a number of factors the incentives that would lead to increased productivity are missing. For example, worker incentives, research and development incentives, saving and investment incentives are all sorely lacking.

The second picture that emerges is one of a nearsighted, security-conscious nation that doesn't want to take chances. The enormous amounts of government regulation are a clear example of our preoccupation with security. We want comfort and a sure thing in a world where sure things mostly do not exist. We have minimized the benefits of risk and magnified the hazards so much that we have immobilized ourselves from moving ahead. Yet progress without risk is impossible.

Years ago, historian Edward Gibbon explained the decline and fall of the ancient city of Athens this way: "In the end, more than they wanted freedom, they wanted security. They wanted a comfortable life. And in their quest for it all—security, comfort and freedom—they lost it all."

Can we escape a similar fate? Yes, provided we make some changes and take a few chances. Admittedly these chances involve the distinct possibility of failure. But our only alternative is to sit back, reminisce about the days when the U.S. was the idol of the world, and watch the American pie continue to shrink.

CHAPTER 2

INCENTIVE—
THE LORD GIVETH AND
THE GOVERNMENT
TAKETH AWAY

*"The fundamental problem is that politicians like to
give things away to voters, and the government
doesn't produce anything to give. They can rob
Peter to pay Paul, but this will lose them a vote
every time they gain one. The trick is to rob Peter
to pay Paul and rob Paul to pay Peter—and
get both their votes."*

—*Thomas Sowell*

One key to greater productivity lies in the creation of incentives. Incentives for saving and investing result in the capital needed for building new plants, acquiring better machinery, and conducting research. Profit-sharing, bonus, and cost-saving incentives give employees the motivation to work smarter and do more with less. The promise of autonomy and the possibility of wealth provide the incentives for individuals to start their own businesses. Indeed, if you expect anyone to do anything with any amount of gusto, you better provide him or her with an incentive. The backbone of American economic growth has been and will be based on individual gains.

As pointed out in Chapter 1, inadequate incentives are a root cause of our productivity decline. And the sad fact is that one of the main destroyers of personal incentive has been the massive amount of governmental growth we have experienced in the past two decades. Between 1967 and 1978 America's productivity growth rate dropped, but the cost of government increased by 212 percent. In fact, one major reason you're working harder and living poorer is simply that government is extracting larger and larger pieces from a shrinking pie. It's the government that subsidizes people for being unproductive, taxes people for being productive, and hires large numbers of us to work for the government. It's the government that competes with industry for borrowed funds and drives up interest rates. It's the government that inflates the money supply by printing more currency and destroys the personal incentive to save. It's the government that has overburdened the small businessman with costly and sometimes meaningless regulations that leave him feeling more like a compliant clerk than his own boss. It's the government that created a mammoth self-perpetuating bureaucracy that has grown out of control and weighs heavier each year on the productive sector of the economy. In fact, government has become so large, so burdensome, and so all-encompassing that it is one of the largest single causes of our economic maladies. It's a classic case of the road to hell being paved with good intentions.

THE PESSIMISTIC AMERICAN

Despite sagging productivity growth, Americans entered the 1980s better educated, better housed, and in better health than ever. The net assets of the average household in 1979 came to $83,500—a statistic unequaled in the history of the world. Yet we find ourselves gripped by a mood of pessimism and fear about the future. In fact many of us feel poorer than ever.

And many who aren't poor are anxious about the future. A 1981 survey of $90,000-a-year executives found that they didn't expect their standard of living to improve in the next two years and many were quite worried about keeping pace with inflation. A third of them were counting on their children to help finance their own college costs and more than a third said they had no confidence that their investments would outpace inflation.

Walk into any bookstore and you'll see stacks of best-selling

doomsday books on techniques for surviving impending financial disasters. We seem to feel as if something horrible is about to
happen to us. Why?

MEET THE NEW HAVE-NOTS

A closer look at economic statistics reveals that all this concern is
more than mere hype and fantasy nightmares. While *average*
statistics show Americans entering the eighties with unprec-
edented wealth, average statistics don't reveal the plight of the
middle-income wage earner struggling to pay the mortgage (if
fortunate enough to have a house) and raise a family. What has
actually happened is that the vast majority of middle-class Americans have been working hard and losing ground for over a
decade. Through a combination of taxation, inflation, and government social programs, wealth is being redistributed toward
the two income extremes.

The richest 20 percent have tax shelters and investments to
protect their incomes from the ravages of inflation. And the
poorest 20 percent are receiving payments from the government
that rise with the cost-of-living index. But millions of middle-
income wage earners, who are the mainstays of the productive
sector of the economy, enjoy no such protections. They have no
shelters from either taxes or inflation and they "enjoy" too much
income to qualify for government handouts. The result? America has become a country where the rich provide for the poor
using the money of the middle class. Or, stated another way,
Middle America is helping the poor and slowly becoming part of
them. In 1950, seven out of ten American families could afford
to buy a medium-priced house. In 1981, nine out of ten American families could not.

But providing for the poor is only one reason that Middle
America is being squeezed. At the same time a number of very
large bills are coming due. For example, we are being told that
our national defense is woefully inadequate. The result is that a
defense build-up greater than the one for the Vietnam war is
being planned. In addition to being expensive and inflationary,

our defenses provide protection for some of our major indus-trial competitors such as Japan and West Germany. Their de-fense burden drains their productive capacity far less than ours because of our willingness to shoulder this huge and costly re-sponsibility. And who pays for this? You and I.

Another bill coming due is the energy bill; this could be the fastest growing burden of the eighties. It's projected that if real OPEC prices increase at a rate of 5 percent a year during the eighties, prices at the gas pump will hit $3 a gallon by 1989. Short-term oil gluts may come and go but energy is going to be an expensive long-term burden.

Other large bills coming due in the eighties are for medical care, cleaning the environment, and supporting a large educa-tional bureaucracy. During the sixties and seventies the federal government involved itself heavily in each of these areas, and the cost of all three has skyrocketed out of control ever since. In 1949 the combined costs of environment, health, education, and defense amounted to 12.4 percent of our total output. In 1979 the combined costs amounted to almost 25 percent of total out-put and the cost will be increasing during the eighties. In fact, a *Fortune* magazine forecast projects that by 1989 the combined costs of defense, energy, education, health care, and environ-ment will equal approximately 40 percent of total output. And who is going to pay for all this? Why, Mr. and Mrs. Middle American, of course. No wonder we feel so poor.

THE RED, WHITE, AND BLUE SECURITY BLANKET

Almost everyone complains about the size and involvement of government in our lives. Yet there is another side to the story. The simple fact is that we have the government we have been asking for. And now that we have it, we realize it costs too much. Think about it. We have asked the government to:

- Provide low-cost education at all levels
- Increase our national security
- Take care of us when we are elderly or unemployed and if we become disabled

- Provide us with low-cost medical care after age sixty-five
- Insure that all products are absolutely safe
- Keep the environment clean
- End all types of discrimination
- Eradicate poverty

And provide numerous other services that would take several volumes to list. We asked for these services when we elected officials who pledged to work for the establishment of the various agencies' programs and services. And they did. To paraphrase the Toyota slogan, "You asked for it, you got it—big government." The only problem—as we have learned—is that big government can be costly, inefficient, and divert productive resources.

Today it's fashionable to get elected by promising to reduce the size of government, but don't hold your breath waiting for it to happen. The simple fact is that too many of us are now dependent on one form or another of the government for our livelihood. For over a decade there have been more people employed by the government than all of the people employed by *all* manufacturing industries combined. And even if you happen to be employed in the private sector your job may, in effect, be a government job. For example, General Motors employs 23,000 people whose sole job is to fill out government forms. The jobs created by the government for lawyers and accountants are obvious—and these are very high-paying professions. Companies stockpile engineers in hopes of luring fat defense contracts and then pass the costs on to the government. With the advent of Medicare and Medicaid, medical incomes have kept well ahead of the inflation rate thanks, in part, to government subsidies. These are just a few examples.

The point is that to a great extent we are the government. We built it, asked for it, and expect it to take care of us from the cradle to the grave. Our attitude toward government is a paradox. We don't want to pay for it but expect it to cater to all of our needs. We are going to have to make some very hard choices between now and the end of the century about the role we want government to play. If we expect the government to still be our red, white, and blue security blanket that provides for the welfare of all in the year 2000, then we had better lower our expectations for the good life in twenty-first-century America.

GOVERNMENTAL INCENTIVE KILLERS

To say that the government destroys personal incentive will come as no shock to you. If you've been struggling to make ends meet in the past decade you have experienced it first-hand. However, some of the governmental incentives that curtail productivity are rather subtle. For example, think of the millions of highly educated, intelligent, competent people who are diverted from the private sector of the economy and opt for careers in the government bureaucracy where jobs have been secure and well shielded from inflation. And who can blame them? The benefits are terrific and the work isn't bad. It's just unproductive. In his essay "The Wealth of Washington" Tom Bethell makes the point vividly:

> Don't work for an oil company—you might get your hands dirty. Work for the Department of Energy and ponder energy "policy," this is much more prestigious. You are a nurse? The pay is low and you change bedpans. Better try and get on a health "task force" and write a memo on "Health Care Delivery Systems." You want to paint a picture? Hard work. Better go to work for the National Endowment and talk about creative partnerships at a meeting. Your salary is assured![1]

Thus many potentially productive people invest their time and efforts in a bureaucracy that costs each American family approximately $2,500 per year. But employing people to expand the bureaucracy is only the tip of the iceberg. Here are some other incentive killers that destroy productivity.

[1] Tom Bethell, "The Wealth of Washington," *Harper's* (June 1978), p. 60.

Ever-increasing Taxes

Economist Milton Friedman has remarked that "There are very few of us who believe that we are getting our money's worth for the 40 percent of our income that is being used to support state, local and federal governments." Government has become such big business that we now work from January through May each year just to pay for it. That fact is particularly ironic considering that the Revolutionary War was started because of a tax on tea. From 1971 to 1981, while Middle America's buying power declined 5 percent, federal income tax revenues increased 200 percent and Social Security taxes increased 300 percent.

Traditionally, the Internal Revenue Service has relied on the honesty and compliance of the American taxpayer for collecting revenue. But in the past several years many Americans have been quietly staging their own taxpayer revolt and failing to report some or all of their income. Estimates are that as many as 20 million Americans are failing to report part or all of their income. And it's estimated that this underground economy is upwards of 300 billion dollars each year.

The majority of these people aren't underworld figures engaged in organized crime. They are otherwise-law-abiding, honest citizens who are fed up with taxation, wrung by inflation, and fighting back in any way they can. They use a number of artful dodges such as demanding payments in cash, padding expense accounts, bartering services, and skimming cash from their businesses. Tax evasion is most prevalent among the self-employed. The IRS estimates that they fail to report some 40 percent of their total income.

As you read this you may be cheering for the tax evaders. Unfortunately, the people who are least able to evade taxes are the ones who need financial help the most. The typical American employee is salaried and has no artful dodges and few tax shelters available. The IRS estimates that if tax evaders were honest, the honest taxpayers' bill could be reduced by 16 percent and collections would remain constant.

To be sure, not all tax resistance is peaceful and passive. According to the FBI, three-fourths of all threats and nearly half of all assaults against federal workers are aimed at IRS employees.

When the subject of taxation is raised most of us think of the large yearly bills we pay for federal income tax, Social Security, state income taxes, and property taxes. However, did you know:

- Federal and state gasoline taxes can add up to 13¢ per gallon or more?
- Federal excise taxes are added to the cost of oil and tires?
- Uncle Sam taxes you every time you place a phone call?
- You may be taxed extra for entertainment and lodging?
- The federal government taxes every barrel of beer $9?
- In most states you are taxed for the privilege of driving an automobile?

On top of it all, working couples are taxed for being married. Is it any wonder we feel so discouraged? Who wants to work for 60 percent of a salary that can't keep pace with the cost of living?

In addition to destroying morale and the incentive to work, higher taxes also destroy the incentive to save, which in turn reduces investment capital. Those of us with modest incomes have become painfully aware that you only lose by saving. But from a national standpoint, the real damage to productivity is done by taxes that discourage the wealthy from saving. Price Waterhouse & Company studied the savings rates of high-income individuals in eight industrial nations. The typical individual in their study earned a $99,000 income, broken down as follows:

Salary	$50,000
Dividends	10,000
Interest	5,000
Capital Gains	34,000
Total	$99,000

The study found that the nations where investment incomes were least taxed were the ones where personal savings were the highest. For example, in Italy and Japan, where there are no capital gains taxes, the personal savings rates were 23.1 and 21.5 percent respectively. Conversely, the U.S. showed a capital gains tax of 26.8 percent, a total investment tax burden of 33.5 percent, and a savings rate of only 6.3 percent. It's also interesting to note that, of the eight nations studied, the U.S. both had the lowest savings rate and was only second to Sweden in the amount of taxes levied on investments.

In 1981, Congress passed sweeping federal budget and tax cuts designed to spur incentives to save and invest. On the surface this appears to be a move in the right direction, but don't get too optimistic. Federal tax and spending cuts may curtail the growth of the national government, but the net effect will likely be an increase in state and local taxation. If this happens, you will still be working from January through May to pay for a counter-productive bureaucracy.

Spiraling Inflation

The story goes that a rich man who was terminally ill was nearing death. He decided to have his body frozen with the hope that a cure would someday be found and he could be thawed and restored to good health. Sure enough, his wish came true twenty years later. The first thing he did was call his broker and ask "How's my IBM stock?" "$35,000 a share" was the reply. "Fantastic!" he exclaimed. Just then the operator interrupted: "Your time is up. Please deposit $500 for another three minutes."

That story isn't so funny when considered in the light of the inflation we have recently experienced. In fact, it's been projected that if prices increase in the next forty years as they have in the last forty, the average family's income will be $124,000, homes will sell for $300,000 to $500,000 (many already do), and bread for $7 a loaf.

The government is forever fighting inflation but inflation

always seems to win. Although it's true that inflation is a worldwide problem, the fact is that the government has been a major contributor and benefactor of escalating prices. It's also interesting to note that our productivity decline began in the mid-sixties, when inflation began to rear its ugly head.

We are told that inflation is a very difficult problem to cure, and there is no doubt about that. However, the governmental cause of inflation is really simple in concept and goes back thousands of years. For example, the Roman emperor Diocletian had many large government spending programs and paid for them by issuing cheaper coins. This lessened the value of the currency already in circulation and resulted in everyone's raising prices. Diocletian expressed shock when he heard that inflation was sweeping the empire. But did he stop government spending and issuing cheap money? Of course not. He denounced "greedy" citizens for raising prices and established price controls. The result was that production of goods slowed down because businesses had their profit incentives destroyed. Shortages of goods developed, people lost faith in the value of the currency and invested in gold. Gold prices soared. Sound familiar? The same scenario has been played out in twentieth-century America. Our recent inflation problems began when the federal government financed the Vietnam war and the Great Society by printing money.

At first the idea of printing money to pay for programs sounds great because it seems as if nobody is paying for it. And "free" programs have terrific voter appeal. But the fact is that everyone who holds money pays for the programs because the printing of new money cheapens the money that you worked hard to earn. The real cost of the programs is quietly stolen from your paychecks and savings and raises your income to put you into a higher tax bracket.

As Abraham Lincoln noted, "you can't fool all the people all the time" and after a while people start to wise up and realize they are being taken. Instead of saving, which could be used for capital formation, they invest in gold, real estate, and collectibles which they hope will increase in value faster than the inflation rate. Everyone demands more money and the inflationary spiral is off to the races. Meanwhile governmental officials decry the misfortunes of inflation and talk about how complex it is. And the printing presses keep on turning.

And everybody loses. Productivity declines because necessary investment capital isn't available because of decreased savings. However, the worst result of inflation is the devastating psychological impact it has on us and our incentive to improve our lot. Inflation confuses us, disorients us, and scares the hell out of most of us. We search for scapegoats, and workers, consumers, and businessmen all waste productive time fighting with each other. Lenin believed that the surest way to destroy a capitalist system was to destroy public confidence in the currency through inflation. On that point, he was certainly right on target.

Demoralizing Transfer Payments

Columnist Kathleen Kroll expressed the anger of many Middle Americans in an article that appeared in *U.S. News and World Report.* Here is part of what she had to say:

> There's something disconcerting about standing in line at the checkout counter behind someone using food stamps—especially when one is paying for one's own order with the family's mortgage money.
>
> I find myself thinking that there must be something terribly wrong with a system which causes me to, even for a moment, consider the advantages of being a food stamp recipient.
>
> While window shopping at a lobster pound and bemoaning the astronomical prices, I spoke to the owner. "See this," he said while fanning food stamps. "The only lobster sales I've had today were paid for by these. Sad commentary, huh?"
>
> Huh indeed. I left, half-heartedly clutching a small package of frozen fish.
>
> All the way home I wondered: "Where did I go wrong? Does this really bother me? Should it bother me? Does it bother anyone else?" It was a long way home, believe me.

It's not that I begrudge the needy. It's just that I begrudge living less well than they do.

"Oh," a friend once said, "you're too proud to withstand the humiliation of public assistance, of food stamps, of Medicaid. It's degrading."

That may have been so at one time. But what could be more degrading than struggling to move to a nicer home, a better neighborhood, trying "to keep up with the Joneses" who just happen to be setting the pace with your tax money?

And where is the incentive for the Joneses to get off welfare, to "live the good life"? They already live it.

Another neighbor summed it up for many of us when she said: "Why should my husband and I have to work 70-odd hours a week to earn $30,000 a year, to live equal to, or substandard to, a welfare family? Ridiculous!"

Where is my piece of the American pie? I finally figured it out. Yup, it seems the system has placed it on someone else's table.[2]

When you take what A has earned and give it to B you destroy the incentive in both A and B. Simplistic as that statement may be, it describes the government's contribution to the productivity crisis. In 1981, one-third of your federal tax dollars went to pay for what the government calls "income security"— outlays for retirement, disability, and other Social Security payments and welfare. And almost everybody is unhappy with the system. Millions of hard-working middle-income families are making do with less while a government bureaucracy redistributes the pie. As comedian Flip Wilson put it, ("We is sometimes the stuckor and sometimes the stuckee, but we is the stuckee an awful lot more than we is the stuckor.")

In 1976, M. Stanton Evans made an interesting point about federal welfare programs. He noted that between 1965 and 1975 the cost of federal welfare programs increased by $209 billion to a total of $286.5 billion a year. Evans then noted that if the 25 million people that the government classified as "poor" in 1975

---

[2] Kathleen Kroll, "A Worker: I Begrudge Living Less Well Than the Poor Do," *U.S. News and World Report*, March 30, 1981, p. 46.

had been given the $209 billion, without government middlemen, each poor person would have received $8000 per year! That would have added up to a very healthy $40,000-a-year income for a "poor" family of five. How much did your family earn in 1975?

Obviously, not all of this money gets to the poor. Much of it goes to bureaucrats whose salaries and status are measured by how many people report to them. Their incentive is to perpetuate and increase the size of the bureaucracy. And God forbid that they fail to spend all of their budget! That only insures that it will be cut. Please don't misunderstand me. I'm not blaming those who work for the government. Most of them are honest, hard-working people. The problem is that the system rewards them for waste and growth rather than for providing efficient services.

In fact, a number of studies comparing services provided by government and private sector organizations revealed that government services cost about four times more. For example, in 1975 the city of New York estimated that it costs $297 per year to collect garbage twice a week from a single-family dwelling in Queens. In nearby Nassau County, a private firm collected garbage three times a week and charged customers $72 per year.

The redistribution of wealth by government goes far beyond welfare. Whenever the government bails out a weak company, wealth is being redistributed. Whenever farmers are paid not to grow crops, wealth is being redistributed. Every time government pensioners receive a cost-of-living increase, wealth is being redistributed. Medicare and Medicaid services are transfer payments that fatten the health care community at the taxpayers' expense. One classic example is the Kentucky pharmacist who collected $328,000 from Medicaid for servicing a town of 750 people! "I think Medicaid has been good to me and I think I've been good to it," he said. When Medicaid was first proposed, the Department of Health, Education and Welfare estimated it would cost $238 million. By 1979 it was costing $20 billion. Indeed, an elephant is a mouse built to government specifications.

Stop and Go Regulations

Voltaire wrote that "A great many laws in a country, like many physicians, is a sign of malady." If Voltaire was correct, we are in deep trouble. Business today is being strangled by regulations that are so inflexible, contradictory, complex, and cumbersome that it staggers the imagination. Yet for all the hundreds of billions of dollars that regulation costs, there is little if any evidence that we are any better off than before we were smothered with red tape and regulation. As economist Murray Weidenbaum noted, "Virtually every study of regulatory experience from trucking to pharmaceuticals to pensions indicates both needless expense and ineffective operations or, worse yet, counter-productive results."

If the vast majority of government regulations are ineffective and counterproductive, it is only reasonable to ask "Why do we have so many?" One reason is that many of these regulations are started when single-interest pressure groups create a hysteria mentality over an alleged crisis. This puts a tremendous amount of pressure on congressmen either to vote for the regulations or be branded as a someone who doesn't care about public security. It's tough to keep a seat in Congress by voting against clean air, safety, and health. As a result new laws are passed, new agencies are established, more bureaucrats are added to the government payroll, and red tape that slows down productivity is created.

Once the regulations are established there are scads of lawyers ready to proceed with litigation whenever there is an indication that a client, or potential client, has been damaged. The oversupply of attorneys in this country is incredible. On a per capita basis we have four times as many lawyers as Great Britain, five times as many as Germany, ten times as many as France, and twenty times as many as Japan. There are, in fact, more lawyers in the U.S. than the rest of the world combined.

Among other things, productivity means getting things done in less time and responding rapidly to changing market conditions. And all of the red tape, regulation, and litigation has placed a huge burden on private businesses. "At least 50 percent,

and probably closer to 70 percent of my time is spent dealing
with the government instead of applying that time to my duties
as chief scientist and chief operating officer of my company,"
says George Lockwood, a pioneering farmer who is attempting
to domesticate abalone. Forty-two federal, state, and local agencies regulate Lockwood, who is attempting to innovate and start
a small business. Lockwood estimates that it has cost his business about $1 million to comply with regulations in only two
years of operation.

Another classic story involves a railroad which developed a
new vehicle that would reduce up to one-third the rates for hauling grain. The Interstate Commerce Commission banned the
vehicle on the grounds that it wouldn't be fair to other railroads
and truckers. The railroad spent millions of dollars and had to
wait four years before it was allowed to use the new vehicle.

Perhaps, however, the most insidious aspect about regulations is that so many of them are contradictory. A Virginia poul-
try processor was ordered by a federal job-safety agency to "Put
in an acoustical ceiling to cut down noise." And he did. Then
along came the Agriculture Department inspectors. "Take out
that ceiling—it's a sanitation hazard." And he did. When the
job-safety people returned they said "No ceiling? Then make
your workers wear earmuffs or you'll be fined." And he did.

Numerous other contradictions abound in the entangle-
ment of red tape. The Environmental Protection Agency re-
stricts the use of pesticides while the Agriculture Department
promotes pesticides for agricultural and forestry uses. The
Energy Department wants rail rates lowered for hauling coal to
encourage the use of coal while the Transportation Department
is pushing for higher rail rates to help the ailing rail industry.
The Environmental Protection Agency is pushing for strict air
pollution controls while the Energy Department wants companies to switch from oil to coal. The net effect of all these
regulations has been to prolong the life of inefficient industries
and prevent the growth of new and more efficient ones.

To be sure, the American public is safer and healthier than
ever. However, it's also true that most of this progress occurred

well before the advent of health and safety agencies.[3] For example, the general accident rate peaked in 1907 at 94.1 fatalities per 100,000 people. The rate then declined steadily until it leveled off at about 20 per 100,000 after 1957. Harvard professors Albert Nichols and Richard Zeckhauser put it best when they wrote "The history of regulation is a history of disappointment."

Frivolous Waste

"Giving the government 40 percent of my salary is bad enough, but what really galls me is what they do with it." That statement echoes the sentiment of most Americans.

Are you captivated by "The Romantic Poetry of Young Karl Marx"? Are you enchanted with "The Folk Rituals of Birth, Marriage and Death Among Urban Polish-Americans"? Do you yearn to "help youth understand how the sky has influenced the humanities discipline"? Well, believe it or not, your tax dollars are paying to further such projects. It's all part of the great giveaway at the National Endowment for the Humanities, which has dispensed nearly a billion dollars in federal funds.

To be fair, a lot of that money has been very well spent. For example, one grant made it possible for the King Tut exhibit to tour the U.S. and a lot of very solid scholarly work has resulted from NEH grants. The problem is that like all government agencies the NEH is rewarded for spending and increasing its budget. Since its creation in 1965, the yearly appropriation of NEH increased from $2.5 million to $151 million in 1981. And as Milton Friedman noted, "If you put a pot of gold at the NEH, people are going to try to get at it." The result has been the financing of some very, very dubious projects, such as "Prizefighting in Boston's Irish Community," "The Life and Times of Rosie the Riveter," and "The Harp Tradition in Uganda."

---

[3] The Occupational Safety and Health Administration (OSHA) wasn't created until 1970, and the Consumer Products Safety Commission was established in 1972.

Although highly publicized, NEH waste is hardly a drop in the ocean of governmental waste. The entire NEH budget is around .015 of a percent of the federal budget and is sure to be slashed in the budget cuts of the eighties. Yet it does serve as a barometer for just how out of control and frivolous government spending has become. Here are some other examples:

- $3.3 billion is spent each year to print forms, directives, and reports created by the government.
- $2 billion is spent each year to file and store all these accumulated papers.
- $29.1 million was spent on advertising for the federal government in 1981.
- $100,000 was spent to study the emotional effects of separating baby monkeys from their mothers.
- $100,000 was spent to study why hermit crabs pick one seashell over another to live in.
- $93,000 went to teach Navajo Indians to be medicine men.
- $100,000 went to tend Amazon parrots.
- The National Institute of Alcohol Abuse and Alcoholism spent millions of dollars to find out if drunk fish are more aggressive than sober fish.
- $2500 was spent to find out why people are rude, cheat, and lie when playing tennis.

In summary, the government has eroded productivity incentives through increasing taxes and through printing-press economics that fuel inflation, transferring wealth into less productive sectors of the economy, and strangling businesses with regulations. The problem is not that these phenomena exist. Taxes, the printing of money, regulations, and transfer payments are necessary in an organized society and promote economic growth when they are appropriately used. The problem is that these programs have been allowed to proliferate unchecked. Elected officials have promised more than the country can deliver and now the bills are coming due.

WHAT YOU CAN DO

There is no doubt that we are going to have to change the role of government in society if we hope to prosper and increase productivity. And changes are already being made. However, you must think of yourself as a footsoldier on a battlefield. You have no control over what the generals or the enemy is doing and your major goal is to survive, live to fight another day, and prosper. Keeping your incentives to work and bettering your standard of living boil down to staying ahead of inflation.

Accept Reality

You may not like giving a large chunk of your earnings to the government. Who does? But the fact is that you will continue to do so for the foreseeable future or run the risk of being fined and imprisoned. The tax and budget cuts of the eighties will offer little relief to the middle-income wage earner. What the tax cuts will ensure is that federal governmental growth will not continue at the rates of the past twenty years. You may not have to pay a higher percentage of federal income tax in the future. But what about state and local taxes? Many local governments will opt for tax increases when federal funds are reduced. And what about Social Security? Who's going to pay that bill?

The other unpleasant reality is that inflation will also be here for the forseeable future, because nobody really knows how to permanently cure it. Ask ten different economists how to cure inflation and you'll probably get ten different answers. Neither bankers, government officials, economists, nor politicians know how to halt the plague of ever-increasing prices. Unfortunately, it's another uncontrollable factor you are going to have to live with.

Take Advantage of Your Advantages

Volumes are written every year telling how to make a fortune in one investment or another. This book isn't one of them. Nevertheless, a great deal of financial success is the result of applying common sense to your own unique situation. For example, do you live in a fast-growing small town? Perhaps real

estate is a good bet. Is your company bringing out a new product, service, or other innovation that could revolutionize the industry? Maybe buying company stock is a smart play. Just be
sure to get the best *objective* information you can before making
investment decisions.

Don't let the life insurance salesman sell you a whole life
policy. Its cash value just won't increase as fast as the inflation
rate. Nor will bank certificates of deposit or government savings
bonds. Company matched savings programs and fixed annuities
(not variable-rate annuities) can also be poor choices. Enlist the
help of a financial planner or someone who has successfully
managed his own money before choosing your investments. Remember that he who knows not and knows he knows not is wise.

New tax laws to encourage saving and investing are being
phased in, and everyone who can do so should take advantage of
them. One of the best new laws is that people, whether or not
they are covered by employer pension plans, are now able to put
up to $2000 (or $2250 if you have a nonworking spouse) into an
individual retirement account. In addition to getting a $2000 tax
deduction for putting money into the IRA, earnings in the IRA
accumulate tax-free. Taxes aren't due until you begin withdraw-
ing funds (no earlier than age fifty-nine and a half without incurring a penalty). If you're self-employed you can now shelter
up to $15,000 per year in a Keogh plan. New opportunities are
also available for savings certificates that pay tax-free interest.
My next recommendation is the greatest reason why you should
put money away for your later years.

Do Not, I Repeat, Do Not Rely on Social Security

If you think Social Security is taking its toll on you, talk to
the people who retired and are trying to live on it in the face of
ever-increasing prices. In 1950, there were sixteen people contributing to the program for every person receiving benefits.
Today there are three people contributing for every beneficiary
and the projection is a ratio of two to one by the year 2030. The
system is clearly in trouble and Congress has pledged that Social
Security won't be allowed to fail. Not having a crystal ball, I can't

tell you what's going to happen. But neither can anyone else. Social Security by itself will offer you a poor retirement at best and maybe none at all. Play this one close to the vest. Plan for your own retirement and if you receive Social Security income, your later years will be that much better.

Get in the Habit of Saving

Erma Bombeck wrote: "The bookstore was bulging with books on how to save money. It seemed strange to me that they were on a table marked 'Current Fiction.'" I know it sounds contradictory to tell you to put money away when you're working harder and living poorer than ever. But the fact is that accumulating a chunk of capital to invest is your greatest hope for getting and staying ahead. I'm not suggesting that you salt money away in a savings account that won't keep pace with inflation. Money market funds are almost as convenient as checking accounts and pay much higher rates of interest. Once you accumulate $1000 you can open such an account.

Resolve to save at least 10 percent of your take-home pay. Saving should be your top financial priority. Put 10 percent of your check away before you do anything else with it. By living in America, you have been conditioned to spend everything you earn and expect instant need satisfaction. Learn to practice a little deferred need gratification. It's one key to becoming successful and getting you ahead in the world.

In searching for ways to save money, begin by keeping a spending log for a month. Every time you spend money write down how much you spent and what you purchased. Once you have a record of where your money is going you will be able to see where your money could be put to better use. Did you really need that banana split last Saturday? Did you have to buy prime rib when chuck can be very tasty? Did you really have to go to the ballgame when you could have stayed home and watched it on television? Once you record and review your purchases, you will find many of them are unnecessary.

Long before there were such things as food stamps and welfare, penniless immigrants came to America and many managed to accumulate fortunes. Their formula was simply to save, sacrifice, and intelligently invest their time and money. These are things that all of us can do and the odds are that you have much more going for you than they did. Think about that before convincing yourself that you can't save. Don't allow yourself to get sucked into the spending psychosis that is so typical of an inflationary economy.

Wean Yourself from Government Dependency

The more all of us rely on government, the bigger it will become, the more productivity will suffer, and the less free all of us will be. However, the opposite is also true. The tide is turning and Washington has gotten the word that voters are fed up with big government. Keep sending the message by supporting and voting for people who, in fact, do limit the size of government rather than those who just talk about it.

As a private citizen keep this in mind: Every time you receive a government check or service you are supporting the existence of big government and a mammoth bureaucracy. I'm not suggesting that you quit your government job or send back your Social Security checks. But work to replace government services with private ones and keep a wary eye out for coming increases in state and local taxes. If you're thinking about changing jobs or launching a second career, look first in the private sector. It's so easy to take what appears to be free money, but in the final analysis it's a terribly expensive drain on the pocketbooks, incentive, and morale of everyone—and that ultimately includes you.

I'll close this chapter with the fable of "The Modern Little Red Hen" because it graphically depicts the government's contribution to our productivity ills. A friend passed it along to me from an unknown source:

Once upon a time, there was a little red hen who scratched about the barnyard until she uncovered some grains of wheat. She called her neighbors and said, "If we plant this wheat, we shall have bread to eat. Who will help me plant it?"

"Not I," said the cow, the duck, the pig, and the goose.

"Then I will," said the little red hen. And she did. The wheat grew tall and ripened into golden grain. "Who'll help me reap my wheat?" asked the hen.

"Not I," said the duck.

"Out of my classification," said the pig.

"I'd lose my seniority," said the cow.

"I'd lose my unemployment compensation," said the goose.

"Then I will," said the little red hen, and she did. At last it came time to bake the bread.

"Who will help me bake the bread?" she asked.

"That would be overtime for me," said the cow.

"I'd lose my welfare benefits," said the duck.

"I'm a dropout and never learned how," said the pig.

"If I'm to be the only helper, that's discrimination," said the goose.

"Then I will," said the hen. She baked five loaves and held them up for her neighbors to see. They all wanted some and, in fact, demanded a share. But the little red hen said, "No, I can eat the five loaves myself."

"Excess profits!" cried the cow.

"Capitalist leech!" screamed the duck.

"I demand equal rights!" yelled the goose.

And the pig just grunted. And they painted "unfair" picket signs and marched round and round the little red hen, shouting obscenities.

When the government agent came, he said to the hen, "You must not be greedy."

"I earned the bread," she said.

"Exactly," said the agent. "That's the wonderful free enterprise system. Anyone in the barnyard can earn as much as he wants. But under our modern government regulations, the productive workers must divide their product with the idle."

And they lived happily ever after, including the little red hen, who smiled and clucked, "I am grateful. I am grateful."

But her neighbors wondered why she never again baked any more bread.

CHAPTER 3

PRODUCTIVITY—
THE JAPANESE WAY

*"The key element in our economic growth is the
Japanese society itself. Our paintings, and
sculpture, our architecture and our gardens
have been designed on the premise that 'less is
more' because less is all there is."*
—*Kyonosuke Ibe*

Incredible! It's the only way to describe Japanese productivity
when you consider the circumstances. Here is a nation with half
as many people as the U.S. has crowded onto a land area the size
of Montana. Japan imports 100 percent of its aluminum, 99.8
percent of its oil, 98.4 percent of its iron ore, 66.4 percent of its
lumber, and only 15 percent of its land area is arable. In 1945,
Japan's industrial capacity was totally destroyed and years later
"Made in Japan" was a catch phrase for shoddy, second-rate
merchandise. Things have changed.

In the 1970s, while the U.S. earned the poorest productivity
improvement record of major free-world nations, Japan set the
pace. Consider these facts:

- Japanese steel outcompetes American steel.
- Japanese motorcycles have eliminated the British motor-
  cycle industry.
- The German camera and lens industry and the Swiss
  watch industry have given way to Japanese superiority.

- Japan is the leading developer, producer, and user of robots.
- In 1980, Japan surpassed the U.S. as the world's leading producer of automobiles.
- If subsidized housing is included, Japanese wages surpassed American wages in 1978 and are growing at a faster rate.
- Due to successful energy conservation, Japan can produce a unit of gross national product at one-third the energy cost of the U.S. unit.
- Illiteracy is virtually nonexistent in Japan.
- Japanese crime rates are a fraction of those in the U.S. and declining.
- In 1977, Japanese longevity surpassed Sweden's to become first in the world.

Additionally, Japan has for years been a leader in consumer electronics, has played havoc with the American photocopy industry, and is now mounting a serious challenge in the world computer industry. Good grief, Charlie Brown! How did they do it?

Today, American executives and consultants are journeying to Japan and treating it with the reverence of an industrial Mecca. Everyone is eager to learn the secrets of Japanese productivity that enabled an industrially destroyed nation to rebuild itself into the world's second largest free-world power in less than thirty-five years.

Actually, there aren't any secrets. The Japanese have simply learned to get maximum productivity from people because people are their only resource. Japanese executives are among the best in the world and their approach to human resources is one of unparalleled excellence. If there's one lesson we can learn from Japan, it's that productivity improvement begins with people improvement. Once you have a trained, organized, and committed workforce pulling together, productivity takes care of itself.

In this chapter we will look at some of the reasons Japan has enjoyed such phenomenal success. We will also look at what we are learning from the Japanese that can be applied to solve our own productivity problems.

THE POOR LITTLE RICH NATION

Economic insecurity is the driving force behind Japan's booming success. Does that surprise you? It would be reasonable to assume that the Japanese should be very smug about their economic success, but just the opposite is true. Japan may be a very affluent country but the Japanese don't see it that way.

From parents, teachers, the media, and every other informative source, young Japanese are told again and again that Japan must cram 115 million people onto a small island and depend on foreign sources for everything from food to oil. As a result, if you ask a Japanese citizen about Japan's prosperity you're likely to hear a real hardship story, like "We are a very poor nation with no natural resources. All of us must work very, very hard."

And very, very hard is how they work. Japanese managers have little trouble motivating employees to work hard because most of them come to the job believing that they, in part, shoulder the burden for Japan's survival. To paraphrase the Datsun slogan, they are driven.

Most Americans are surprised to learn that the Japanese are rather uneasy about their lot. After all, most of us hear and read success stories and predictions of how Japan will surpass the U.S. in per capita GNP by 1990. But the insecurity is very real and understandable. Imagine, if you would:

- Crowding the U.S. population into two states the size of Montana.
- Removing all of our oil and mineral resources and just about all of our agricultural resources.
- Putting the gigantic defense umbrella that protects the U.S. into the hands of a foreign power.

- Having experienced total destruction of the U.S. in your lifetime through conventional and nuclear war.

Would these conditions and experiences increase your concern about America's future? Now you're beginning to understand the Japanese pangs of insecurity. A fifty-year-old Japanese citizen has experienced all of these things in his nation in his lifetime.

In addition to explaining the Japanese capacity for hard work, insecurity also explains their superior capacity for self-denial. Personal consumption in Japan takes a smaller percentage of total income than in most developed countries. The Japanese save 20 percent of their income and government policies stress the need for investment and productivity. Japan, compared to other advanced countries, lags in such areas as highways, hospitals, housing, schools (not education), and recreational facilities.

Other indicators of self-denial in the name of economic growth abound. Cities are overcrowded, lengthy commutes are common, and Tokyo is the world's most polluted city. In one sense, Japan is a nation of workaholics. Perhaps Carnegie-Mellon president Richard Cyert summed it up best when he remarked "It's the old syndrome, when you're number two, you have to work harder. I wish we Americans would get a little of that 'We're number two' spirit. If we don't we're going to be." In fact, if current trends continue, Japan will lead the world in gross national product by the year 2000.

WHY IS JAPAN SO PRODUCTIVE?

Insecurity may be the driving force behind Japan's success, but it's hardly a sufficient explanation. Many other resource-poor, hard-working, insecure nations remain destitute. Obviously, Japan works smarter.

The following are some of the major contributors to Japan's superproductivity. As you read each of these factors, ask yourself "What lessons are here that we can learn and profit from?" For years, Japanese executives and government officials have let America teach them to work better. Now it's the students' turn to teach and our turn to sit back, listen, and learn.

National Commitment Is Strong

The most striking factor about the Japanese is their strong sense of national purpose and clear-cut goals for every person, group, organization, and industry. Everyone's role is related to helping achieve the ultimate goal of a more prosperous Japan. In a sense, Japan is one gigantic program of management by objectives. Each worker works for the company who, in turn, works for the industry, who, in turn, works for Japan. Japan, Inc. (as Japan's triumverate of government, banking, and industry has been enviously labeled) gives the impression of being one gigantic team.

And teamwork has been a major key to Japan's success. Management, government, labor, and the banks have all worked together in a rather simple, straightforward plan to build a better Japan. Here's how the plan was set up:

1. In the government, Japan's Ministry of International Trade and Industry (MITI) worked with businesses and developed policies to guide industrial growth.
2. Japan's banks and the Ministry of Finance saw to it that the capital was supplied to the businesses to enable them to grow.
3. Business and labor were given a relatively free hand to develop without government intervention in a free-enterprise, capitalistic environment. Social programs and governmental regulations were minimized or deferred.
4. Top priority was given to building first-class modern industries with the best technology available.

Management, labor, and the government all pulled together with a common plan. And the plan worked.

Capital Formation Is Assured

As we saw in Chapter 1, capital formation is an essential ingredient to increasing productivity. And the Japanese have come up with a great way to assure that banks have a ready supply of capital to lend to businesses.

Japanese workers receive approximately 40 percent of their yearly income in two bonuses. The size of the bonus is based on how well the company does, which gives everyone an incentive to work better. But the real national advantage is that workers become accustomed to living at a level less than their income. Consequently, the average citizen saves 20 percent of his income, which supplies a ready source of capital for banks to lend to businesses.

The result is that Japanese firms rely more heavily on bank loans than on selling stocks and bonds for raising capital. And bank loans put far less pressure on businesses to look good today at the expense of ignoring long-term investments. The average Japanese company raises only one-sixth of its capital needs by selling securities compared to one-half in the United States.

The growth of Japanese capital has been a key factor in their success. Available capital has made investing in new plants, retooling old ones, new industries, and basic research all possible. In fact, one study by the New York Stock Exchange attributes Japan's economic growth between 1973 and 1979 to the fact that capital stock increased at a rate of 7.2 percent. The study also claims that the U.S. growth rate would have equaled Japan's during that period had our capital stock increased at an equal rate.

Knowledge Is Power

The pursuit of knowledge is a near-obsession with the Japanese. They realize that a high-technology, industrial nation needs information like a car needs gasoline. Consequently the Japanese are the most avid learners in the world. This unending thirst for knowledge exhibits itself in many ways.

Most important, Japan is the world's best educated nation. In addition to having a thorough grounding in Japanese, millions of Japanese are fluent in English and many speak three and four languages. In international testing programs Japanese youth score higher than American youth, whose scores continue to decline. On a per capita basis, Japan graduates over twice as many scientists and engineers as the U.S. and the level of mathematical and scientific instruction in Japan is reputed to be the highest in the world.

Japanese education is rigorous and tightly controlled by the Japanese Ministry of Education. A premium is placed on academic achievement, and the environment (like Japanese business) is extremely competitive. In addition to mastering the very difficult Japanese language (which involves memorizing almost 2000 characters), math, and science, Japanese children must take courses in ethics that stress proper social behavior, work, and community obligations. Unlike the U.S., Japan sees nothing inconsistent about teaching moral values in public schools and the constitutional separation of church and state.

But the Japanese appetite for information doesn't end with their formal education. Training is a regular part of every employee's job until he retires. Japanese workers are always on the lookout for new ideas, new techniques, new books, or any type of information that will enable them to increase productivity and improve themselves. Japanese executives will be the first to tell you that much of their success has come from applying knowledge that was learned from Western nations, most notably the U.S.

The ability to listen and learn also pays off handsomely for Japan in the area of international trade. No other country equals the Japanese in defining what the world will buy. Instead of developing new products and then trying to sell them, the Japanese listen very carefully to the customer and then give him the product that *he* wants.

Competition Is Strong

Although the spirit of teamwork permeates the Japanese culture, it should be pointed out that fierce competition is also a part of Japan. Competition for entrance into top schools and colleges is very rigorous. And competition between firms and industries is extremely heavy. Those that emerge as winners are encouraged and supported in their efforts to expand internationally.

What happens to the losers? I can assure you the government doesn't bail them out. Japanese banks take a merciless approach to dying products and industries and refuse to finance them. Weak companies make better use of their resources or go out of business. Japanese competition is a battle where the strong survive. And this internal competition helps Japan decide which products, companies, and industries are most likely to succeed in the world market place.

❄ A Holistic, Paternalistic Work Culture

Large Japanese corporations offer employees much more than wages. They offer a way of life and a large dose of paternalism.

About 35 percent of Japan's labor force enjoys the security of guaranteed employment until age fifty-five. When business is poor everyone receives lower salaries or bonuses instead of being fired or furloughed. Most workers are employed directly out of school and remain with the company for the length of their careers. Such a practice offers several advantages:

1. The workers develop strong company loyalty because of job security and the fact that salary increases are based on seniority.
2. Companies can invest in the continuous training and development of workers with the confidence that it will pay off.
3. Workers are eager to learn and accept new ways to increase productivity. A new robot or computer won't put them out of work and will likely increase their income.
4. Employees can be evaluated over a long period of time to discover their strengths and how the company can best use them.

Decisions by consensus and extensive participation are another major component of the Japanese work culture. It's a long, tedious process that may involve scores of individuals and would drive many American managers up the wall. Everyone affected by a decision is given the opportunity to have a voice in making the decision. The goal is to find an alternative that everyone can agree on and live with. Once agreement is reached, decisions are much more readily accepted and implemented because everyone is in agreement. No one attempts to slow down or sabotage the plan. The willingness to achieve consensus through compromising is one of the most important native characteristics of the Japanese.

This isn't to say that Japanese management is soft and permissive. In a Japanese organization there's no doubt about who's boss and bosses demand large amounts of work, loyalty, and discipline from employees. But every worker's opinion is regarded as important and he is consulted on decisions that will affect him.

To the Japanese, a corporation's most important role isn't to make a profit but to provide for the wellbeing of its workers and society as a whole. Japanese managers place much more emphasis on providing a work environment that most of us would think of as one big family. Japanese organizations downplay the status distinctions between managers and workers, which helps to promote a team atmosphere rather than one of "us versus them." Typically, Japanese managers don't have private offices. They feel that the open offices nurture a feeling of togetherness.

Company identity is very strong. It's common for employees at all levels to wear company uniforms and workers often begin their days by singing the company song and doing exercises. Most companies have a ceremony to welcome new employees and the ritual is attended by the new recruit's parents and other relatives. Lifetime employee training stresses the importance of individual growth and improvement through self-discipline. New employees are often housed in company dormitories and company financing is frequently provided for workers wanting to buy their own homes. Company social clubs provide for off-the-job needs, offering everything from short courses in the tea ceremony to wedding arrangements. In short, the employee's life revolves around the company.

It should be pointed out that all of these characteristics are descriptive of large Japanese corporations and that not everyone in Japan works in such an environment. Japanese society also consists of a large number of persons who are self-employed as farmers, shopkeepers, scholars, writers, lawyers, artists, and the like. Japan is an essentially free society and anyone who works for a large, paternalistic corporation does so by choice.

Managers Learn Through Experience

The extensive training given to Japanese managers is one reason they are so good. Young trainees take part in a lengthy program that may last up to one year and places a heavy emphasis on learning coupled with a healthy dose of hands-on experience.

New trainees typically begin learning about their company by attending a series of lectures given by company executives. For a one- or two-week period, new recruits are schooled in such areas as company background, products, production, sales, and basic business skills.

Realizing that lectures can often be boring and ineffective, many companies require employees to compile a company handbook after hearing the lectures. This forces them to assimilate the knowledge and express it themselves. Another orientation exercise is to distribute employee handbooks to trainees and tell them the company is dissatisfied and wants it revised. Teams of five or six employees are then asked to write a revised handbook by the next morning. In addition to providing the company with fresh ideas, this gives the trainees experience in working as a team against a tight deadline.

Following the orientation period, management trainees usually spend several months involved in practical work experience. Manufacturing-oriented companies require trainees to work various production jobs to enable them to understand the inner workings of the company. Thus, a new trainee may work around-the-clock shifts alongside regular production workers as part of his training. Later he may be transferred to sales and service and asked to work in these areas. Still later he may be assigned to a financial job, inventory control, purchasing, personnel, or some other division. Rotating future managers through a number of training assignments gives them broad experience in understanding how the pieces of the organization fit together and the problems associated with each department. The experience also teaches them how to communicate, work, and empathize with people from all areas of the company. Later on as managers they will probably settle into one functional area and stay there throughout their career.

Live-in training is also another important aspect of most Japanese training programs. During the training period, new employees live together in company residences or external training centers. In addition to making a successful transition from student life to company life, trainees are expected to learn and experience teamwork, punctuality, human relations, and social rules. Through live-in training future managers are also expected to learn self-sufficiency, a positive attitude, and consideration for others. Live-in training lasts from a few days to several months, depending on the company.

Most companies require new employees to keep a diary of their experiences and impressions throughout the entire training program. At the end of the program, participants are asked to submit a written report based on the diary.

By the end of the training period, the company and the future manager both know a lot more about each other than at the start. The trainee has been observed in various work situations and management can use this information to identify which work area would be best for the new manager. And the new manager has been indoctrinated, has experienced the company from many different viewpoints and been absorbed into the corporate culture. He hasn't had the specialized training of his

American counterpart. But why should he worry? Once he is assigned to a functional area he will continue learning about it for the rest of his career.

Patience and Futurism

One quality that the Japanese have an abundance of is patience. Unlike the Americans, they haven't been crippled by wanting everything now. Japanese executives and governmental officials aren't interested in the quick payoff or the fast yen. Rather, they think in terms of five, ten, and twenty years ahead, and their ultimate aim is to build a solid prosperity and stability that will serve Japan for generations to come. And they are reaslistic and pragmatic enough to realize that the future belongs to those who plan for it, work hard, and invest in it. The seeds of today's Japanese success story were sowed more than thirty years ago.

Unlike American firms, Japanese firms don't suffer from short-term pressures from Wall Street. As pointed out earlier, most of the businesses are invested in or partly owned by banks and banks are much more interested in solid, long-term growth than in inflated stock prices and fast dividends. This, coupled with the savings of the Japanese people, has contributed immensely to Japan's success by making long-range investments possible. And those investments are paying off handsomely today.

BUT THERE ARE PROBLEMS TOO

While Japan's economic growth is remarkable, it's also a nation with many problems on the horizon. Most notably, the Japanese are keenly aware of their dependence on foreign nations for oil and other resources. Consequently, large sums of money are being invested in research and development of solar and nuclear power. Also one project that is attempting to harness the energy created by the ocean's waves is under way.

But resource shortages aren't Japan's only problems. Japan will enter the twenty-first century with one out of every four adults aged sixty-five or older. Keeping a prosperous, growing economy and providing for so many elderly people will be a challenge that won't be easily dealt with. Japan hopes to solve much of this problem by substituting computers, robots, and other automated equipment to do many of the tasks now being done by workers. But computers and robots can't do it all. An aging population poses a serious threat to the lifetime employment concept that many Japanese corporations practice. The traditional Japanese retirement age of fifty-five will, no doubt, be raised to sixty.

Still another problem is the pressure mounting for Japan to provide more for its own national defense. Japan spends less than 1 percent of its GNP on defense, compared to the U.S. 5 percent. In the past several decades, Japan has been protected largely by the U.S. and has been able to concentrate most of its efforts on building a strong economy. However, the sagging U.S. economy and the Soviet arms build-up are leading Japanese conservatives and some Americans to call for a Japanese arms build-up. And defense build-ups are very expensive.

In the interest of building a strong industrial base, Japan has had little left over to provide for social services such as sewers, housing, and roads. In an attempt to keep the economy growing and provide necessary social services, the Japanese government has been using debt financing since 1975; things now seem to be getting out of hand. Japan's 1980 deficit was 33 percent of national spending, compared to 10 percent in the U.S. And as we Americans have learned, deficit spending is great stuff until the bills come due.

Finally, Japan's growing wealth will likely create a new breed of worker who, having known only affluence, will perhaps not be as ambitious and hungry as his parents, who endured the hardships of war and destitution. There are already signs that some young Japanese, like young Americans, place a high value on individualism, leisure, and self-fulfillment.

Despite the problems, however, Japan has momentum and will continue to show solid gains in productivity for the forseeable future. With the world's best-educated labor force, fine executives, and a sound economic strategy, continued prosperity is inevitable.

JAPANESE STRATEGIES WORTH ADOPTING

As you may have gathered, I have a tremendous amount of admiration and respect for the Japanese. Yet it would be foolish to believe that the U.S. can make wholesale adaptations of Japanese business characteristics and be successful. Japan is a homogeneous, group-oriented culture and America is a heterogeneous culture that places a high premium on individualism. There's a lot of truth to the adage that it took the Japanese to build Japan.

There are also many characteristics of Japanese corporations that we wouldn't want to copy. For example, the selection of managers is limited to men who are chosen before they are hired. There's little or no opportunity for workers to move up through the ranks. And Japanese corporations have no women executives. Obviously, such practices are incompatible with the American ethic of equal and unlimited opportunity.

Despite the vast cultural differences between us, Japan has been successful in applying Western management techniques and concepts. All of which leads me to believe that many Japanese practices can be successfully transferred to the American business scene. Some American companies and American-based, Japanese-owned operations have been successfully applying management techniques that are a mixture of Japanese and American characteristics. In his book *Theory Z*, William Ouchi describes such organizations.

The hybrid or Z type organization isn't nearly as paternalistic as the Japanese firm but displays a holistic concern for employees. In short, the Z organization attempts to increase the quality of work life for the worker without imposing the loss of freedom that results from a traditional paternalistic operation. The hope is that there is evolving a new type of organization that combines Yankee ingenuity with the Japanese facility for teamwork, two-way loyalty, and participation. Leading firms such as IBM, Sony, Honeywell, Kodak, Honda, and Intel are a few of many companies moving in this direction with success. The evidence is mounting that much of what's good for Japan can also be good for the U.S.

Historically the Japanese have built a lot of their success by emulating successful practices in other countries. The following key points of the Japanese success story we would do well to emulate. Fortunately, movement in some of these directions is already under way.

Governmental Support of Industry

It must seem very strange to the Japanese that American business and government have such an adversarial relationship. Most government activities related to business don't tell it how to succeed but what not to do. In Japan, the government feels an obligation to help industry grow so that Japanese citizens can live better lives. The Ministry of International Trade and Industry promotes industrial growth by pointing out and encouraging industries and products that will be the most profitable for Japanese businesses. It has no formal power like Communist central planning, and the businesses are privately owned. But it does provide invaluable services.

For example, MITI can provide tax incentives, import protection, or direct subsidies for research and development. It recently pledged $300 million over a ten-year period to the development of futuristic computers. But it also lowered trade barriers and allowed cheap Korean textile imports to flood the market and compete with Japan's inefficient textile industry. MITI helps concentrate Japan's business efforts in areas where success is most likely. Why can't our government have such a service? Entire governmental departments have been created in the past few decades for housing, energy, and environmental protection. Why can't we have one for industrial growth? Most companies give half or more of their incomes to the government and if profits decrease, government revenues decrease.

If we hope to turn this productivity mess around, government and industry are going to have to get together, cooperate, and provide the direction and leadership for industrial growth.

The way things now stand, there is no formal organization coordinating government and industry.

Savings Incentives

During the past decade U.S. banks really took it on the chin, though bank financing is essential because it provides a stable supply of capital essential for long-range growth. But the banks can't lend what people and businesses don't save.

Fortunately the rules are changing, and incentives are being created to encourage rather than penalize savers. Saving for rainy days and retirement is becoming a better investment once again and banks are showing signs of becoming competitive with other investments. But we still have a long way to go. More tax breaks to people and businesses coupled with savings incentives are needed to create the climate to build America's capital. All the motivational and productivity improvement techniques are futile without capital formation. If you doubt me, ask the Japanese.

Lifetime Employment

The Japanese system of lifetime employment isn't a long-standing tradition. Rather, it was imposed on Japanese companies by General MacArthur during the occupation period following World War II. Because the system has worked so well, Japanese companies have elected to continue the practice and consider it to be one of their major strengths.

We all know what happens to American workers when hard times arrive. Chrysler responded to its financial crisis by laying off 28 percent of its blue-collar workers and reducing white-collar salaries only 5 to 7 percent. Mazda of Japan, on the other hand, reacted differently to a decline in sales. Senior managers had their pay cut 20 percent, middle managers had their wages frozen, and production workers received regular cost-of-living increases. Japanese workers aren't loyal and dedicated to the company simply because they're Japanese. They're loyal because they know the company isn't going to abandon them when the going gets rough. If American corporations want loyal and dedicated employees, management must realize that loyalty is a

two-way street and must begin with the company pledging its
commitment to workers.

Japanese corporations with plants in the U.S. have established policies preventing layoffs and establishing company
bonus plans in which everyone shares in both good and hard
times. Sony and other Japanese companies with U.S. plants report that American workers are excellent and nearly as productive as their colleagues in Japan. In fact, in 1981, the Sony plant
in San Diego staffed with American labor and Japanese management, set the all-time company record for productivity.

Humanized Work Environments

Many of the ways to improve the quality of work life have
been practiced in Japan for years with success. And there is
growing evidence that many of their attempts to humanize work
can be successfully transplanted.

For example, in 1974, Matsushita Electrical Industry Co.
bought a television factory in Franklin Park, Illinois, to make
Quasar and Panasonic television sets. The new management
almost immediately began making changes to humanize the
work environment. Workers' names were placed on the walls
at their work stations and some of the worst tasks were automated. Fixed-speed production lines were replaced with a
system the workers could control. Whenever a worker spotted
a problem he could stop the assembly line and fix it. Before
the changes, quality inspectors had found up to 140 defects
in every 100 televisions coming off the line. Five years after the
changes, the reject rate is down to about five per 100 and warranty claims have been reduced eightfold.

Select Team-Builders for Management

There is mounting evidence that the adversarial relationship between management and labor is going out of style. Perhaps the competition of the Japanese has forced us to realize
that only by management and labor working together will
everyone be able to prosper. Whatever the reasons, team-
building managers are going to be more in demand than ever.

Traditionally, Americans have managed through confrontation and managers were chosen for their rugged, individualistic personalities. Our role models of leaders have been of the Teddy Roosevelt, George Patton, or Vince Lombardi variety. But managing by consensus is the mode of the future and calls for a different breed of leader.

The Japanese don't look for the flashiest individual to lead. Instead they look for those who have the knack of getting people with diverse interests and viewpoints to work together. Team-builders know how to create a situation where each individual works for both his own good and the good of the organization. And they're very adept at persuading, massaging egos, and getting people to trust them.

Hands-on Management Training

Japanese managers often complain that American managers are too logical, analytical, and don't rely enough on gut-level feeling or managing by the heart. And much of the criticism is well founded. A lot of American B-school training (discussed in Chapter 4) is pure logic with little attention paid to the feelings side of management.

Getting a feel for managing—or anything else—can only come through experience. This is probably why Japanese management training provides such broad exposure and is a practice most American companies could profit from. We need to allow our future managers to experience more of what a company is about before we slot them in a division or specialty. Seeing the big picture helps every new manager better understand where his job fits in and how he can best contribute.

The superior quality of Japanese goods and services is another characteristic we need to emulate. Improving quality is the subject of Chapter 7.

It's clear that both Japan and the U.S. are learning a lot from each other in the race for industrial supremacy. Through this healthy competition let's hope both nations emerge as winners.

2

Organizational Problems and Solutions

CHAPTER 4

THE MANAGERIAL MALAISE—WHY JOHNNY CAN'T LEAD

*"At some time in the life cycle of every organization,
its ability to succeed in spite of itself runs out."*
—*Richard H. Brien*

What's the greatest single cause of poor productivity? Inflation? Lazy workers? Unions? The government? According to a survey of executives, it's none of these. In fact, the managers blamed themselves and named poor management as the single greatest obstacle to productivity. The results of the poll, conducted by the newsletter *Productivity*, were a surprise to the surveyors, who felt that management would place the blame elsewhere.

It's encouraging to see managers squarely shouldering the responsibility, and it's likely that their observations are right on target. The greatest key to improving productivity won't be found on the factory floor but in American offices—where more than half of us, including managers, work. If we are going to turn this crisis around, management is going to have to commit itself to being more than a privileged, elitist culture.

In Chapter 2, I took the government to task for creating a self-perpetuating mammoth bureaucracy. But the plain, unfortunate fact is that most bureaucracy in the U.S. exists in the

73

private sector and is growing all the time. The percentage of white-collar employees is increasing and their efficiency is decreasing.

One study conducted by Theodore Barry and Associates, a management consulting firm, concluded that white-collar employees are unproductive at least 50 percent of the time and about 10 percent less productive than their blue-collar colleagues. The study also pointed out that most workers spend much of their time waiting around for things to do. And many office workers, according to the study, don't have a firm idea of their job's goal. If people have to wait around for things to do and don't know their job's main goal, it's obvious that management has dropped the ball.

American government is bureaucratic and inefficient, but much of American industry has become just as bureaucratic and equally inefficient. Think for a moment about the firm you work for. Has it added new layers of management in the past decade? Has the volume of internally generated paperwork and reports increased in the past decade? Has the number of secretarial and administrative assistants increased in the past decade? Are you spending more time at meetings than ever? If you work for a large private corporation you probably answered yes to all or most of these questions. We have become largely a nation managed by bureaucrats. And all of this red tape is strangling productivity.

MANAGERIAL MYOPIA

Like most of us in America, management has become very nearsighted and preoccupied with making the most of today and letting tomorrow take care of itself. This has been a popular approach to managing for almost twenty years. But tomorrow has arrived and it isn't taking care of itself.

"American managers are too worried about short-term profits and too little concerned about their workers," noted Akio Morita, Chairman of Japan's Sony Corporation. "These two mistakes are interconnected and go a long way toward explaining productivity problems."

Morita's observations are both perceptive and accurate. Unlike the Japanese, most American managers don't work with the assumption that either they or their workers will spend an entire career with the company. With turnover as high as it is there is less incentive to invest in the long-range development of people. Why bother if they're here today and gone tomorrow? Or, why bother if they're here forever and I'm gone tomorrow? These are unconscious assumptions that cause managers to pay less attention to developing the long-range potential of employees.

But failure to consider the long-range potential of workers is just the tip of the iceberg. At the same time, managers are under immense pressure to make today's profit picture look as bright as possible. Necessary long-range investments such as buying new plants and equipment or funding basic research lower today's bottom line. Investing in the future thus becomes a lower-priority item. Decisions to innovate and update are postponed in the name of squeezing that last drop of profit out of today's income statement.

The American automobile industry is a classic example of management opting for short-term results at the expense of long-range prosperity. After the 1973 Arab oil embargo, it became obvious that skyrocketing energy costs were going to make gas-guzzling autos no longer practical for the vast majority of Americans. However, just as most of America failed to recognize and deal with the energy shortage, so did the auto industry. Instead of committing itself to a long-range policy of developing high-quality, fuel-efficient cars, the auto industry scaled down existing models and hoped for the best. The result was that fuel-efficient foreign autos accounted for nearly 30 percent of the U.S. auto market in 1980. Opting for the short term in 1973 put Chrysler on the endangered species list and posted record losses for Ford and General Motors in the eighties. Unfortunately, short-term thinking is more the rule than the exception in the corporate offices of America today.

Why is American management so nearsighted? Is it ignorance? Stupidity? Laziness? Actually it's none of these, but rather a number of other factors. One of the biggest pressures comes from Wall Street, where the idea is to make today's financial statements shine and increase the market value of company stock. As Andrew Fuller of Microdata Corp. remarked, "When you're down, you can't sell future performance worth a damn on Wall Street."

But the biggest reason managers opt for short-term results is that their financial and career incentives are frequently based on short-run performance. Promotions, bonuses, stock options, and other perks are based on today's profits. Economic incentives tied to long-range company growth are rare or nonexistent. And managers, being human, are going to behave in their own best interest.

A third factor is that the U.S. economy has been on the skids in recent years. Whenever people begin to feel pessimistic about the future the natural reaction is "To hell with tomorrow—let's take care of today." A manager who takes a loss in profits while choosing to invest in research or new equipment may find himself looking for a job. And what good are long-term results to him if he is fired, retired, or working for another company? Doing the right thing may be self-satisfying but it doesn't buy groceries.

A final factor contributing to managerial myopia and a number of other ills is the way we have been training and educating managers in the past two decades.

WHAT DID YOU LEARN AT THE B-SCHOOL, JOHNNY?

In the past two decades, enrollment in both undergraduate and graduate colleges of business administration has mushroomed. In 1960, the MBA (Master of Business Administration) degree holder was relatively rare. Only 4643 such degrees were granted that year. By 1970 the figure jumped to 21,599, and in 1981 over 54,000 MBA degrees were handed out to promising future captains of industry. Newly minted MBAs armed with their sheepskins, calculators, and a head full of techniques have been calling a lot of the shots. And no doubt a lot of the decisions made are the result of the way they have been trained to think.

Management by Numbers

Business schools have changed a lot in the past twenty years. In the late 1950s they were criticized for not being academic enough and failing to teach scientific, rational, logical, and analytical approaches to managing and running organizations. Taking the criticism to heart, B-school deans and faculty worked very hard to upgrade academically and change the nature of graduate and undergraduate degree programs. The application of computers and mathematical techniques was introduced into the curriculum. Students learned to program computers, work calculus problems, and solve hypothetical business problems using operations research, financial analysis tools, and other techniques. Many of the tools and techniques of the physical sciences were applied to business problems and taught to students. In fact, many B-school faculty members have degrees in disciplines such as mathematics, engineering, chemistry, and physics. And some B-schools went so far as to teach only numbers courses to their students.

The problem is that business never will be an exact science. There are simply too many variables and too many factors operating to make even the most sophisticated techniques very useful. The result is that students in B-schools spend most of their time learning narrow techniques of limited applicability. And what is applicable is only applicable to solving short-run problems. As financial consultant Michael Thomas has remarked, "A lot of what is preached at business schools today is absolute rot. It is paper management. It is not the management of hard resources and people. Business schools teach that business is nothing but the numbers—and the numbers only for the next quarter."

Most B-schools don't have a complete numbers orientation. But business courses are more technique-oriented today than ever. And when you teach people techniques, they are going to use them to solve problems—even if it's the wrong problem. As psychologist Abraham Maslow said, "If the only tool you have to work with is a hammer, you tend to see every problem as a nail."

Narrow, specialized, technique-oriented training may be useful in some entry-level positions, but it's no preparation for a lifetime career in management. While you may think that this is a critical indictment of the way we educate our managers, keep in mind that business schools are giving industry what it has been asking for. When the recruiters come to the campus seeking potential managers, the first thing they want is people with specific skills.

One of the unfortunate byproducts of teaching management by numbers is that management today is drowning in numbers. Inundated with reams of computer printouts and other data, top management's attention is diverted from long-run, important issues to urgent and sometimes meaningless details. The ship floats adrift while the captain tries to plug leaks in the hull. Too little attention is paid to strategic long-term planning as managers are deluged with numbers from their own accounting and budget directors. And what are all those numbers about? Why, the next quarter's profits, of course.

Risk Avoidance 101

Young MBA graduates frequently see themselves as an elite caste that has been trained to walk into corporate offices and assume positions of leadership. Nothing could be further from the truth. Growing numbers of seasoned executives see them as inexperienced amateur technicians who don't understand the management of people or resources. While they are very bright and ambitious, their training for management is sorely lacking in several respects.

Most notably many young MBAs are reluctant to become line managers and assume positions of direct responsibility. Robert Lear, executive in residence at Columbia University, made this point most vividly when he told graduating MBAs "None of you want to be horses. You want to be jockeys, bookies, have the hay concessions for the stables, or best of all, the management consultant to the racetrack. That's why none of you will ever be CEO of a major corporation."

Perhaps the biggest void in B-school training is that students aren't trained to think as entrepreneurs and risk-taking innovators. Rather they are preoccupied with learning complex techniques and analyzing detailed cases. MBA candidates are given little, if any, encouragement or opportunity to display any creative thinking. Yet all businesses begin and prosper with new ideas and established businesses die without them.

It's bad enough that so little attention is paid to innovation, but the problem is compounded by the way B-school students are trained to make decisions. The two criteria are: maximize short-term profits while minimizing risk. Or, stated another way: Protect yourself at all times; take the money and run. Any company can increase short-term profits with such a strategy. But the price of short-term risk avoidance is long-range stagnation. The auto and steel industries are cases in point.

Risk avoidance isn't prevalent only in the B-school. What is being taught is a mirror reflection of the way decisions are being made in corporate offices. The following real example is typical of the decision-making mentality in many of today's skyscrapers:

> It's much more difficult to come up with a synthetic meat product than a lemon-lime cake mix. But you work on a lemon-lime cake mix because you know exactly what the return is going to be. A synthetic steak is going to take a lot longer, require a much bigger investment, and the risk of failure will be greater.

Where would we be today if men such as Thomas Edison, Henry Ford, and other innovators had made decisions from that perspective?

Lessons from Learned Men

Another major problem is the tremendous gap between the world of academia and the world of the practicing manager. Many B-school professors have no interest or experience in working with the problems of everyday management. Yet they train the business leaders of tomorrow. Universities typically reward faculty members for publishing scholarly articles in academic journals and presenting scholarly papers at professional academic meetings. And God help us if we are counting on scholarly papers to solve our productivity problems. Most academic business research is overspecialized, highly technical, and unreadable to all but a handful of other specialists. It is true that publications such as *Harvard Business Review*, Indiana University's *Business Horizons*, and some others do provide interesting insights and very useful information for practicing managers. But these periodicals aren't scholarly journals in the true sense. Rather, they are classified as professional journals.

Like all other bureaucracies, universities have their own set of rules for advancement. And young faculty members seeking promotion or tenure have to play the game. Most important is publishing in select journals. Good teaching is paid lip service. Every school wants it but very few reward it. Scholarly research is the name of the game. The only problem is that most of it has little or no relevance to the real world. The attitude of the pure academic researcher is "Please don't disturb me. I'm playing with my mental blocks." Yet these are the people that many B-schools are most likely to hire, tenure, and reward.

TOO MANY CHIEFS

It's bad enough that today's manager suffers from myopic pressures and inadequate training. The third and perhaps greatest cause of the managerial malaise is simply that we have too many of them. Time after time corporations have seen fit to add layer upon layer of management to their ranks with the hope of providing more growth, direction, and leadership for the company. The swelling of the ranks of middle managers and specialists has been a very common characteristic of practically every large organization. In just thirty years, Swift and Company increased its managerial ranks over 400 percent, while in the same period the number of workers increased only 50 percent. The rule of thumb for managing growing, complex organizations has been to increase the number of managers, often to the demise of the company. While it's true that adding layers of middle management is sometimes necessary to improve coordination, there are a number of definite liabilities.

Communication Breakdowns

Everytime a new layer of management is added the chief executive officer is removed another notch from the bottom of the organization. Most top managers only know what they are told by others. And every time a message passes through a level of management parts of it are selected, filtered out, and distorted. By the time information travels through the bureaucratic maze it's likely to be entirely different from the situation being reported. The result is that many top-management decisions are made on the basis of information that is nearer fiction than fact. Billy Carter was once asked what he felt was his brother's greatest mistake as president. Billy replied that Jimmy's greatest mistake was thinking that Washington, D.C., was the real world. Men at the tops of large pyramidal hierarchies rarely know what is really happening. And everybody else in the company knows that they don't know.

Management by Activity

As staff specialists and middle managers are added to the organization they create committees, reports, rules, policies, and procedures to carry out stated objectives. And too often all of this red tape snowballs into a sequence of activities that becomes an end in itself. Committees become standing committees. Meetings become weekly meetings. Reports become semiannual reports regardless of their utility. One day management realizes how overworked it is. There is just too much to do! But does it cut back and question existing activities? Not usually. Instead it hires more managers and specialists to help with all this new work. And you can guess what happens. The cycle repeats itself. More managers and specialists are hired—and create more rules, more committees, more reports, more policies, and more procedures. Everybody becomes so busy being busy that the major, important goals are lost in the shuffle of memos, meetings, and computer printouts. This is best illustrated by what I call the bureaucratic cycle.

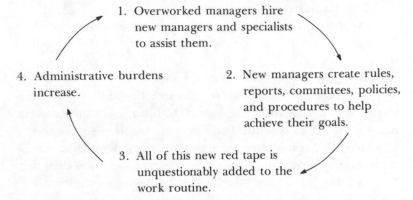

1. Overworked managers hire new managers and specialists to assist them.

2. New managers create rules, reports, committees, policies, and procedures to help achieve their goals.

3. All of this new red tape is unquestionably added to the work routine.

4. Administrative burdens increase.

Managers spend a great deal of time creating work for each other. Much of it is needless and counterproductive. Precious time that could be devoted to developing employees, new products, or long-range planning is wasted on meaningless activities.

As an activity becomes part of the routine it tends to become more important than the purpose it was intended to serve. And the older an activity becomes, the more it gains in respectability. What starts as a temporary activity becomes a habit, then a procedure, and finally some activities become so entrenched that they are believed to be indispensable. Bosses push subordinates to do activities rather than produce results. New ideas and creative approaches to doing things are swept aside by those caught in the activity trap. Employees are evaluated in light of their types of activities rather than the results they produce. Filling out forms correctly, being at all meetings on time, and preparing reports according to a prescribed format become yardsticks for performance rather than being innovative or doing a job well.

Managing by activity is the most dehumanizing aspect of bureaucracy and it hurts the organizations that create it. People fall into a rut, go through the motions, and pray for Friday. They become bored, feel alienated, and many leave for greener pastures or psychologically retire. The company loses a tremendous source of productive potential as people caught in the activity trap aren't able to grow in their jobs. Everybody loses.

Corporate Gamesmanship

Large, complex, inflated managerial hierarchies increase the chances for all sorts of political games, intrigue, and one-upmanship. Ambitious managers frequently devise ingenious schemes to expand their base of power and increase their chances of advancement. And many of these schemes are counterproductive. For example, department heads in large organizations often view other heads with contempt and see them as threats to their realm of authority rather than as teammates. Every bureaucracy has its little fiefdoms and rulers who jealously guard their territories. Conflicts between departments frequently evolve into zero-sum games where someone ultimately wins and someone loses. Thomas Martin, author and college president, summed up the situation well when he described administrative maneuvering as an endless game of bureaucratic "tit for tat" and wrote: "Everyone knows that the name of the game is to let the other guy have all of the little tats and to keep all of the big tits for yourself."

But all this political game-playing wastes a lot of time and energy. Worse yet, most of these games hurt productivity and can destroy an organization when carried to extremes. It's naive to believe that you can remove political game-playing from organizations. However, increasing the layers of management only invites such problems and increases the odds of their severity.

Diluted Decisions

Risk avoidance, as pointed out earlier, is a serious problem with today's managers. Perhaps it's because we have become too specialized and too knowledgeable. Inventor Charles Kettering once warned that knowledge frequently breeds caution. The more we know about a situation the more obstacles we see and the more inclined we are to know why something can't be done.

Frequently, the people who get things done are those who fail to realize it can't be done and do it.

Whatever the reasons, bureaucracies and bureaucrats develop all sorts of techniques for avoiding decisions. Here are some of the more common ones:

1. Say no to any proposals or innovations that have a large possibility of failure. It's the easy way out. If he says yes, the manager has to explain why and sell it to people above him. If he approves, he will have to do additional work. If the project fails, he will be held accountable. But saying no is safe and fail-proof because the innovation will never be tried and soon be forgotten.

2. As an alternative to saying no, delay a decision. As C. Northcote Parkinson noted, "Delay is the deadliest form of denial."

3. Appoint a committee or (better yet) several committees to study the problem. Committees are a great way to diffuse accountability and pass the buck. Everyone becomes a little responsible and no one becomes totally responsible. No one person can be held accountable if things go wrong and no one can totally get the credit if things go right. Every decision becomes everybody's business and everyone spends his time coordinating and checking with ten other people before making a move.

True, committees can be a very positive vehicle for motivating people through participation. And we do need more participation at all organizational levels. However, too often we have participation without accountability.

4. Hire a consultant to study the problem. The manager then tells the consultant what he wants done and pays her a fee to write a report recommending his desires. If things go wrong, the manager can always say that he acted on the basis of highly paid, expert advice. Like committees, consultants have their proper place and can be extremely useful. Unfortunately, they too are often used as vehicles for buck-passing.

The net result of decision delays and avoidances is that red tape is created, opportunities are missed, and managers spend much of their time busily conferring with each other and wondering why they are so overworked.

The Creation of a White-Collar Elite

One reason we have too many bureaucrats is the fact that we have trained and educated so many people for white-collar jobs. And the supply of such workers creates its own demand. This phenomenon is best explained by what is known as Bunk Carter's Law: "At any given time there are more important people in the world than important jobs to contain them." When we have so many people trained to assume important jobs it becomes necessary to create important jobs for them. All of which leads to increases in department heads, staff specialists, and vice-presidents whether they are needed or not.

Until recently, white-collar workers haven't been subjected to massive firings and layoffs like their blue-collar colleagues. When an executive fires blue-collar workers to raise factory productivity, he dismisses someone from a different working class, someone with different values, education, and background. But firing white-collar workers to raise office productivity hits much closer to home. It's far more threatening to fire someone performing a similar role in a similar job. If a manager can fire workers beneath him, it means he can be fired by those above him. The result is that white-collar workers are less likely to be dismissed than their blue-collar colleagues when the business falls on hard times.

Social status and occupational prestige are the driving forces behind the creation of the white-collar elite. We see white-collar and professional jobs as being of a higher order than blue-collar work. And this is one societal value that can only hurt productivity. As long as we believe that it's better to be a second-rate manager than a first-rate plumber, we will have more second-rate managers and more poor plumbers.

THE BASICS OF EXCELLENT MANAGEMENT

While many companies suffer from the managerial malaise, a number of others are extremely healthy and very well run. Several years ago McKinsey and Co., a management consulting firm, studied management practices at thirty-seven well-managed organizations with the hope of finding what practices all of them had in common. Of those thirty-seven companies, ten were heavily focused on in the study: IBM, Texas Instruments, Hewlett-Packard, 3M, Digital Equipment, Proctor & Gamble, Johnson & Johnson, McDonald's, Dana, and Emerson Electric. The findings were most interesting.

Above all, the study found that high-quality managers work hard to keep things simple. Goals, strategies, organizational structures, and communication are all kept as simple as possible. While many of these companies use the formulas, tools, and techniques that are taught today in B-schools, they don't use them as substitutes for sound management. In fact, some managers described MBA graduates as bright planners but not the type to implement programs. And they told horror stories of having learned this the hard way.

Additionally, the study found eight basic attributes that all well-managed operations had in common. These attributes are simple in concept and require neither high IQs, high technology, nor high finance to implement. However, they do require managers to invest their time, effort, and—most of all—ability to think for themselves. Here they are:

1. Management Is Action- and Results-Oriented

Managers don't allow themselves to fall into the trap of overanalyzing and questioning new products and ideas. Complicated procedures for evaluating ideas are avoided. They gather data, implement the idea, and develop it rather than waiting for perfect information and a perfect plan. New ideas are tried, tested, and perfected. Those that work are pushed. Those that don't are quickly dropped. The key idea is _do it_, _fix it_, _try it_.

This is quite in contrast to the way bureaucracies frequently operate. For example, McKinsey found one company that required 223 separate committees to approve a new idea before it could be put into production!

To insure a results orientation, companies set a few, well-defined goals for their managers. One Texas Instruments executive explained that after experimenting they have found that more than two objectives are no objective for a senior manager.

2. Structure Is Simple and Staff Is Small

All of the ten major companies in the study are multibillion-dollar operations. Yet' they managed to avoid bureaucracy by organizing into small autonomous units. Within the units, activities are further broken down into small manageable work teams. The companies also take pains to avoid bureaucracy by keeping staffs small. For example, fewer than a hundred people run Dana, which does over $3 billion in sales each year.

3. Well-Managed Companies are Customer-Driven

They don't look for new insights and ideas by poring over marketing research data or asking their scientists what's new. They begin their search for new products and ideas by talking with their customers. Top managers at IBM and Digital Equipment spend at least thirty days per year conferring with top customers and both companies compensate their managers, in part, on the basis of customer-satisfaction surveys. Successful companies view the customer as a central part of their business and realize that most new product ideas come directly from the customer.

4. Productivity Improvement Is Through People

In addition to improving productivity through new equipment, good companies stress productivity through motivating employees. Production teams are formed and given the autonomy to set their own target dates. The results have been excellent and employees generally set challenging but attainable goals for themselves. Teamwork in meeting goals is stressed and outstanding production is recognized and rewarded. In addition to bonuses, badges, medals, pins, and other nonmonetary rewards are used as incentives. At Texas Instruments, outstanding production teams are recognized by being invited to describe their success to the board of directors.

5. The Spirit of Entrepreneurship Is Encouraged

Well-managed companies encourage innovative risk-taking by their managers and give them the autonomy to do so. For example, plant managers at Dana make their own purchasing decisions and start productivity programs on their own. The results of these programs have been excellent in improving productivity and reducing grievances.

As a further incentive to encourage entrepreneurship, divisions are allowed to reinvest most of their earnings in their own operations. The companies realize that division managers aren't likely to act like entrepreneurs if they have to give most of their earnings to the corporate hierarchy.

Most important, new ideas are sought and encouraged at all staff levels. For example, Texas Instruments has created a group of "listeners"—138 senior technical people whose purpose is to assess new ideas. Staff members are encouraged to bring new ideas to one of the listeners for an evaluation. If the idea is approved by the senior technician, he can authorize start-up funds for product experimentation. One new product that resulted from this was TI's profitable Speak 'n' Spell device.

6. They Stress Doing One Thing Well

All the major companies studied stressed one key business value with religious zeal. At IBM and McDonald's it's customer service. At Proctor & Gamble it's product quality. At 3M and Hewlett-Packard it's new-product development. At Dana it's productivity improvement. Whatever the key value, it is stressed over and over and over until it becomes the focal point that everyone in the corporate culture identifies with. The outstanding companies don't have monthly or yearly themes. They have one theme and stick to it.

7. They Do What They Know Best and Stick To It

All successful companies in the study knew their strengths and built on them. They resisted temptations to move into areas and acquire businesses they knew little about. As Robert W.

Johnson, former chairman of Johnson & Johnson said, "Never acquire any business you don't know how to run."

8. Controls Are Few but Tight

Managers are given lots of freedom in day-to-day operations but a few variables are tightly controlled. This allows top management to keep a rein on the direction of the company without smothering it with red tape. For example, when Rene McPherson became president of Dana, he threw out all of the company's policy manuals. In its place he substituted a one-page philosophy statement and a control system that required divisions to report costs and revenues each day. Too many controls create overly cautious and risk-avoiding managers who, in turn, can cause a company to lose its vitality and growth.

How does your company measure up against those eight characteristics?

In another study, the American Management Association, in cooperation with McBer & Co. of Boston, analyzed more than 2000 managers over a five-year period. From this they found nineteen competencies that directly contributed to managerial performance. Here are the characteristics that, according to the study, contribute to making a manager effective. The characteristics are centered around five clusters:

Entrepreneurial cluster
   1. An interest in efficiency and doing things better
   2. A bias toward action

Intellectual cluster
   3. Logical thought—sees events in sequences
   4. Conceptualization—ability to put unrelated pieces together and see the big picture
   5. Diagnostic use of concepts and models

Socioemotional cluster
   6. Self-control
   7. Spontaneity
   8. Perceptual objectivity

Use as check list for review of Gen'l Managers performance.

   9. Accurate self-assessment
10. Stamina/adaptability

Interpersonal cluster

11. Self-confidence
12. Developing others
13. Concern with impact
14. Use of unilateral power
15. Use of socialized power
16. Use of oral communication
17. Positive regard
18. Managing group processes
19. Knowledge—the special information a manager needs to do his job effectively

Not surprisingly, the results of both studies have much in common even though their purposes were different. Both studies stress the need for action-oriented, innovative, risk-taking management. Both studies stress that the manager needs to be able to think for himself—not just logically, but creatively, objectively, and conceptually as well. Both stress the need for management to be able to communicate, motivate, and develop others. And both studies stress that good managers involve themselves only in managing activities that they have special knowledge about.

PRESCRIPTIONS FOR THE MANAGERIAL MALAISE

It's been suggested that the turtle is the best-equipped creature to become a modern manager. It has a strong back, thick skin, keeps its ears close to the ground, eyes wide open, moves slowly to avoid being trapped, knows when to stand perfectly still, doesn't stick its neck out unless it plans to move, and lives longer than most mammals. But on the other hand, the turtle isn't agile, lacks charisma, has no followers, and is usually found alone rather than as part of a group.

Our problem is that we have too many managerial turtles. Improving productivity in organizations must begin with changing the way we train and motivate our business leaders to think and act.

Bifocals for Managerial Myopia

The successful manager of the future will be able to meet short-term pressures while not losing sight of long-range goals. He should think of his role as one of dual commitment to two time frames. As Northrop's Chairman Thomas Jones put it, "We tell our guys they're supposed to take care of short-term profits with their left hand and long-term performance with their right."

Telling managers to be more long-run oriented may make them aware of the problem, but it isn't enough. As long as the company rewards short-term performance, that's all it's going to get. There are a number of things companies can do to ensure that a commitment to long-range improvements is more than mere lip service. Here are several:

1. The most important thing is to link executive incentives to long-run performance. For example, a manager could be paid a base salary and two bonuses. The first bonus could be immediate and based on short-term performance. The second could be based on long-range decisions made by the manager and paid on the basis of long-term performance at a later date. This would encourage managers to meet the short-run pressures and take long-range, innovative risks.

Some companies already have incentive systems for long-term performance. Johnson & Johnson awards stock credits to higher-level executives. The value of the credits is based on short-term performance. However, they can only cash in the stock on leaving the company. Thus they collect later on long-term decisions made now. For lower-level executives, J & J has discretionary bonus systems allowing bonus money allocation for smart risks and long-range decisions.

2. Another possibility is to review managerial performance over an extended time period, say every five years. Managers could be asked to set growth and earnings objectives for that

time period and a bonus system which pays them on the basis of how well those objectives are met could be created.

3. Nonmonetary incentives must also be set up. Managers are only human and usually have rather large egos. Therefore one very good incentive strategy is to reward managers who take solid, long-term risks with status and recognition. Certificates of merit, pins, and membership in an exclusive company club for long-range thinkers may all sound corny. But they do work as positive motivators. Public praise is also an invaluable non-monetary reward.

4. Another cure for managerial myopia is to change the internal accounting system for reporting earnings. For example, one idea is to allow funds that managers allocate to long-term projects, such as capital investment and research, to be deducted from future earnings at much later time periods. This would reduce much of the pressure to look good today at tomorrow's expense. And the long-run investment costs could be deducted from earnings during the time periods when the investment is paying off.

5. Finally, the company needs to identify those strategic factors that are most associated with its particular long-run growth and link them to managerial incentives. For example, is your company's long-range growth and prosperity most dependent on new-product development? If so, pay the largest bonuses and give the greatest recognition to managers who contribute most in that area. Is it customer service? Reward managers who come up with new and better ways to aid the customer. Does your company's future growth depend on increasing its market share? Then reward managers who find ways to get a bigger piece of the action. The basic law at work here is that organizations get what they reward—not what they ask for. Reward the type of behavior that's most important and you'll get the type of behavior that's most important. And be sure to allow for failure. If managers aren't given the right to be wrong, the climate for innovation and risk-taking will be destroyed.

Wholesale Changes in Business Education

Highly specialized, narrow education is a poor way to train tomorrow's managers. The business education of the future must be broader-based, holistic, and more realistic in nature. Managers need this type of training much more than technical sophistication and short-run gimmickry. In the past twenty years B-schools have achieved greater respect from their academic colleagues, but none of their colleagues are faced with the problems of managing a company. To provide the leadership that is crucial to our nation's long-run prosperity, business education is going to have to change in the following ways:

1. Entrepreneurial thinking needs to be stressed. As the studies revealed, risk-taking, innovative, action-oriented managers are the most effective. More than anything else, management training needs to stress that a manager is much more than someone who facilitates, mediates, and calculates. *The primary job of a manager is to make something happen.* 〒

2. There must be an increased emphasis and understanding about the nature of implementing solutions to problems. Most of our young business leaders have no earthly idea of what it takes to manage a business. And neither do many of the people who teach them. Newly graduated MBAs can analyze problems and recommend a ton of solutions. But putting the solutions into effect is where their training is woefully inadequate. Business training must place less emphasis on analyzing problems and more on putting solutions into action.

One way to stress the realitics of managing is to require students to serve an internship working for a company and implementing a new product or service. Another is to require students to work in industry before returning for an MBA degree. Still another alternative would be to hire successful executives to teach courses in B-schools. All the plans and techniques in the world are worthless if you can't implement them. It's much like the plight of the man who knew forty-eight ways to make love but didn't have a woman.

3. Human skills must be given greater emphasis in B-school

curricula. Teaching technique-oriented management only results in highly skilled bureaucrats. Students should spend more time learning what it takes to motivate people and keep them motivated to perform. Case role-playing and team-building exercises, when properly carried out, can portray real-life situations and give students practice in dealing with types of problems they will be likely to face as managers. It's a trite idea but truer today than ever—the ability to deal effectively with people is a most crucial management skill.

4. Other necessary managerial skills that have been ignored need to be taught. Most business training is left-brain oriented while right-brain skills are all but ignored. Yet management requires a lot of right-brain skills. Being able to put unrelated pieces together and see a problem, the ability to think up new ideas, and grasping the big picture are all necessary skills for managers. Yet most business training emphasizes analysis rather than synthesis. Many creative and conceptual skills can be learned and developed. In Chapter 12 you will learn how.

Other crucial skills that have been ignored need to be stressed. For example, time management is a skill rarely found in a B-school course or curriculum. Yet a manager who can't effectively manage his time is doomed to failure. And remember the McKinsey study on what makes excellent management? You won't find anything like it covered in most business curricula. Yet this type of basic information is most vital.

5. B-schools must refocus and change their reward systems for their faculty. Instead of rewarding faculty for publishing a narrow, scholarly, irrelevant treatise in an obscure journal, why not give greater rewards for writing or consulting that contributes to the solution of real business problems? Professors should be encouraged to work and consult with businesses in order to gain a greater understanding of real-world business problems. Many of them already do, but far too many don't.

6. Finally, management training needs to become more philosophical. Managers need to have a broad understanding of what their values are and what they are hoping to achieve for

themselves and their organization—not just for the next quarter but rather for the next quarter-century. A manager without such a frame of reference runs the high risk of falling into the activity trap and never climbing out.

Bureaucratic Red Tape Must Be Cut

The bureaucratic cycle has resulted in a huge increase in meaningless activities and overinflated staffs. And trimming down the red tape is essential to restoring sound management.

How do you cut red tape? Above all you must work hard to make things simpler and eliminate *anything* that isn't absolutely essential. Here is an exercise that can help you simplify your job:

1. Begin by answering the following question: What are you paid to do? Be careful to answer this in terms of results, not activities. You aren't paid to read *The Wall Street Journal,* go to meetings, or visit clients. You're paid to get results, not perform activities. If your job is only activities, your job is expendable.

2. Make a list of the activities you perform in your job. Then consider each activity and ask "What's the worst thing that will happen if I don't do this?" If the answer isn't too bad, it's an activity that can be eliminated. Scratch it off the list.

3. Take remaining necessary activities and list each step taken to complete the activity. Break the activity down into as many detailed pieces as possible. It helps to construct a flow diagram showing the sequence of steps involved doing the activity.

4. The next step is to question every detail of the activity. Which details are unnecessary? Which can be combined? Which ones are being done somewhere else? What else could be substituted? How can you do it faster and easier?

5. Complete steps 3 and 4 for all remaining necessary activities. It's a long, tedious process, but if everyone in an administrative job performed this exercise a whole lot of red tape could be cut and a whole lot of money could be saved and a whole lot of time and effort could be put to better use.

Some organizations have been experimenting with work

simplification to increase white-collar productivity and have reported excellent results. For example, Intel Corp. reports an estimated saving of at least $2.5 million a year and the elimination of 153 jobs.

If you are an executive attempting to trim the bureaucracy, begin by reassuring people that they won't be fired if their job is eliminated. In fact, one crafty employer paid a bonus to anyone who could find a way to eliminate his own job! Now, that's working smarter.

Displaced workers can be retrained for a new, productive job that makes use of their aptitudes, interest, and abilities. That's what Japanese corporations do. Why can't we?

Work simplification techniques are also useful for examining office procedures and activities involving numbers of people. For example, Intel reduced the number of steps for hiring an employee from 364 to 250 and cut the number of Xerox copies in an accounts payable department by almost 30,000 per month.

Eliminating the bureaucratic fat from today's skyscrapers is the greatest key to improving managerial and white-collar productivity. Trim staffs are better equipped to respond to changing conditions and managers are free to perform the essential tasks of motivating workers and making things happen.

HOW TO WORK SMARTER WITH YOUR BOSS

These are tough times to be a manager; if you are one, you know what I mean. The normal demands of a difficult job have been complicated and compounded by all the problems previously discussed. You may not have enough clout to cut red tape or create the organizational changes that will improve the overall management of your company. But all of us can help our bosses and ourselves to work smarter by consciously striving to create a harmonious working relationship.

Establishing a good working relationship with your boss doesn't mean becoming a political gamesman or apple-polisher. It means making a deliberate and conscious effort to work with your boss with the goal of helping your boss, your company, and yourself achieve the best results possible.

Most of us don't consciously try to improve our relationship with the boss. Many feel powerless to do anything about it and others think of the relationship as one of parent to child. It isn't. The relationship between you and your boss is one of two adults who are mutually dependent on each other. If you consciously practice the following guidelines, you will realize that you can improve both your and your boss' effectiveness:

1. Know your boss. What is he paid to do? What are his priorities? What are his strengths? What are his weaknesses? What's his work style? Does he like to delegate or does he remain involved in every activity? Does he prefer conflict or shrink from confrontation? Does he like things in writing or deplore paperwork? Is he better in the morning or the afternoon? What pressures are on him? What does he need from you? How can you make his job easier and more productive? Before you can establish a good working relationship you have to gather as much information and understanding about the boss as you can.

2. Take a self-inventory. What are you paid to do? What are your strengths and weaknesses? What's your work style? Do you require close supervision or do you prefer to work alone? Do you need frequent feedback or is a periodic review enough? What do you need from your boss? How can the boss improve your job? What do you want from your job? Gaining self-awareness can be rather difficult and sometimes painful. You may find it helpful to ask several friends or colleagues to help you get an external viewpoint.

3. Once you have gathered information about yourself and your boss, try to make adjustments in the working relationship that are mutually beneficial and meet the expectations of both of you. Each is a fallible human being and neither is very likely to change. However, once you have uncovered the weaknesses, pitfalls, and blind spots the chances are you can work around them and make adjustments to minimize their impact. If your boss is forgetful, follow up important face-to-face communications with a memo. If he likes to be involved with all decisions, keep him posted about yours. If either you or he is not at your best in the mornings, confer about important issues at later times. If you

need more frequent feedback, ask him for it and explain why. Like every other good relationship, a good working relationship accommodates individual differences. The key is to build the relationship on your individual strengths and work around your individual weaknesses.

4. Keep your boss informed. A good working relationship takes much more than good, open communication. But without good communication it's impossible. Bosses need to hear both good and bad news; if your boss only wants to hear good news, the odds are he won't be your boss very long. Managers are in the problem-solving business and need to hear about successes *and* failures. Be alert for potential problems and point them out to your boss before they escalate into major crises. It can save both of you a lot of future headaches.

5. Don't promise more than you can deliver. This is a sure way to get yourself labeled as undependable and unreliable. And no one wants a subordinate who can't be trusted. It may impress the boss to tell him that you can have the report on his desk a week early, but you will only hurt yourself by failing to meet an early deadline.

6. Respect his time as a precious resource. Most bosses today are very much overworked. Don't waste their time with trivial problems. If you have a problem you want to discuss with the boss, write it down and list some alternative solutions before meeting with him. This will make the meeting more efficient and tell the boss that you have thought through the problem before taking his time. And showing respect for the boss' time increases the odds that he will respect yours.

The managerial malaise is a difficult disease but the cures aren't impossible, immoral, or fattening. Curing it involves a lot of changes, and change is always tough. But until we eradicate the plague of short-term, risk-avoiding, bureaucratic thinking from our large corporations, American productivity will continue to flounder.

CHAPTER 5

TURNING ON TURNED-OFF WORKERS

"Every C.E.O. I've ever talked to, once pushed into a corner with two martinis, will tell you that though the myth is that he stands with the reins of power in his hands, his big question is not 'How shall I drive this marvelous chariot?' but 'How the hell can I get these goddam horses to move their asses at all?'"

—*Geoffrey Hazard*

"Take this job and shove it!"

"Try to imagine how little I care."

"Why should I worry about going to hell? I already work there five days a week."

Does that sound like you? If you work for a living, you may see yourself in those statements, because today's American worker is becoming more and more frustrated with his job. In fact, the situation has deteriorated to such an extent that fewer than half of all Americans report being very satisfied with their jobs and 60 percent would prefer to have a different job.

At first glance, all this discontent seems confusing. Today's workers are very well paid and have more benefits than at any time in American history. Yet survey after survey reveals increasing worker discontent. And almost everyone agrees that worker attitudes play an important factor in declining U.S. productivity. While it's true that satisfied workers aren't necessarily productive, it's also true that worker discontent can lead to absenteeism, high turnover, unnecessary conflicts, and a host of other counterproductive problems. Perhaps the impact of turned-off work-ers was best illustrated by the boss who was asked "How many people do you have working here?" His reply: "About half."

The problem isn't that people are apathetic or that the work ethic is dead. In fact, while today's worker is dissatisfied, it's also true that his job is more important to him than ever. The decline of close family ties, church membership, and small communities has resulted in work becoming a more important place to satisfy needs that used to be satisfied off the job, such as status, self-fulfillment, and friendship. And it's the demand to satisfy these needs through work that's causing a lot of worker frustration.

To define the problem as lazy young people or social misfits is a grave mistake. And the number of turned-off workers has become so large that it would be economic suicide to fire or ignore them. It's another crucial problem that all of us are going to have to work together to solve.

THE OLD GUARD VERSUS THE NEW BREED

The key to understanding the turned-off worker begins with a look at how workers have changed in the past several decades. Today's labor force is far different in its composition and its values from the labor force of the 1950s. For example:

- The typical worker of the fifties was a man who worked and had a wife who stayed home and cared for children. Today only about 15 percent of workers are of this kind and the typical worker of the eighties is almost as likely to be a woman as a man. In the majority of today's house-holds there are no children or the wife works.
- The typical fifties worker believed that working hard to be a good provider was his most important role as a man. Today's younger worker probably has a working spouse (although many are single) and sees the role of breadwin-ner as a burden to be shared.
- The worker of the fifties had experienced the Great De-pression and World War II. He believed that sacrifice, hard work, and self-denial were the keys to security and

economic wellbeing. Contrast this to today's new workers, who grew up in times of prosperity, Vietnam, and Watergate. Not surprisingly, they are less likely to believe that hard work pays off, that self-sacrifice is necessary, or that authority can be trusted. Today's younger worker is much less likely to be the organization man who sacrifices himself for the good of the company.

- Fifties workers believed in discipline, organization, and following orders without questioning, but today's new workers are better educated. And education makes questioners out of people. The new breed wants to know why it's done that way and why they have to do it.

- Finally, the traditional worker believed in a fair day's work for a fair day's pay. And that's where the problems begin. The new breed demands much more than a fair day's pay. As labor relations analyst John R. Browning put it, "They want nothing less than eight hours of meaningful skillfully guided, personally satisfying work for eight hours' pay. And that's not easy for most companies to provide."

OLD INCENTIVES DON'T WORK AS THEY USED TO

Years ago, motivating people to work was much simpler and management had a number of basic tools that could be readily applied. But the workforce has become so diverse and values have changed so much that the traditional motivational incentives have lost some or all of their effectiveness. Young people today come to work with very different expectations and motivations; it's the failure to recognize this fact that is creating so many disenchanted younger and older workers. Here are some of the basic motivational tools management has traditionally relied on:

The Big Stick

Fear, traditionally the big stick of management, is very simple in concept. The manager doesn't have to play amateur psychologist but simply demands that workers perform or else. In leaner times fear was an effective but distasteful motivator. But today fear has lost practically all its clout for the following reasons:

1. The fear of being fired has been diluted by the two-income family. If one wage-earner gets fired, there is another income.

2. Social programs and unemployment benefits virtually guarantee that no one is going to starve if he loses his job. In fact, 20 percent of all households have no wage-earners but live on pensions and welfare programs.

3. The plentifulness of skilled and high-technology jobs in the labor market is such that many young workers have other options. Getting fired is no longer always an economic disaster. What many young workers fear more than dismissal is meaningless work that leaves them feeling empty.

4. The new breed perceives job security as a right rather than a privilege. This attitude is completely alien to traditional workers, who were grateful just to have a job. Younger workers feel that the company *owes them* job security. And this is simply a natural byproduct of a generation reared during prosperous times. Nevertheless, it's difficult to motivate someone to work by promising job security when he feels it should be given rather than earned. All workers think job security is important, but it's more of a demand than an incentive.

5. Fear has always been a rather expensive way to motivate people. The worker has to believe that he will be caught and punished if he doesn't do the job. And this in turn means that elaborate and costly control systems have to be formed to keep a close check on workers.

One of the classic modern examples of fear motivation was practiced by the W. T. Grant Co. on its store managers. The Steak and Beans program, as it was called, attempted to motivate store managers with a host of negative incentives. Store managers who failed to meet their credit quotas were hit in the face with custard pies, had their ties cut in half, were forced to run around their stores backward and to push peanuts with their

noses. There was even one unconfirmed report of a district manager being required to walk around a hotel lobby dressed in
nothing but a diaper! The W. T. Grant Co. went bankrupt in
1977.

Money

Money is still very important to people and always will be,
and many of our traditional incentives are tied to money in one
form or another. Everybody wants more and most people will
tell you that they don't have enough.

For most of us money is still a very effective incentive. However, for a growing percentage of younger workers, money has
little effect on motivating them to work harder. Their attitude is:
"Work until you have enough money to pay the bills and then
opt for leisure time." All of this is very puzzling to those who
hold traditional values.

One example is the young machinist who wanted to take
three days' vacation to go deer hunting. His supervisor refused
his request because the department was very pressed and being
forced to work overtime and on Saturdays. The machinist, who
had a record of tardiness, came to work thirty minutes late and
the harassed supervisor told him "If you are tardy one more
time this month, you'll be suspended for three days without
pay." You can guess who was late the next morning. The
machinist perceived the monetary "threat" as his chance to go
deer hunting and showed up tardy. The machinist was suspended, went deer hunting, and got what he asked for. And
management applied the "proper" disciplinary policy. But the
work didn't get done.

Another reason money has lost some of its clout is that most
jobs don't have monetary incentives directly linked to productivity. Seven out of ten jobs in the U.S. have no direct relationship
between money and performance. And study after study has
concluded that simply paying someone a higher salary or increasing fringe benefits has no effect on motivation to work.

In many jobs today, money causes people to hold back efforts rather than work harder. When each of us goes to work, we make an unwritten psychological contract with our employers in which we agree to give time and effort in return for certain rewards such as money, meaningful work, security, status, acceptance, and the like. We also demand that we be rewarded fairly, as *we* perceive it, relative to our peers. Whenever we feel someone is being paid more for doing what we perceive as the same or less work, motivation can only suffer and we tend to hold back our efforts and do the minimum. Worse yet, in many salaried jobs the most highly paid people are the most recently hired ones. All of this can have a disastrous effect on company loyalty and the motivation to work.

Reliance on Technology and Structure

Another traditional management technique to ensure productivity has been to create a work situation where individual motivation really isn't important. Work has been automated or workers organized into assembly lines where they have little control over their jobs and are forced to do repetitious, boring tasks. While this may have been effective in a manufacturing-oriented economy, most of us no longer work in manufacturing. Over 70 percent of us are in government and service-oriented jobs where productivity isn't as easily and directly measurable. In a service job, productivity is much more than simply output per manhour. It's the overall picture of how well things get done. And service organizations and jobs depend much more on such human factors as employee dedication, motivation, and a willingness to give without holding back. As more of us assume white-collar service jobs, structure and technology will become less important and human motivation and incentives will become more important.

The Belief That Hard Work Pays Off

At one time management could simply assume that most workers came to the job believing that hard work and sacrifice paid off. This was a correct assumption. However, a decreasing percentage of younger workers believe in the value of hard work. While they are willing to work hard under the right conditions, they're too smart to believe that sweat and elbow grease automatically guarantee success. Younger workers are much more likely to be dedicated to self-fulfillment and leisure pursuits than company loyalty and hard work for its own sake. And if they don't like the job or the way they're being treated, you can count on them to leave—or, worse yet, retire psychologically and continue to draw a paycheck.

In summary, management has relied on tools such as fear, money, work structures that don't depend on motivation and traditional worker values to ensure productivity. Yet all of these tools aren't properly suited to the needs of many of today's workers. Pollster Daniel Yankelovich was right on target when he wrote "I can sum up what's happening in the American work force today in a single phrase: a growing mismatch between incentives and motivations."

WHAT EVERYBODY WANTS

Motivating anyone is a very complicated business. And the job has been further complicated by the fact that the workforce today is more diverse than ever. Yet for all the differences in race, sex, education, and age, almost all of us would like to satisfy several very strong needs through our work if given the opportunity. Here are four.

To Feel Free and in Charge of Our Own Life

Everyone likes to be the captain of his own ship and to feel that he has control over his present and future. And work is one way we try to exercise control over our lives. Traditional values hold that work is an unpleasant necessity and most people are lazy and will avoid it if they can. But is this really true? One research study found just the opposite and suggests that we have an inherent need to work. In the study, small children were given the opportunity to obtain an equal number of marbles with or without working for them. The results revealed that the majority of children wanted to work for their marbles rather than have them given to them. Researcher Devendra Singh concluded: "The important thing appears not to be that human beings get food, water and shelter, but that they get these things in ways that convey to the individual that he is important, that he does control what happens to him." It's when people feel controlled, rather than in control, that they are likely to lose the motivation to work.

To Do Something That's Meaningful to Us

According to Victor Frankel, the greatest drive in life is meaning. Frankel came to this conclusion while being held prisoner in a Nazi concentration camp. He observed that many fellow inmates when subjected to atrocities and inhumane conditions died unprotesting while others clung to their lives with an almost unreal tenacity. He concluded that those who felt that their lives had meaning, worth, and a purpose to be served were far more likely to survive.

You don't have to observe anything as drastic as concentration-camp victims to reach the same conclusions. Look at the actuarial statistics on death and retirement and you'll find high rates of illness and death occurring shortly after retirement. On the other hand, those who never retire and remain active and productive all their lives tend to live much longer. Creative professionals such as Arthur Fiedler, Grandma Moses, George Bernard Shaw, and others are only a few examples. They live longer, healthier lives because their work has meaning and it isn't taken from them like persons forced into retirement.

All of us can't be great artists or composers, but everyone likes to feel that he is doing something that's important and useful as *he* sees it. Look at the people at work around you and talk to the people you feel are the most motivated. More often than not they are driven because they feel what they are doing has meaning and importance.

If you examine your own feelings about your job you will likely find that you like doing things about the job that give it meaning and make a contribution. On the other hand, the things that turn you off will very likely be those tasks that you perceive as time-wasting and meaningless. Everyone likes to feel that what he does counts for something.

To Be Appreciated, Accepted, and Valued as an Individual

One turned-off worker I know has a cartoon drawing of the Peanuts character Linus hanging on his office wall. In the picture Linus says "Doing a good job around here is like wetting your pants in a dark suit—it gives you a warm feeling but nobody notices." In addition to being an economic-technical system every organization is a social system, and most of us have a very strong need to feel appreciated and accepted as one of the group. In addition, we have a strong need to feel that our efforts don't go unrecognized by the people we work for. Nobody likes to be taken for granted. And the boss who takes people's efforts for granted is in for hard times.

Very often strikes, grievances, work slowdowns, and conflicts appear on the surface to be over issues such as salary, working conditions, and benefits. But many of these areas of conflict are really caused by people who feel that their efforts aren't being recognized and appreciated. It isn't socially acceptable for an adult to say "You hurt my feelings by not recognizing the loyalty and effort I've given you." But it is socially acceptable to complain, be apathetic, strike, grieve, or resign over an issue that is symptomatic of the problem. With the loosening of family and community ties in our society, the worker's need to be appreciated, recognized, and accepted on the job is greater than ever.

To Feel Good About Ourselves

This is the most important need of all. Each of us carries around in our brain an image of who we are, and this image is the single greatest factor in deciding how we behave. In short, how you see yourself determines who you are. Believe you are a healthy, worthwhile, valuable, responsible person and you will tend to become that person. Unfortunately, however, a negative self-image determines behavior just as much as a positive one.

Obviously everyone's self-image is a mixed bag of positive and negative beliefs. But it's the negative beliefs that cause problems. The more I read, observe, and research human behavior, the more I'm convinced that many of the world's people problems are caused by those who feel unworthy, inadequate, and unsure of themselves. The insecure boss is most likely to be a tyrant and the insecure worker is most likely to be a poor performer. People who feel comfortable with themselves and their work usually perform well under the right conditions.

A smart boss can capitalize on a worker's need to feel good about himself because achieving meaningful goals is one key to improving anyone's self-image. "My basic job as a manager is to convince every worker that he is better than he believes he is," said one very successful executive. "And I prove it to him by giving him challenging tasks that cause him to stretch and grow. As he achieves his goals, I point out his progress and encourage him to climb bigger mountains. And every succeeding mountain he climbs makes him feel better about himself."

There is a whole lot more to building a positive self-image than achieving goals. Self-image depends on many factors, including how autonomous we are, how other people react to us, and whether we feel our work is meaningful. These are all factors a boss can have some control over in motivating people to work smarter.

THREE KEY RULES OF MOTIVATION

People can only be motivated by appealing to unsatisfied needs. You can't want what you have if you already have it. Therefore, as Abraham Maslow pointed out many years ago, "A satisfied need is not a motivator of behavior." Yet the needs mentioned in the preceding few pages tend to be insatiable. Most of us would like more autonomy, more recognition and appreciation, more meaningful work, and to feel even better about ourselves. And these are the needs that will have to be appealed to if we want to turn on today's turned-off workers. The threats, direction, and control of the past just won't work unless people feel they have no choice but to comply. And most of us have plenty of choices. True motivation to work without holding back comes only when people feel that it's in their own best interest to do so. With that thought in mind, here are three cardinal rules for motivating people to work harder.

Rule #1—Treat People the Way You Want Them to Become

Time and again it's been shown that people will change their behavior to meet others' expectations. And if you're a boss, how you treat employees tells them how to behave. Continually checking on them tells them they aren't to be trusted. Barking out directives and orders tells them they aren't to think for themselves. Frequently pointing out errors tells them they aren't very competent. And you can count on them to live up to your expectations.

But there's also a positive side. Giving people latitude to do the job their way tells them you respect their maturity and judgment. Paying particular attention and giving recognition for a job well done tells them you appreciate their efforts and their work doesn't go unnoticed. Structuring their jobs to help them get what they want out of work tells them you care about them as people and believe in their potential. And positive expectations, more often than not, lead to positive results.

Rule #2—You Get What You Reward—Not What You Ask for

This rule may sound like an elaboration on the obvious. But look around you and you can find all sorts of examples of poor performance because the right behavior is punished or ignored and the wrong behavior is rewarded. Organizations of all types frequently fall into the trap of asking for A and rewarding B. And B is what they get. The machinist who wanted to go deer hunting is one example. He was rewarded for coming in late rather than doing the job.

Other common examples abound. Universities tell faculty that good teaching is most important—but promotions, tenure, and merit increases are given for research and writing. The result is publish or perish. Managers are told that long-range planning is important but the rewards are for looking good in the short run. Employees are told that they are paid to get results but those who look busy and court the boss' favor are the most likely to get ahead. Workers are asked to work hard but their salary is based on showing up five days a week and punching a clock. Students are told that learning is most important but the rewards are for performing well on tests. (I could fill the rest of this book with examples of how all of us ask for A, reward B, and wonder why we get B.)

People can be turned off by a number of factors. But turning them on to work requires that they clearly understand and see the relationship between what they do and how they are rewarded. Perhaps they can't even verbalize it, but sooner or later almost everyone learns what is being rewarded. And rewarded behavior is what a company or a boss is going to get.

Rule #3—Know the Person

Turning on turned-off workers is an individual matter that has to be tailored to the needs of each person or group. And discovering someone's needs begins with finding out as much as you can about him. Consider each individual you're trying to motivate and ask yourself "What does he want? What's meaningful to him? How does he respond to praise?" Ask him what he wants from his job, career, and life. People won't always give you an answer like "I want to be praised," "I want to feel better about myself," or "I want to be more accepted by others." Yet asking the person what he wants can provide useful insights. Try to find out what his life is like off the job. He may be satisfying somewhere else needs that you're trying to appeal to. The more you know about an individual the better you're able to empathize and understand what makes him tick and what he's looking for in his work. And everybody is looking for something in his work or he wouldn't be there.

REWARDS THAT WORK

Assuming you know what someone wants from work, there are a number of specific rewards that can be tailored to appeal to almost anyone. The key points to keep in mind are:

1. The rewards must appeal to unsatisfied needs.

2. The person being motivated should clearly understand the relationship between performance and rewards. Desirable behavior and the subsequent rewards should be as specific as possible. For example, don't say "Increased effort on your part will be taken into account when giving merit raises." Aim for something more concrete, such as "Improve your output by 10 percent and I'll guarantee you a minimum 15 percent merit increase."

3. Deliver the rewards rapidly after you get the desired performance. Otherwise you run the high risk of being branded as untrustworthy and future efforts at motivating may be futile. With those key points in mind, here are ten types of rewards that can be tailored to turn someone on. None of them will work for everyone, but at least one of them will work for almost everybody.

Money

Although it may have lost some of its clout as a motivator, money is still the number-1 <u>incentive</u> for most workers and probably always will be. The reason is simply that no other reward is capable of satisfying such a wide range of needs. In addition to buying the groceries and paying the rent, money buys education, opportunity, dignity, prestige, power, and peace of mind. No, money isn't everything and it may not buy happiness (although some will debate that point). But at the very least it's a sure cure for many of life's miseries.

Money works best as a motivator for someone trying to satisfy basic needs. Young, achievement-oriented workers who are striving to save for the down payment on a house, workers who have suffered financial hardships, or employees with children nearing college age are all prime candidates for being money-motivated. And with the U.S. standard of living continuing to decline, money is sure to become increasingly important as an incentive. Indeed, man lives by bread alone when there is no bread.

Part-time workers also respond well to money rewards, because this is usually their only reason for working. They have no long-term career commitment and other rewards are less likely to work.

Money can also be used as an incentive to lower costs of absenteeism, safety, and operations. Parson Pine Products, Inc., of Ashland, Oregon pays workers "well pay," extra pay for not missing work—just the opposite of sick pay. Employees are also paid two hours' extra pay each month if they don't have an accident. Workers are also allowed to share in profits that the company earns over 4 percent after taxes, with each individual's share being determined by his performance rating. Top-ranked employees generally receive 8 percent to 10 percent and time is taken to explain to all employees how they can affect business costs and to work with them to reduce these costs.

The best way to use money is with other rewards such as recognition. For example, Xerox Corporation has two cash merit programs that combine money and recognition for personal achievement. The Special Merit Program awards an employee a lump sum of cash (between 5 and 10 percent of his annual salary) for significant contributions to the company. The President's Award is given for the most outstanding contributions to Xerox. In addition to receiving a lump-sum cash award of up to 50 percent of the employee's salary, the recipients are honored in an annual awards ceremony held at corporate headquarters.

When using money as a motivator, there are several points to remember:

1. Use it to reward results. Most jobs have little or no rela-

tionship between payment and performance—the main reason money isn't the motivator it once was.

2. Like every other reward, money loses its effectiveness if you use it too much or too often. The second piece of cake isn't as satisfying as the first unless time is allowed to pass between servings.

3. Don't rely on it totally. You may not always have the funds available to provide money incentives. Thus, it's necessary to develop a package of other rewards.

Recognition

According to author Laurence Peter, "There are two kinds of egotists: Those who admit it, and the rest of us." It's incredible how hard people will work and dedicate themselves if they feel they will be recognized, appreciated, and praised (either publicly or privately) for a job well done. It gives a boost to our social and esteem needs and few, if any, people fail to respond to recognition in one form or another.

Employee of the month, secretary of the year, clubs for high performers, changes in title, publicity such as newspaper write-ups are all effective forms of recognition that can be used as rewards. Various awards, trophies, publicly announced bonuses, certificates of appreciation, and status symbols (such as a private parking space or a carpeted office) can also be given to recognize superior performances.

Using money and recognition as the principal reward, Mary Kay Ash has constructed a giant multimillion-dollar cosmetics empire. On Awards Night 8000 women who sell Mary Kay cosmetics are lavished with applause, praise, and gifts ranging from pocket calculators to pink Cadillacs. Queens of sales and recruitment are crowned and presented with flowers and scepters, accompanied by standing ovations and musical fanfares. No doubt much of the success of Mary Kay Ash has been her ability to understand the kind of recognition that's most meaningful to the people who sell her products.

While it's important to give the highest recognition to the

highest performers, it's also important to keep in mind that *everyone* needs some type of positive regard for his work. Workers who fail to get the boss' attention through positive efforts often resort to negative performance. People need to be recognized, and if they can't get your attention one way they are likely to get it another.

Time

With today's new breed, leisure time and not having to punch a clock are very important; for many this is more important than money. "I want more time to go fishing" or "Time with my family and friends are most important" are words most bosses would have been shocked to hear in 1950, but such statements are common today.

Instead of requiring workers to punch a clock, why not establish a daily or weekly production quota and allow them to leave once the quota is met? It would surely reduce a lot of time- and energy-wasting behavior that comes from waiting around for the five-o'clock whistle to blow.

If employees must work on an hourly basis, why not let them choose when they wish to put in their time? Flexible working hours can be used as a reward for higher performers. More about flextime in Chapter 6.

Still another way to reward with time is to reward high performers with extended vacations. An extra few days or a week's vacation can be a positive reward for those wanting more leisure time.

Advancement

Fail to have this reward available to your high performers and you're sure to lose them. Year after year companies lose their most valuable, promising employees because they feel their future is limited. Try to see to it that everyone is given assignments that set the stage for future promotions. For most highly educated workers, the opportunity to advance, grow, and climb the company ladder is very important.

Workshops and Seminars

Sending employees to training and development seminars is also an excellent reward. In effect the company is telling the worker "We want you to grow and develop and are willing to invest in your future." When choosing a seminar as a reward be sure to choose one that's meaningful to the worker. For example, is he motivated by the need to grow and achieve? Send him to a skills seminar on leadership or one tailored to developing job skills. Is she motivated by self-fulfillment? Send her to a workshop on physical or mental health improvement. Is she trying to be a career person and homemaker? Send her to a time-management seminar. Better yet, choose a number of acceptable topics for seminars and let her choose.

Meaningful Assignments

In any organization there are necessary tasks to be done; some are more satisfying than others. For example, an employee may enjoy starting new projects or helping new workers develop but abhor recordkeeping and paperwork chores. The idea is to find the productive tasks the person likes most about his job and give him more of them as a reward. At the same time he can be excused from some of the tasks he least enjoys. In effect, you are saying to the worker "Tell me what you like to do best, do it well and I'll give you more assignments you enjoy. At the same time, I'll excuse you from the tasks you least enjoy."

Obviously, not all jobs have the potential to be satisfying. But for those that do this can be an effective way to increase motivation and productivity.

Food and Other Slight Distractions

Don't laugh, it works! Research studies indicate that attempts to persuade people are more effective when presented in conjunction with a modestly distracting positive reward. For example, Fran Tarkenton, former NFL superstar quarterback, was known to give candy to his teammates after they made a good play. Obviously Fran was good at more than passing and scrambling. He also knew how to motivate.

When making a request you can increase odds of its acceptance if you do it over lunch, drinks, or a cup of coffee. Salesmen and great lovers have known this for years. Distracting, positive rewards are another, healthy addition to your motivational tool kit.

Social Activities

Parties, weekend trips, banquets, and company-sponsored vacations are all excellent rewards for a job well done. These forms of reward work best when motivating people to cooperate, achieve group goals, and promote company spirit. For example, it's common for public accounting firms to celebrate the end of tax season by rewarding the staff with a very nice vacation. An airplane is chartered and employees and their spouses spend several days basking in the sun at a seaside resort or a mountain retreat. In addition to being nice rewards, social activities can be great vehicles for generating company loyalty.

Social Acceptance

One of the strongest needs of most people is to be accepted by colleagues at work. And a smart boss can motivate workers by creating a team-building environment where workers are dependent on each other to get the job done.

One classic example is the R. G. Barry Corporation of Columbus, Ohio, a manufacturer of footwear. In 1969 the company decided to try to increase job satisfaction and productivity through the creation of group incentives. Production workers were organized into teams ranging from eight to twelve employees, each team responsible for completing total manufacturing of a product from cut stock to finished product. Rewards were given for team performance rather than individual performance and employees were allowed to participate in company decision-making activities.

The results were terrific. Absenteeism and turnover dropped 50 percent. Total output jumped 35 percent. Defective products were reduced two-thirds. Training costs decreased 50 percent. And from 1969 to 1973 wages increased 35 percent.

The reason the new system worked so well was that group incentives created peer pressure. As one worker put it, "Before, everyone was on his own and no one cared about helping his fellow employee. Now everyone is dependent upon everybody else. I know in my case I think twice before taking a day off because I know if I do it will affect my team."

Contests and Campaigns

Everybody likes to be a winner, and there's a little of the competitor in most of us. Another way to get improved performance is therefore to make the task fun and provide fitting rewards.

George Schmidt, president of Industrial Motivation, Inc., of New York, has put together a thirty-day cost-reduction campaign that has been used by 2000 companies with great success. The program is called "Buck-A-Day" and asks each employee "What can you do in your own job, in your own area to save one dollar a day?" Most employees can't relate to cost savings of thousands or millions of dollars but everyone can relate to saving the company a dollar a day. The program asks employees for money-saving ideas and proclaims the campaign month BAD (Buck-A-Day) Month. Large BAD posters urge workers to "Join the BAD guys." Employees are rewarded for their money-saving ideas with items such as BAD-guy coffee mugs, rubber dollars, vests, paycheck stuffers, and other items which cost $13 to $16 per employee. (You could probably make this program even more effective by supplementing the rubber dollars with real ones. Why not give the employee a chunk of the hundreds of dollars a year he's saving the company?)

According to Schmidt, pilot studies on the program revealed that the program paid for itself more than tenfold. One company reported a cost saving of $73,000 for every thousand dollars spent on the program. Another company that made wires coated with semiprecious metals received a suggestion from one employee to vacuum workbenches. The result is that the company saved $90,000 in salvaged metals from this one idea. BAD has been so successful that companies are now purchasing Schmidt's follow-up program, Son of BAD.

Raffles and poker games have been successfully used by some companies to reduce tardiness and absenteeism. In one case, each employee was issued a playing card every day of the week upon arrival at work and at the end of the week the worker holding the highest poker hand received $20. After the program was started, absenteeism dropped 18 percent.

In a St. Louis hardware company, employees who came to work on time for a month were eligible to participate in a drawing with one prize awarded for every twenty-five eligible workers. People with perfect attendance for six months were eligible to draw for a television set. Both tardiness and absenteeism dropped substantially and sick leave cost dropped 62 percent.

Many managers dislike the idea of having to induce people to come to work with games and prizes. But business is business. If a drawing saves the company more than it costs, it's worth it. It's also a good way to boost morale.

Frequent, Positive Feedback

What's a pat on the back for a job well done worth? If you ask Emery Air Freight Corporation, they will tell you it's worth a $2 million cost savings over three years. And according to the 3M Co., positive feedback saved the company $3.5 million in 1977. Numerous companies are jumping on the behavior-mod bandwagon with programs that systematically provide employees positive feedback. And many of them are getting significant gains in productivity, cost savings, and improved morale.

The basic principle is to monitor employees' performance on a frequent basis and praise them every time they show improvement. For example, at Emery Air Freight the goal was to answer all customer inquiries within ninety minutes but the goal was only being reached 30 percent of the time. In an effort to boost performance, customer service reps were asked to record how long it took to answer each inquiry on a log sheet. Management then checked the log sheets on a daily basis and rewarded a rep with praise every time his daily performance improved. Reps who didn't improve were praised for their honesty and accuracy in filling out the log sheets and reminded of the goal.

The results? After a few days of feedback and praise, service reps were meeting the ninety-minute goal 90 percent of the time. Emery also applied the same principle in the shipping department and found that container packing efficiency soared from 45 percent to 90 percent.

In addition to being an excellent reward, positive feedback gives the direction and encouragement so necessary for nudging people on to improved performance. And almost everyone wants to improve if given the opportunity and encouragement.

So there you have ten effective rewards that can be used to motivate individuals or groups at work. One question frequently asked is "How can I tell if a given reward will work?" The only way you can be sure is to try it and see. If you get more of the behavior you want, the odds are that the reward is working.

Also it's important to know that once you have established a pattern of rewards for the behavior you want, it isn't necessary to reward the person every time he performs well. Research in behavior modification indicates that intermittent rewards can be most powerful in shaping behavior. For example, people get hooked on gambling because the rewards are intermittent. Spend some time watching people at the race track, the slot machines, playing cards, or at the Bingo tables and you'll see what I mean.

You Don't Have to Be a Boss to Be a Motivator

As you read this you may be thinking to yourself "That's all very nice, but it doesn't apply to me because I'm not a boss." You may not have the clout to give raises, promotions, or time off to your colleagues. But you do have the ability to give certain rewards and influence everyone you work with. Most bosses will tell you that formal authority is very overrated as a motivator. The real ability to turn people on to work comes from informal leaders who may or may not be bosses. Every organization needs informal leaders to provide the spark that makes work more productive and enjoyable. Here are five ways you can help turn people on to work no matter what your position is:

1. You can give praise and recognition wherever you see good work. Everyone needs to know his efforts are appreciated. A well-placed compliment or encouraging word can be just what someone needs to spur him on to greater efforts and successes. If someone at work appears discouraged (and we all get discouraged), make a special effort to find something positive about his work to praise. It can make all the difference in the world.

2. You can suggest motivational rewards to those with the authority to implement them. A good boss is always looking for new ways to make employees more interested, productive, and enthusiastic. It's a never-ending challenge and most bosses need all the help they can get. Why not provide it? Whenever you read or hear about how a company successfully motivated workers, ask yourself if it can be adapted to your workplace. If it can, pass the idea along to your boss. Look over the ten rewards and make a list of five ways any one or a combination of them can be adapted where you work. If only one out of every twenty ideas works, the effort will pay for itself many times over. It will also be very beneficial for you because people who learn how to motivate and influence others greatly increase their chances of success, growth, and advancement.

3. You can organize social activities to promote company spirit and teamwork. We all work for social as well as economic reasons. Perhaps you're just the person to organize a softball game, monthly party to celebrate employee birthdays, company picnic, weekend cook-out, bowling league, wine and cheese party, dance, or whatever. Don't wait for the boss to suggest such activities. He may be too busy. Take the initiative and tell him what you would like to do. Most bosses will love the idea and probably offer to support it any way they can.

4. You can think up new ways to make work more enjoyable and productive and suggest them to your boss. How about a contest that gives a prize to the person who comes up with the best way to reduce the photocopy budget? Or another contest that rewards the best ideas for managing time at the office? Or how about a monthly productivity competition between offices where the winning office is treated to lunch? Flex your creative muscles and you can find all sorts of ways to keep people interested and motivated.

5. Most important of all, you can set an example for other people through your own efforts and excellent work. Motivation by example speaks louder than anything else and any enthusiasm you generate for your own work will be highly contagious.

A FINAL WORD TO TURNED-OFF WORKERS

You need more than just a paycheck from work. You need to feel that you're growing, using your talents, accomplishing something, being appreciated, and gaining control over your life. If you feel dissatisfied, bored, or resentful with your career, it doesn't mean that you're a lazy, useless bum. It probably means that you have to get in touch with who you are, what you have to offer and see how it matches up with what your job has to offer.

Consider yourself first and ask yourself "What are my lifetime goals?" What do you want to accomplish for yourself and others? What are your special talents and strengths? What are your weaknesses? What things do you enjoy most? What types of things do you enjoy least?

Now look at your job. What's turning you off? Is it the nature of the work or is it things surrounding the work such as working conditions, your boss, your salary, lack of recognition, or administrative hassles? If you don't like the nature of the work, get out of it and find something that better matches your talents.

If your work is unsatisfying, perhaps you can restructure your job and your life to make work more satisfying. If you feel you aren't being recognized for your efforts, seek out people who will praise and encourage you. Focus on the positive aspects of your job rather than dwelling on the negatives. Try to look for ways to structure your workday to make it more enjoyable for you. If your job is stress-producing, work off the stress after work with a leisure activity you like. Learn to praise and reward yourself with compliments and special treats when you do a good job.

It's a short trip from the cradle to the grave. Spending half of your waking hours as a turned-off worker is no way to go through life.

CHAPTER 6

HUMANIZING THE WORKPLACE

"Job satisfaction?? I didn't know those two words went together!"

—*Anonymous*

The story goes that a tourist in Mexico at a woodcarver's shop was admiring a hand-carved chair. "How much is this chair?" she asked. "Fifty pesos," said the woodcarver. Hoping for a matched set of chairs and a quantity discount, the tourist then asked, "How much for four chairs?" "Two hundred fifty pesos for four chairs" was the reply. Surprised that the price per chair for four chairs was more than the price of one chair, the tourist asked why. The woodcarver answered, "But, senorita, it is very boring to carve four chairs that are exactly alike!"

One issue you will hear a lot about in the next few years is improving the quality of work life. Basically, quality of work life (QWL) refers to how well a job or the job environment matches the needs of its workers. The purpose of QWL programs is to produce more humanized jobs that increase worker satisfaction. Jobs are redesigned, organizational relationships are changed, and the work environment is altered to make work a better place for everyone. And if you think that's a very ambitious undertaking, you're right.

123

As pointed out in Chapter 5, workers have changed a lot in the past few decades. And this means that industry is going to have to change to fit the needs of the modern-day worker. The organizations of the future must offer a lot more than a day's work for a day's pay. They are going to have to be places where people cannot only be productive but also grow and develop as complete human beings. In short, management is going to have to look at employees from a holistic point of view. It may be simpler to take the point of view that a worker is only hired for his skills and paid to deliver them. But the fact is that every employee is a total person with a variety of needs, roles, goals, and expectations that companies of the future are going to be expected to address and fulfill.

A MOVEMENT TAKES HOLD

The term *Quality of Work Life* has been around for some time. But during the late 1970s the idea really gained momentum. In 1972, the first international QWL Conference attracted only fifty people, mainly academics. No union officials and few managers were present. Contrast this with the 1981 Conference, which had more than 1500 delegates, including 200 unionists and 750 practicing managers.

Case histories of QWL programs are multiplying like rabbits. In 1972, only about twenty-five such cases were documented, but by 1981 more than a thousand had been reported. These studies demonstrate that QWL programs are indeed capable of improving product quality and productivity, reducing absenteeism and turnover, and increasing job satisfaction. It's hard to pick up a business magazine or newspaper and not read about how X corporation has been reborn by letting workers manage themselves and have a greater voice in running the company. No doubt there are plenty of success stories, but these stories should be read keeping several things in mind.

The first precaution is to realize that QWL is no "open sesame" or quick fix to an organization's productivity or morale problems. Whenever success stories begin to appear lauding new programs there's a natural tendency to see the programs as panaceas for an ailing business. Yet the reason the successful programs succeed is that they are given a high priority and commitment by top management and are consistent with the beliefs and values of those running the organization. QWL programs frequently mean making fundamental changes in operating philosophy and a long-term commitment.

The second word of caution is to realize that many QWL programs don't work for a number of reasons. Lack of management commitment is one reason. Employee apathy is another. Failure to understand the philosophy the programs are based on is another. QWL is something that almost everyone in the organization must understand, believe in, and be committed to in order for it to work. Otherwise the programs will become just one more faddish technique that will waste everyone's time and effort.

Fundamental Assumptions of QWL

Basically, QWL assumes that a job and the work environment should be structured to meet as many of the worker's needs as possible. This is quite a departure from the philosophy of a fair day's work for a fair day's pay. QWL seeks to motivate people by appealing to higher needs such as esteem, recognition, self-improvement, and growth as well as more basic needs. The fundamental idea is that workers are human resources who need to be trusted and developed as human beings rather than exploited like pawns on a chess board.

QWL also assumes that work should be meaningful and fulfilling and that the job shouldn't put the worker under undue stress. Furthermore, the job should not be threatening, dangerous, or degrading but should enhance a worker's sense of dignity and self-esteem. Finally, QWL assumes that a job should contribute to a worker's ability to grow in other life roles such as private citizen, spouse, and parent. Former GM Chairman Thomas A. Murphy capsuled the QWL philosophy when he said "We should try to treat our people the way we would like to be treated. That in my judgment will be good for the individual and good for business."

As you read this you're probably thinking "That's all great pie-in-the-sky stuff, but what does it have to do with productivity?" The answer, in a direct sense, is nothing. But research on numerous QWL programs indicates that improved productivity seems to be a byproduct that can result when the quality of work life is improved. The relationship is by no means direct or absolute, but growing numbers of companies that have implemented QWL programs are reporting significant productivity gains. It would be a mistake to jump on the QWL bandwagon if your only hope is to increase productivity. The primary focus on these programs should be to make work more satisfying.

HOW TO HUMANIZE WORK

To make work more satisfying you can change only two things: the work itself or the environment. What follow are five basic ways a job can be changed to make the work itself more satisfying. As you read these techniques, think about a job in your company and see if you can think of ways to make it more satisfying. Better yet, see if you can apply these strategies to your own work.

Increase Variety

The first way to increase satisfaction is to bring new tasks to the job with the hope of reducing monotony and making the job more challenging. For example, a secretary who has only taken dictation and typed might be given basic information and asked to compose letters and reports for the boss. In addition to increasing the secretary's value to the company, the new assignments develop administrative ability and reduce boredom.

Do a Whole Task

One of the drawbacks of specialization of labor is that people frequently can't identify with what they do. It's difficult to put hundreds of right front fenders on automobiles as they pass through an assembly line and point with pride to the finished product and say "I did that." When a job is broadened enough, workers begin to feel that their contribution is something they can take pride in and responsibility for. Giving people a sense of closure where they can complete an entire task or major part of a project is essential to keeping them motivated and satisfied.

Make It Meaningful

Every job is important or should be eliminated. The key point here is to make the worker understand how what he does is important to others. For example, some years ago St. Regis Paper Company received customer complaints about seams tearing and bottoms dropping out of about 6 percent of grocery bags made in three plants. Traditional efforts to increase inspection and change production methods had little or no impact.

Management then decided to go directly to the bag-machine operators. Customer complaint letters were circulated to the operators to show them the seriousness of the problem. It was also decided to have the bag operator's signature stamped on the bottom of the bags with the following inscription: "Another quality product by St. Regis. Personally inspected by _____ [operator's signature]."

The plan worked beautifully and the number of defective bags dropped from 6 percent to .5 percent. Because they understood the significance of their work, bag operators began to take pride in what they did. Some even took their nameplates with them during coffee breaks because they wanted to be personally responsible for bags having their signatures.

Increase Autonomy

Letting workers do the job their way and giving them greater freedom is fundamental to creating a sense of responsibility. QWL recognizes that narrow procedures and prescriptions can hurt morale and productivity and seek to provide only the minimum necessary controls. Workers are held accountable for results rather than performing activities. Timeclocks are replaced with flexible work schedules. Assembly lines are replaced with work teams who divide the tasks among themselves. The basic idea is to make the worker feel he is in control of his job rather than vice versa.

Provide Frequent Feedback

Everybody who works invests a lot of time and effort into a job. Therefore, most of us like to know how we are doing. Frequent feedback is a very potent reward and also a way people can correct their own behavior. It's important that workers receive total feedback about positive and negative aspects of their performance. Negative feedback alone ultimately results in turned-off workers.

Continuous feedback, if possible, is best in many jobs. For example, operators of bottling machines are given continuous feedback through panels on the machinery to let them know how the work is progressing. If things are going well, the feedback is an immediate reward. If production is slow, they know that adjustments have to be made to get back on course.

WAYS TO HUMANIZE THE ENVIRONMENT

In addition to enriching the job itself, QWL programs seek to humanize all factors that surround the job. Here are some of the more popular methods that are being adopted today.

Share Power

One of the most prominent features of QWL programs is the overwhelming emphasis on involving workers in decisions that affect them. A videotape is circulated through the Xerox Corporation in which the president states "I pledge to you that management of this company at all levels will listen to you and put your ideas to work."

The traditional view that workers are paid to work and not think is giving way to a totally different approach to managing employees. The new emphasis is that people will be responsible and productive if given the proper incentives and a climate in which they can gain a voice in decisions that affect their jobs and lives.

The R. G. Barry Corporation is a classic example of successful participative management. In one instance the company was faced with deciding where to locate its new plant in Columbus, Ohio. One possible site was selling for $100,000 and was located near a bus route that would be convenient for half of the workers who relied on buses to get to their jobs. Another site being considered was priced at only $10,000, but no bus routes passed nearby. The company allowed the workers to vote on the new site and 75 percent voted for the less-expensive location. They decided that transportation could be arranged through car pools and it was worth it to save the company $90,000.

Using a participative management philosophy, R. G. Barry has expanded its footwear business from sales of $4.6 million twenty years ago to $127 million in 1980. Absenteeism is around 2 percent and turnover averages 10 percent in an industry where 100 percent turnover isn't rare. President Gordon Zachs credits the growth and success of R. G. Barry to building trust and respect among the workers—whom the company calls "associates"—and sharing decision-making power with them. As Zachs put it, "By sharing you make better decisions and your people are more likely to be committed to your success."

General Motors is another example of a company learning to benefit from worker participation. Its greatest success story comes from the Tarrytown, New York, plant where labor-management disputes were the rule, quality was poor, and grievances on the books numbered as high as 2000. After small-scale testing over several years, GM launched a QWL program on a plantwide scale in 1977. The company committed $1.6 million in training with the main goal of gaining worker involvement. By December 1978 there were only thirty-two grievances on the docket. Absenteeism plummeted from 7.25 percent to between 2 and 3 percent. Quality performance at Tarrytown changed from one of GM's worst plants to one of its best.

Another QWL group reports successful participation at a

Cadillac plant in Detroit. In this program workers get together to discuss gripes with supervisors. The result? Grievances on the books have fallen from 3000 to fewer than seventy. Perhaps GM vice-president Alfred Warren summed it up best: "American business has treated its employees like children. We've found they behave differently when they participate."

The concept of worker participation and trust is hardly new. Management scholars have been advocating it for years and it is one of the key features of Japanese management. But today participative management is taking factory floors and offices by storm. Quality circles, problem-solving groups, and self-managed work teams are spreading rapidly throughout American industry. It seems strange that after years of adversity, turmoil, and bloodshed management and labor have finally stumbled onto a simple truth: It's much better to work with people than to work against them.

Allow Flexible Work Schedules

One of the most popular outgrowths of the QWL movement has been the change in the traditional forty-hour workweek. For many Americans, nine-to-five is becoming a thing of the past and being replaced by more flexible approaches to working hours. Today over one-fifth of all American employees work unorthodox schedules and the trend is clearly on the upswing.

Flexible approaches to working hours have been created to help companies and employees better meet their needs. For example, there are more single parents in the labor force today who need flexibility to care for their children. Increasing energy costs demand that workers be given flexible hours to take advantage of car pooling and cut commuting time. Companies with expensive plant and equipment need to schedule innovatively to make the best possible use of resources. Shutting down a plant or expensive machinery every night can be very costly indeed. Two-career families are increasing and need flexibility to be able to schedule time together. These are just a few of the reasons

Americans are saying adieu to rigid work schedules. But what are these new schedules and how do they work?

Flextime

No doubt the most widely used alternative to the standard work week is *flextime*. In fact, you probably know someone who works such a schedule. In a typical flextime arrangement, all employees have to be at work during a core period, for example from 10 A.M. to 3 P.M. However, starting and quitting times fall into a range. Thus, an early-bird worker may choose to come in at 7 A.M. and leave at 3 P.M. and a late riser would prefer to arrive at 10 A.M. and leave at 6 P.M. Most flextime arrangements demand that workers put in eight hours per day, although this isn't universal. For example, one company only asks that workers be at work from 10 A.M. to 3 P.M. daily and work a total of eighty hours in every two-week period.

Flextime is one work innovation that seems to be good from just about every standpoint. Needless to say, it's very popular with workers who enjoy the freedom of not having to conform to a rigid schedule every day. But additionally, flextime is beneficial for the organization. Research studies investigating the impact of flextime on organizations report increased morale and productivity along with reductions in absenteeism, tardiness, and turnover. Perhaps the greatest benefit of flextime is that workers take more responsibility for their jobs and realize that getting things done is more important than showing up at a certain time each day.

The Compressed Workweek

A more radical departure from the standard nine-to-five is the compressed workweek. This approach to work scheduling simply reduces the number of days worked each week by working more hours per day. Thus, instead of working eight hours five days a week, an employee might work thirteen hours three days a week and enjoy four straight days of leisure. In the four-day workweek employees put in four ten-hour days. The benefits of compressed schedules to the company is they often permit better plant and equipment usage and unpopular shifts are more easily covered. Employees benefit by getting larger blocks of free time and having to commute less often.

Several variations of compressed schedules are worth noting. One is the weekend schedule. Firestone and Goodyear were having trouble getting workers to work weekend shifts. To solve the problem, they paid employees thirty-six hours' wages for working two twelve-hour days. Thus workers who worked weekends were given the rest of the week off. Hospitals have also used this type of scheduling as an inducement to get nurses to work weekend shifts.

Another variation which looks promising is the five/four, nine-hour plan. This plan calls for an employee to work eighty hours every two weeks and approximately nine hours each day. Such a schedule gives employees a three-day weekend every other week if the tenth day is scheduled on a Monday or Friday. The workday is only lengthened by one hour, by adding a half-hour to the beginning and end of each day.

Research on the benefits of compressed workweeks is a mixed bag and not as overwhelmingly positive as flextime is. Complaints of employee fatigue and inconvenience for car poolers and parents of small children have caused some companies to abandon the idea. Still other companies report improved productivity and job satisfaction as a result of switching to compressed workweeks. To be sure, the two-, three-, or four-day workweek isn't for everybody. Compressed schedules work best when the workers are young, single, and without small children.

Job Sharing
Another increasingly popular work alternative is to have two people arrange to perform one full-time job and share the salary, responsibility, and benefits. Job sharing can boost productivity by providing the company with two full sets of skills for the price of one full-time employee.

The concept is also popular in many industries as an alternative to laying off workers. In 1980 United Airlines, due to decreased business, decided to lay off 200 flight attendants. The Association of Flight Attendants proposed job sharing and 270 attendants paired off and arranged their own schedules. In this case, 125 jobs were saved.

While it can be very advantageous, job sharing can also create headaches. Both parties sharing the work must be responsible, compatible, and clearly understand their respective duties. This doesn't always happen. Additionally, job sharing puts a greater burden on managers because more people must be trained and supervised.

Create Autonomous Work Teams

Human beings are social creatures. But for too long, too many jobs have been organized without keeping that thought in mind. Another QWL idea that has been meeting with great success is to divide workers into autonomous teams.

Serious study of autonomous work groups began somewhat by accident. A group of researchers studying coalminers in England noted that technical improvements in mining at the Durham coal mines led to decreases in productivity because the workers were separated from each other and unable to interact socially. This finding led to the formation of the Tavistock Institute to study work groups and learn how work teams should be created to foster greater productivity and job satisfaction. Results of the research have found that it's possible to reduce costs, increase productivity, and improve the quality of work life if the following guidelines are kept in mind for organizing work teams:

1. Give each team a manageable piece of the business for which they are collectively responsible. The work should be big enough to give the team a sense of achievement but small enough to be attainable and not overwhelming.

2. Arrange the work to foster cooperation and social interaction between team members. Every worker should hold a piece of the puzzle and only by all of them contributing their piece can the job be successfully completed.

3. Allow every team member to learn all jobs necessary to make a complete product. By learning additional jobs, boredom is reduced, each worker is more valuable to the company, and team resources are strengthened.

4. Every team must have the resources, training, tools, and technical skills necessary to do the job. Without these key ingredients no work system can be effective.

5. Give teams enough information to enable them to evaluate their own performance. Each team must know how it contributes to the total organizational effort so it can provide meaningful feedback to itself. Teams need to have specific goals and benchmarks for measuring output, quality, and other meaningful performance indicators.

Many of the hundreds of QWL success stories center around the successful implementation of autonomous work groups. Here are just a few:

- At Texas Instruments, 600 electronic assemblers were put into groups and held responsible for setting their own production goals. Assembly-line time per unit went from 132 to 32 hours. Absenteeism and turnover also dropped. In another situation at Texas Instruments, maintenance workers were reorganized into nineteen autonomous work groups that set their own goals and scheduled their work. The reported results were astounding. Turnover dropped from 100 percent to 9.8 percent. Personnel requirements were reduced from 120 to 71 and estimated annual cost savings were $103,000.

- The optical laboratory of a national corporation shifted its work orientation from an assembly-line operation to business-oriented work groups in a last gasp effort to boost productivity. Numerous other techniques had been tried and the company decided to try work groups before closing the operation. Within three months after the implementation of work groups, operating costs, turnover, and the number of grievances all declined. After five years the work groups reported a 92 percent increase in productivity over the old assembly-line system.

- A General Motors parts plant in Flint, Michigan, has been successfully employing autonomous work groups. The groups are given authority to make major decisions on how their jobs will be performed. Workers neither answer to foremen nor punch timeclocks. Despite the lack of supervision, parts made by the groups pass inspection 99.5 percent of the time.

Provide a Total Package

In addition to worker participation, flexible schedules, and autonomous work groups, other features of QWL are aimed at improving the work environment to match the total range of worker needs. Efforts are being made to ensure that all work areas are clean, safe, and healthy from both a physical and psychological standpoint. Opportunities for growth and development through such things as company-paid educational programs, employee counseling, and physical fitness facilities are also being added. Efforts are being made to create a climate where employees can enjoy a feeling of belonging and a sense of community and teamwork. Employee rights to privacy, free speech, dissent, and fair treatment in all work-related activities are being recognized. New incentives and methods of compensating employees are being tried. The environmental aspect of QWL focuses on what's good for the employee and tries to create a work situation that's in balance and harmony with a worker's other roles in society. Workloads are balanced so as to be reasonable and not in conflict with other needs for family, recreation, and community service.

GROUND RULES FOR SUCCESSFUL QWL PROGRAMS

More and more companies will be adopting QWL programs in the coming years. Many of them are going to be disappointed, disillusioned, and dismiss the ideas as wastes of time and money. Yet it doesn't have to be that way. There are a number of points every organization needs to keep in mind when considering the adoption of QWL programs. Perhaps the most important point is to realize that it's not for everybody. If the company doesn't have the time and money to commit to the project, QWL will be a waste. If management at all levels isn't receptive to power-sharing, forget it. If the company tries to implement QWL by thinking of it as a series of unrelated projects, failure is almost assured. QWL is a fundamental change in work that involves building trust, providing training, and dealing with power issues. Companies and consultants who have worked on successful and unsuccessful endeavors all have one common message: "If you're going to do it, do it right." With that key idea in mind, here are some other ground rules for successfully putting QWL to work:

1. Make sure management understands what QWL is about and is willing to make a large, long-range commitment. QWL is not a motivation or productivity-improvement technique. Nor is it a substitute for managerial competence or administrative discipline. QWL requires a genuine belief in the values and rights of people in a trusting business partnership. It recognizes job security as a right of all employees and frequently allows them to share in the profits and savings they contribute to. Unless there's something in it for everybody the program is doomed.

2. Enlist the help of a consultant in organizational development. He or she can look at your organization and give you an objective reading of where your company stands today with respect to QWL and what you can reasonably expect to accomplish. Many consultants use surveys and feasibility studies to assess an organization. It's important to get an accurate reading of what's possible before jumping in with both feet.

3. Train and retrain *everybody*. Inadequate training causes many QWL programs to fail. No doubt training is expensive, but to launch into QWL without adequate training is the most costly route of all. Particularly, training is needed at *all* levels in participative problem-solving and communication skills. In addition, workers usually require training in new job skills and quality control (more about that in Chapter 7).

One common training pitfall is to ignore the necessity for training middle management in participative skills. Most participation efforts fail not due to a lack of top-management support or worker enthusiasm but because the people in the middle haven't been properly trained and informed. Like the proverbial chain, participative management is no stronger than its weakest link, and the entire process can be destroyed at any level in the hierarchy.

When training employees, don't present new skills as abstract concepts. Find an immediate problem and have the workers solve the problem by applying the new skills. If workers can actually see that the new skills really work in their jobs, they will be much more enthusiastic about learning them. As a popular proverb states:

I hear, I forget
I see, I remember
I do, I understand

Once again, be sure to enlist the aid of a consultant for training.

4. Don't use QWL to avoid or circumvent unionization. Otherwise the union will lobby against the programs and cause ultimate failure. Many QWL programs run the high risk of being torpedoed by unions who perceive them as threats to their existence. If the sincere purpose of management and the union is to make work a better place for workers, then QWL programs can be a joint, cooperative effort where everybody wins.

5. Begin QWL efforts on a limited scale that focuses on the solution of specific problems. Trying to make wholesale, sweeping changes is blueprint for frustration and failure. Although major changes may be the grand plan, the best changes are made gradually, smoothly, and systematically. Large changes are best made by starting with a series of small successes. Carefully choose areas, problems, and groups where the initial chances of success are high.

It's also important to resolve immediately minor misunderstandings that develop. As programs are instituted, mistrust, misunderstandings, and doubts will surely appear. Resolve them *quickly* or little problems can grow into monsters that will destroy the entire program.

6. All QWL programs should be voluntary. Forcing people to participate isn't participation and is one sure way to damage new programs. Not everyone will want to participate at first, but as people begin to see the value and successes of QWL efforts, the enthusiasm will spread and more people will participate. A well-designed QWL program has something in it for everybody; when people realize that fact, most will be eager to participate.

7. Realize that QWL is a never-ending process. Once again, let me emphasize that we aren't talking about one-shot, quick-fix techniques but making fundamental changes in the way we work. Once QWL takes hold and gains momentum, workers have the power to affect the quality of their own work life. And that is a power that neither unions nor management is likely to take back from them.

CHAPTER 7

GOING AROUND IN QUALITY CIRCLES

"Quality control is not just a little room adjacent to the factory floor, where occupants make a nuisance of themselves to everyone else. It is a state of mind with everyone from the president to the production trainee involved."

—*Norihiko Nakayamo*

If you want to improve productivity, improve quality. Think about it. If every person and machine did things right the first time, the same number of people could handle much larger volumes of work. High costs of inspection could be channeled into productive activities and managers could take all the time they spend checking and devote it to productive tasks. Wasted materials would become a thing of the past. In fact, it's been estimated that attention to quality can reduce the total cost of operations anywhere from 10 to 50 percent. Philip Crosby said it: "Quality is free. What costs money are the unquality things— all the actions that involve not doing jobs right the first time."

Japan learned this lesson the hard way. In the years immediately following World War II, Japan found itself with the reputation as the world's foremost exporter of junk. Being a proud people and eager to rebuild their economy, Japanese leaders realized that they couldn't build a first-rate economy on second-rate merchandise and decided to do something about it.

139

Japan's transition from junk merchant to quality producer began in 1950. In that year W. Edwards Deming, an American statistician, began teaching basic concepts of statistical quality control to Japanese engineers stressing ways to reduce product defects. The basic concepts were passed on to workers at all levels of Japanese companies. But most important, Deming lectured to top executives stressing that quality doesn't originate on the factory floor but begins with a commitment from the top and filters down. Deming assured the Japanese that their quality could be the best in the world if they followed his advice. They did, and the rest is history.

Today Deming enjoys the stature of a national hero in Japan. He holds the Second Order Medal of the Sacred Treasure bestowed on him by Emperor Hirohito. And every year the prestigious Deming Award is given to a Japanese Company for gains in quality.

In 1962 Japanese workers began attacking quality problems in small, informal groups called *quality circles*. Employees at all levels learned the basic tools of statistical quality control and other problem-solving tools by participating in the circles. This chapter will examine quality circles and how to make them effective. But first let's take a look at quality from a broad perspective.

QUALITY—MYTHS AND REALITIES

A wise philosopher once noted "It ain't the things we don't know that hurt us. It's the things we think we know that ain't so." Such a statement applies very well to quality. Because of past experiences many of us harbor a lot of false beliefs about what quality is and how to go about improving it. Here are three of the most common ones:

Myth #1—Quality Control Means Inspection

Most traditional quality control systems are set up to inspect raw materials or finished products and separate the good from the bad. With a system like this it's no wonder quality is so costly.

But as Dr. Deming emphasizes, you can't inspect quality into a product. It has to be built in. All inspections can do is tell you which items to throw away. Inspection doesn't stop the waste of time, energy, raw materials, and effort because they've already been expended. A good quality control system continuously monitors the entire organization for problems so that corrections can be made before they develop into costly errors. Effective quality control is preventive in nature.

Myth #2—Improving Quality Slows Productivity

In our busy, hurry-up world everybody wants everything yesterday. But the fact is that quality doesn't slow productivity—expediency does. Working at a feverish pace only increases the chances of mistakes and poor workmanship. Think of it this way: If you can't find the time to do it right the first time, where will you find the time to do it again? Japan is living proof that if you pay close attention to quality, productivity improvement will naturally follow.

Myth #3—Quality Control Is Techniques,
Programs, and Slogans

Improving quality takes a lot more than simply organizing workers into quality circles, teaching them statistical techniques, and posting slogans reminding them to "Do it right the first time." Above all, quality is an attitude. It's a long-range, continuous commitment at all organizational levels to learn to do things better. And this commitment has to begin at the very top. All of the slogans, techniques, and speeches about quality are useless unless management backs them up with a long-range investment of time, money, and support. Like every other productivity-improvement program, quality must have a long-run focus. There's no quick fix.

THE QUALITY CIRCLE CONCEPT

Quality circles have taken American industry by storm. It's the most popular "made in Japan" technique that industry is adopting with fadish enthusiasm. Companies such as General Motors, 3M, RCA, Hughes Aircraft, American Airlines, and General Foods are just a few of the giants that have jumped on the QC bandwagon. But what are quality circles and why is everyone so excited?

A quality circle is a group of employees who meet regularly during working hours to identify, study, and eliminate work-related problems. The circle usually consists of ten or fewer people who work closely together on the same job. Before any circle begins functioning all participants are given specific training to help them spot and solve quality problems. Joining a quality circle is strictly voluntary and no one is forced to participate. Every circle has a leader, usually a supervisor or the worker's immediate boss.

The philosophy behind quality circles is based on very humanistic assumptions about people:

1. Each worker will assume the responsibility for his or her own work quality and wants to do a better job.
2. Each worker is the best expert at finding and solving his or her own quality problems. Those who do the job know the most about the job.
3. Improvements in quality must come through trained and committed people.

In one sense quality circles are a QWL program and quality circles have indeed resulted in improvements in worker morale, personal development, and enthusiasm. However, another important purpose of circles is to improve quality and productivity. A major emphasis is on learning quality control techniques and applying them to solve problems on the job.

The greatest advantage of the quality circle is that it taps the vast amount of brainpower at all levels of the organization. Once employees are trained and given time off to devote to problem-solving, they come up with all sorts of creative ways to do a better job. Here are a few examples:

- A quality circle of line operators at Texas Instruments increased output of an assembly-line operator from 10,000 to 18,500 units per day. As a result the company saved $1.2 million annually.

- A circle of clerical employees in a corporate mailroom reduced misdirected mail by 50 percent and saved the company $62,000 per year.
- A circle of skilled machinists was losing time locating precision tools. They studied the problem and solved it by building a portable tool cart with space for the appropriate tools. The cart could be quickly moved and the spaces were designed so that tools could be rapidly removed and replaced without misplacement. Estimated annual savings were $157,000.
- By studying the causes of failing solenoids a circle of Japanese operators at an auto parts plant reduced the failure rate from 7 percent to 1 percent in a nine-month period. They pinpointed the failure to three main causes:
  1. Improper soldering irons
  2. Poor quality coil wire
  3. Inadequate operator training
  The company cooperated by changing the irons, buying better quality wire, and allowing the group to set up its own training program.
- A circle of typists in an insurance company studied the problem of typists' errors. The problem was attributed to poor knowledge of linguistics and errors were reduced by scheduling an hour of training each week on title policy and procedures.
- Employee suggestions from quality circles in a large manufacturer saved the company $750,000 the first year by providing ideas for reducing scrap materials.

In addition to improvements in quality and productivity, quality circles can produce a host of other benefits for the company and the worker. By participating in circles, workers and supervisors improve communication and gain a new sense of respect for each other as they work together to solve common problems. The result is that worker attitudes improve and the "we–them" relationship between workers and the supervisor is replaced by an attitude of "all of us working together." Workers improve their self-image as they learn new techniques and see their own ideas used to improve productivity. Job satisfaction increases as everyone works together in a friendly, open atmosphere. The bottom line of a well-implemented quality circle program is that it creates a thinking, caring workforce of people who take pride in their work because their needs are harmoniously meshed with company goals. It's truly a win-win situation.

HOW QUALITY CIRCLES ARE ORGANIZED

When quality circles are being set up, it's important that they be organized subordinate to the regular chain of command as illustrated in Figure 1. Any attempt to bypass the regular management structure is asking for trouble. It's also important that no attempt be made to bypass the union if workers belong to one. Enthusiastic union support isn't necessary, but union leaders should be kept informed and asked to participate.

Most organizations begin their venture into quality circles by establishing a steering committee to investigate the QC concept and decide whether it will benefit the organization. The services of a management consultant can be most helpful here. The committee should have a manager from every major department, and it's a good idea to have a local union representative as well. Assuming the committee decides to adopt a QC program, it develops plans and policies for the program and appoints a coordinator.

The three key positions in a QC program are coordinator, facilitator, and group leader. The coordinator's job is administrative. He keeps the steering committee posted about how the circles are progressing and communicates the steering committee's wishes to the managers and facilitators. In essence, he is the liaison of the program in the various departments. He also has the job of selecting people to serve as facilitators.

The facilitator's job is the most crucial to the success of the QC program. His job is to sell and publicize the concept, get people to volunteer for circles, train leaders, help circle members solve problems, keep department managers informed about

Figure 1.   Quality Circles Organization

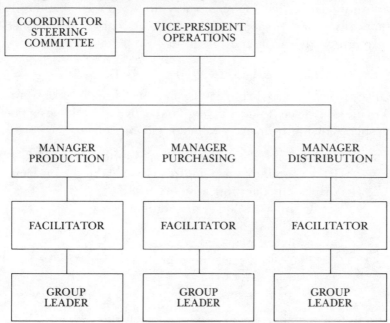

the circles, and anything else that will help the program. He initially conducts training sessions and helps members solve problems without getting directly involved. Instead he works as a catalyst and helps members solve their own problems without giving them the answers. Once the circles are established and functioning it isn't necessary for the facilitator to attend circle meetings. Successful facilitators can come from white-collar or blue-collar ranks. What's most important is their being excited about the program and enthusiastic about helping people reach solutions to problems.

The group leader is usually the foreman or immediate supervisor of the circle members. However, inside the circle he has no formal authority. Any objectives he wants to accomplish must be sold to the group. While the facilitator is usually an impartial observer at meetings, the group leader is an active participant. Group leaders must understand clearly that once inside the circle their opinions carry no more formal authority than any other members of the circle. Decisions are reached through participation and consensus.

QUALITY CIRCLE TECHNIQUES AND TOOLS

Once quality circles begin operating, they usually take a systematic approach to identifying and solving problems. The problem-solving format typically goes like this:

1. Choose a specific problem. Why is it important?
2. Gather specific data and information about the problem.
3. Analyze the data for possible causes.
4. Decide upon a solution or solutions.
5. Plan the "how" of the solution.
6. Do it! Put the plan into action.
7. Check it. Did it solve the problem?
8. Make sure it stays fixed.
9. Choose another specific problem and repeat the cycle.

Before members begin to work on problems they are taught statistical and problem-solving techniques to help them spot and solve problems effectively. Here are some of the more common ones. They are simple, practical; you can probably use some of these techniques in your own job even if you don't belong to a circle.

Check Sheets

In their search to spot problems or investigate causes of problems, circles frequently have to gather raw data and organize them in a presentable fashion. Usually there're plenty of data around in company records—such as inspection reports, scrap records, rework records, customer complaints, purchasing invoices, cost accounting records, personnel records, and the like. Or circle members may have observed problems and need to collect their own data. Whatever the situation, a simple, effec-

Figure 2. Typical check sheet for tallying data

Defect	Week				Total
	1	2	3	4	
Soldering	///	//	₩₩	₩₩ ₩₩	20
Alignment		/		//	3
Wiring	///		//		5
Scratches	/		//		3
Bad Parts	///	////	₩₩	///	15
Other	/				1
Total	11	7	14	15	47

tive way to organize data is to draw up a check sheet (such as Figure 2) and tally the data.

The check sheet in Figure 2 is from a circle of workers who assemble short-wave radio receivers. At an April QC meeting workers concluded that receiver defects were usually attributable to five major causes:

1. Poor solder joints
2. Faulty alignment
3. Wiring errors
4. Cabinet scratches
5. Faulty components (transistors, capacitors, resistors)

Before taking action the workers decided to inspect finished receivers carefully and tally the defects on the check sheet during the month of May. At the end of May, the check sheet (Figure 2) gave them the data to prove their claims. Using the data from the check sheet, the workers calculated the percentage of defects by category and ranked them:

DEFECT	NO. OF DEFECTS IN MAY	PERCENT
Soldering	20	43%
Bad parts	15	32
Wiring	5	11
Alignment	3	6
Scratches	3	6
Other	1	2
Total	47	100%

Now they knew where most of their headaches were coming from and they used another simple statistical tool to present it.

The Pareto Chart

The Pareto Chart is a simple device for portraying visually where major quality problems are. It's based on the principle that most headaches come from relatively few areas. For example, the Pareto diagram in Figure 3 points out that 75 percent of short-wave receiver defects were due to either faulty components or poor solder joints.

Armed with this information, the workers in the circle broke into two subgroups. One group studied component defects and found most were caused by a faulty audio capacitor. The other group found the poor solder joints caused by inferior-quality solder that failed to melt properly. An appeal was made to management for a higher grade of capacitors and solder. The request was granted and quality improved dramatically within two months (Figure 4).

In addition to helping spot major problems, Pareto charts have several other uses:

1. They make an effective visual aid for making presentations. The old cliché about a picture being worth a thousand words applies very well here. Circle members or management can glance at the chart and quickly grasp the nature and magnitude of the problem.

Figure 3.   Pareto Chart

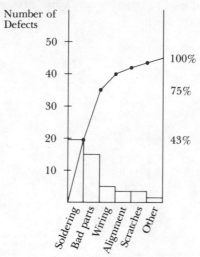

2. They make an excellent motivational tool. Keeping the charts prominently displayed reminds everyone of what the major problems are and encourages them to think about ways to solve quality problems.

3. Pareto charts can illustrate the before-and-after of quality improvement. For example, Figure 4 showed circle members how their efforts in spotting faulty capacitors and poor solder had resulted in a drastic improvement in quality. The before-and-after charts were forwarded to management, who quickly heaped praise and positive feedback on the circle; the members took pride in their success and resolved to do even better.

Cause-and-Effect Diagrams

More often than not quality problems are complicated and difficult to define. And any one problem can be caused by a number of factors. To help clarify problems and spot their causes, quality circles use a very handy tool called a cause-and-effect or "fishbone" diagram.

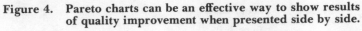

Figure 4.   Pareto charts can be an effective way to show results of quality improvement when presented side by side.

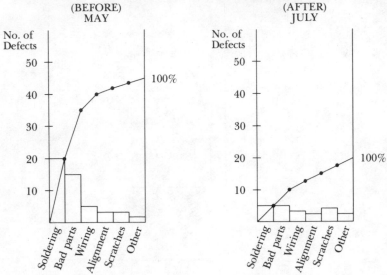

As a problem-solver, the cause-and-effect diagram visually portrays a result and its possible causes. Figure 5 is an illustration of a completed cause-and-effect diagram. It also shows how this useful tool can be applied to solve a problem that many of us face every day at the office—bad-tasting coffee. Here's how a fishbone is constructed in a QC meeting:

1. Define the main quality characteristic or problem. Draw a large line on a chalkboard or flip chart (this is the backbone of the diagram) and a box at the end of the line:

Write the main problem or quality characteristic in the box.

2. Conduct a brainstorming session. In the session, ask all circle members to think of as many potential causes of the problem as they can. Everyone should participate; any criticism of ideas is forbidden. Be sure to write down all ideas. (Details for conducting a brainstorming session are in Chapter 12.)

3. When circle members have finished brainstorming, group the numerous causes into several major categories or causes. Major causes may be such things as materials, manpower, method, machinery management, and customers. Add the major causes to the diagram in boxes parallel to the backbone and add the minor causes by clustering them around the major causes. Thus the skeleton of a "fishbone" looks like this:

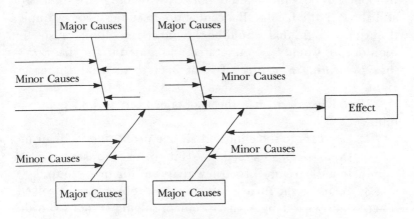

Figure 5.   Cause and effect diagrams are useful for solving all kinds of problems

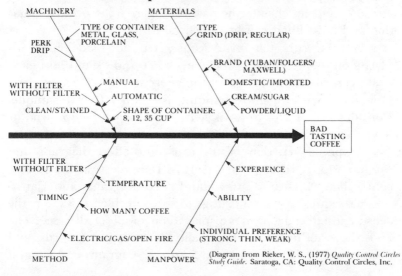

(Diagram from Rieker, W. S., (1977) *Quality Control Circles Study Guide*. Saratoga, CA: Quality Control Circles, Inc.

4. When all the causes have been written on the diagram, the group evaluates and discusses each one. The most likely causes are circled and these are the ones that will get special attention.

The great thing about the fishbone is that it can be applied to almost any problem-solving situation. It can also be used to evaluate good effects as well. Instead of defining a problem, a fishbone can be constructed to portray why things are successful and show all the factors that contribute to success. For example, if output is high, that would be the effect and all the causes for high output would be enumerated and added to the diagram—thus presenting a picture of what it takes to make things go right.

If you decide to use the fishbone, keep several points in mind:

1. Don't try to solve more than one problem on a diagram.

2. Don't overload a diagram. If a group of causes begins to dominate a diagram, draw a new diagram for that group.

3. Focus on the future and how the problem can be solved. There's always a danger that problem-solving sessions can degenerate into gripe sessions where people and circumstances are blamed for past mistakes. Don't let this happen. History is history and nothing can change the past. Emphasize the present situation and how things can be improved in the future.

4. Make sure that every cause is understood before it's placed on the diagram. If members can't understand how each cause contributes to the effect the exercise will be meaningless. One way to insure understanding is the 5-W/1-H technique. Consider each factor and ask why, what, when, where, who or how it contributes to the effect.

A special variation of the cause-and-effect diagram won Sumitomo Electric of Japan the 1978 Deming Award. The concept called CEDAC (Cause and Effect Diagrams and Cards) doesn't require special meetings to solve problems. Rather, the cause-and-effect diagram is displayed on a wall for all to see. The know-how to improve the quality is written on cards and everyone is invited to add causes to the diagrams and suggest improvements by writing them on additional cards. New suggestions are tried and the results are recorded. The advantage of this approach is that workers can make suggestions any time without having to attend meetings.

On Error Training

Another innovative approach to quality circles has recently come out of Sumitomo Electric. On Error Training (OET) is based on the idea that the perfect time to train the group is when an error occurs. Its developer, Ryuji Fukuda, formulated five rules of OET:

1. *Himself (or Herself) Rule.* The person who has made an error must take care of it. If a worker discovers that he has made an error, he calls the group together to discuss what went wrong.

2. *Quickly Rule.* Discovered errors must be dealt with within thirty minutes.

3. *Actually Rule.* The error must be corrected on the spot and not dealt with later at a QC meeting. By waiting for a meeting, critical information may be forgotten.

4. *Support Rule.* The supervisor supports the worker by pointing out that the problem belongs to the entire group. Blaming and finger-pointing isn't allowed.

5. *Don't Speak Rule.* The worker who has made the error must try to find a solution while the group is gathered. Even if he has the answer, the supervisor can't speak until the worker has finished discussing the situation.

OET isn't universally applicable. In many instances it's just too costly to shut down production to look at an error. Nevertheless, OET has worked well for Sumitomo Electric. One group using OET reduced its reject rate by 90 percent in one year. And one of Sumitomo's cable-manufacturing plants hasn't produced a single defect in over four years.

Quality Control Charts

Measuring quality is essential because the very word *quality* means conforming to a specified standard. One of the oldest and most useful tools for monitoring a quality characteristic is the quality control chart. The chart specifies the ideal standard and the deviations that can be tolerated. The quality characteristic is measured periodically and plotted on the chart.

For example, let's assume you work at an auto assembly plant and are responsible for seeing that autos receive a quality paint job. You know that a good paint job requires that the paint temperature never exceeds 90 degrees or falls below 50 degrees and that the ideal paint temperature is 70 degrees. Therefore you measure the temperature hourly and plot it on a control chart that would look like this:

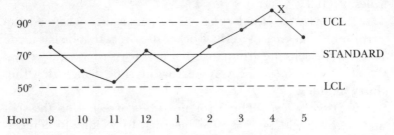

As long as the temperature falls within the upper and lower control limits (UCL and LCL) paint temperature is no problem. However, once the temperature transgresses the limits, adjustments have to be made to bring it back to within the prescribed range. In our example X marks the spot where the temperature went out of control. The painting process has to be stopped until the temperature is correctly adjusted.

Quality control charts come in various formats. Whatever their nature, the basic advantage of a control chart is that it sets an ideal standard, prescribes limits, and provides a method for monitoring and measuring quality on a continuous basis.

Check sheets, Pareto charts, cause-and-effect diagrams, brainstorming sessions, on error training, and control charts are some of the basic tools used by circles for spotting and solving quality problems. The next time you're wrestling with a problem, go back and review these tools. Will a fishbone diagram help you think through the problem and its causes? Can you brainstorm some solutions with a group? Will gathering data and plotting them on a Pareto chart help you pinpoint the majority of your headaches? What part of your job is important enough to be regularly measured and monitored on a control chart? All of us can use these tools to help us do things better in our jobs, in our homes, in our hobbies, or wherever else we want to improve quality.

Making Quality Circles Work

Like every other innovative work program, quality circles are going to have their share of successes and failures. Many of the failures can be avoided by following basic guidelines and avoiding common pitfalls. The ground rules for successful QWL programs at the end of Chapter 6 apply very well to quality circles. In addition, here are some specific recommendations that will help insure a successful QC program.

1. Don't bypass any levels of management by creating a separate structure or independent chain of command for circles. Failure to work through the regular chain of command is asking for failure. And make sure that all levels of management are kept informed.

2. Give circle meetings a high priority. Don't put off or postpone meetings and be sure that meetings are held in a pleasant, private, quiet environment, free of distractions. Providing a well-lit, comfortable, private meeting room tells workers that management is serious about the program. On the other hand, holding meetings in the center of the company cafeteria communicates a lack of support. Be sure to hold meetings during regular work hours and pay workers who attend.

3. Be very careful in choosing facilitators. They are the key to successful QC programs. In the beginning the facilitator must be a salesman who sells the concept to the group. Then he becomes a teacher who trains volunteers in the mechanics of circle operation. Later, as the circle begins to solve real problems, the facilitator works as a coach and adviser at the meetings. Finally, the facilitator acts as a consultant members can call on if they need help when a tough or unexpected problem arises.

Good facilitators are:

- *People-oriented.* They realize that everyone is created differently and accept everyone's strengths and weaknesses. They expect the best from everyone and build the group by drawing on the strengths of individual members.
- *Nondirective teachers.* They don't tell circle members answers to problems but encourage people to think and find solutions of their own.
- *Knowledgeable* about the tasks circle members perform.
- *Stimulating and encouraging.* He asks more questions than he answers in order to stimulate personal growth of the members.
- *Someone members will trust.* People who join circles are participating in a totally new approach to work that may, at first, be strange and frightening to them. The facilitator must be someone in whom they can place their trust.
- *Neutral.* Facilitators can't become directly involved in circle activities because they aren't circle members. They can encourage, train, monitor meetings, and advise but should be careful to never impose their ideas on group members.

4. Be sure to train members before allowing them to begin solving problems. A common mistake is to have workers locate a problem and then try to teach them the appropriate skills. This is inefficient and time-wasting. Provide the training up front. Most QC training falls into two categories. One category deals with human resources topics such as participative problem-solving communication, interpersonal skills, and motivation. The other category teaches the mechanics and organization of circles and the statistical problem-solving tools.

5. Once the program begins several *don'ts* should be kept in mind:

- Don't allow circles to work in problems outside their realm. There's no point in solving problems over which members have no control.

- Don't allow circles to become too large. Instead, create new circles.
- Don't mishandle employees psychologically. There's no place for put-downs, personal attacks, or ridicule in quality circles. When people make mistakes the correction should be constructive and encouraging. Any criticism must be concerned with ideas, not personalities.
- Don't promise what you can't deliver. The whole program is voluntary, and if members start to lose trust you'll find circle leaders talking to empty rooms at meetings.

6. Get more information. If you're seriously interested in quality circles, you need to know a lot more about them than I can tell you in one chapter. Talk to other people who have used circles or find a consultant who has worked with companies implementing QC programs. The following organizations can provide you with more information:

International Association of Quality Circles
P.O. Box 30635
Midwest City, OK 73140

American Society for Quality Control
161 West Wisconsin Ave.
Milwaukee, WI 53203

CHAPTER 8

GRAY POWER—AMERICA'S UNTAPPED RESOURCE

"How old would you be if you didn't know how old you was?"

—*Satchel Paige*

America is facing a gray population explosion. By the year 2000 the estimated number of Americans over age sixty will jump 35 percent to over 45 million. In 1900, U.S. life expectancy was only forty-six years for men and forty-eight for women, but in this century we have increased the average life expectancy almost twenty-five years. Furthermore, older people are living longer. Today's sixty-five-year-old U.S. male has a life expectancy of over seventy-seven years and his female counterpart can expect to live until she is eighty-three. Declining birth rates coupled with advances in medical care have set the stage for a much older population.

While lifespans have been increasing career spans have been decreasing. As we become better educated, Americans spend more years in school and less on the job. And early retirement is part of the American dream. Today's average retirement age is sixty-two and many public and private pension plans encourage early retirement and penalize those who continue to work.

At one time, almost every man between ages fifty-five and sixty was actively employed in the labor force but today a sizable

158

portion of that age group is already retired. And many of the early-retired are some of our most intelligent, creative, and potentially productive people.

If we look far into the future, the picture looks even more drastic. Starting in the year 2010, the baby-boom generation will begin reaching age sixty-five, and those born after the boom will bear the brunt of keeping America productive and providing for a large number of retirees. Today the number of workers to retirees is about three to one but in the next century the ratio could drop to less than two to one. What's going to happen when a huge population of older citizens expects a relatively small labor force to provide for them? What's going to happen to our already sagging productivity if more Americans retire earlier and live longer? How will a huge percentage of retired Americans cope for the last twenty-five or more years of their lives on pensions if inflation continues (as it is likely to)? Can we afford to keep relegating our workers to early rocking chairs? Not if we hope to survive and prosper. If we fail to harness the resources of a graying America we will surely become a decaying America.

Fortunately, the situation is far from hopeless and there are a number of things the government, organizations, and we as individuals can do to insure that a grayer America remains productive, strong, and free. But the key to preventing an American age crisis begins with planning now. In this chapter we will look at the resources older workers can provide and how companies can capitalize on them. And we will also look at a number of ways you can prepare to make your later years both productive and enjoyable.

FACTS AND FALLACIES ABOUT AGING AND OLDER WORKERS

For years our society has worshiped at the fountain of youth and we have dealt with aging much the same way we have dealt with death—by denying or ignoring it. As a result most of us don't know very much about what happens to us as we age, and what we do know is usually negative and highly exaggerated. One

classic (and very humorous) example of the negative stereotype
of aging is the following verse that was passed on to a friend of
mine on his fortieth birthday:

YOU KNOW YOU ARE GETTING OLDER WHEN:
Almost everything hurts. What doesn't hurt doesn't work any
    more.
It feels like the morning after the night before, and you haven't
    been anywhere.
All the names in your little black book end in M.D.
You get winded playing chess.
You look forward to a dull evening.
You still chase women but have forgotten why.
You turn out the lights for economic, not romantic, reasons.
Your knees buckle and your belt won't.
You are 17 around the neck, 42 around the waist and 126 around
    the golf course.
You sink your teeth into a steak and they stay there.
You try to straighten the wrinkle in your socks and find you aren't
    wearing any.
A little old gray-haired lady tries to help you across the street. She's
    your wife.

Many of us harbor serious fears about growing old. We
automatically associate old age with growing senile and spending
our final years as invalids confined to nursing homes. But the
fact is that only 10 percent of Americans over age sixty-five show
signs of senility. And 80 percent of us who live past age sixty-five
will never be a patient in a nursing home.

In addition, recent studies reveal that intelligence or learning capacity doesn't deteriorate until at least age seventy and that
most older people have no serious memory defects. Furthermore, today's older citizens are healthier and far better educated
than their parents. This trend is likely to continue.

Studies comparing the productivity of older workers with
younger ones reveal some very interesting facts. While they
aren't as quick as their younger colleagues, older workers:

- Have fewer accidents at work
- Have less absenteeism
- Display sounder judgment
- Have greater maturity
- Are more emotionally stable
- Are more loyal and reliable
- Have lower rates of drug addiction
- Are more satisfied with their jobs
- Experience less stress on the job

The strengths of younger workers are that they learn more quickly, are more flexible, and have a greater willingness to take risks and try new ideas. But on balance, older workers are just as capable and productive if they are given the opportunity, training, incentives, and a job suited to take advantage of their strengths.

But perhaps the most important fact that comes out of studying older people is that we all age differently. Consequently it's a mistake to judge and stereotype people on the basis of age. As Dr. Robert Butler, director of the National Institute of Aging, put it, "The aged are a more diverse, heterogeneous group than any other. We become more complicated as we grow older."

Don't worry about medical science creating a nation of elderly invalids. It isn't likely to happen. If taken care of, the human body is good for a maximum of about eighty-five years for most of us. After that our cells are programmed to self-destruct and we rapidly deteriorate and die. But until that time, the odds for sound physical and mental health are good. In the coming years, more of us will be reaching the maximum lifespan—and in better health.

THE BENEFITS OF CONTINUING TO WORK

The clear trend is that Americans are going to be extending their career lives in the future. This is good for productivity and older Americans. The companies and the nation will benefit from the contributions of millions of experienced, reliable, dedicated workers. But the greatest benefits will be to the older workers themselves. Why should older people want to continue working? Here are several reasons:

- *To stay ahead of inflation and maintain a decent standard of living.* Retiring on fixed incomes is a thing of the past. Plain old work is still one of the best hedges against inflation.
- *To feel in control of their lives.* Few of us want to spend the later years of our life at the mercy of government programs and handouts or, worse yet, being supported by our children. Working longer decreases the chances of becoming an economic dependent. Continuing to work also gives us the sense that we have some control over what happens to us.
- *To have a sense of purpose and worth.* For many of us, our sense of identity and worth is directly related to our work. Retirement can be a real psychological blow to our self-esteem. And people who retire with dreams of utopian leisure often wake up to find that a perpetual holiday is more like a nightmare. Continuing employment is one way to maintain a feeling of purpose and worth that everyone needs.
- *To live healthier, longer lives.* Retirement is frequently followed by poor health and premature death. More than cancer or heart disease, inactivity may be the biggest killer of all among the elderly. And employment is one way to keep our bodies and minds active. What we don't use, we lose.
- *To satisfy social needs.* All too often, retirement results in isolation. At one time we could retire and spend our remaining years in contentment surrounded by children and grandchildren. But today most American families are scattered throughout the country, with sons and daughters often living thousands of miles away. Continu-

ing work provides us with the people contact everyone needs to feel happy and fulfilled.

A 1979 Harris poll revealed that 46 percent of retirees said they would like to be working—a remarkable statistic when you consider that the Social Security System is going broke. And 48 percent of all fifty-to-sixty-four-year-old employees stated that they intend to extend their working lives. It's clear that America's gray power is a growing resource that's waiting to be tapped.

STRATEGIES FOR HARNESSING GRAY POWER

First of all, we must stop forcing and encouraging our older workers to retire. Mandatory retirement is a waste of valuable human resources that we can no longer afford. It wastes talents that take decades to develop, places greater burdens on the economy, and is a slap in the face to the dignity of older people. While it may be necessary to evaluate older employees more closely, simply to strip someone of a career at an arbitrary age is a big mistake.

In addition to ending mandatory retirement, we have to start providing incentives and programs that will make it worthwhile for older workers to continue working. Why should someone over age sixty-five have his Social Security income reduced if he earns more than a meager sum each year? Why not let him draw the amount he is entitled to regardless of income? To do otherwise is to penalize him for working.

Corporate and other retirement plans also need to be reevaluated. In many of these plans, an employee with twenty or more years of service can retire at a minimum of half-pay. All of which causes many productive people to retire and seek work elsewhere. Why not allow them to draw their pensions and remain in their present job? In many cases it costs the organization less to do this than to hire and retrain a new, inexperienced employee. Obviously, this option isn't the answer for every job or every company. But we need to rethink our policies toward older workers and provide them with programs and incentives tailored to benefit them and the company. Too many of our current retirement policies and programs are outdated and counterproductive.

Fortunately, there are a number of things that are being done by progressive organizations and people to harness gray-power productivity. The following are some of the more successful programs that may be useful in your organization. Or, if you're an older worker, perhaps you can profit from knowing about and participating in some of these programs.

Create Permanent Part-time Positions

As we saw in Chapter 6 the rigid nine-to-five, clock-punching approach to work seems to be fading. Flexible approaches to work (such as job-sharing and flextime) are becoming increasingly popular and many flexible approaches can be tailored to meet the needs of older workers.

Creating permanent part-time positions is one excellent way to harness gray-power productivity; large retail outlets have done this for years. For example, Macy's department store employs older part-time workers and has found them to be a very stable work force. Macy's has no mandatory retirement age and many full-time workers adjust to retirement by taking part-time positions.

Phase-in Retirement

Phased retirement programs are another option that some companies are using with success. Many of us, after retiring, wish we had our old jobs back. Polaroid therefore created a rehearsal retirement program. The program allows an employee to retire for three to six months to see how it feels. If the worker doesn't like it, he can have his old job back.

In order to help older workers adjust to retirement, the Wrigley Company helps sixty-five-year-old workers gradually adjust. If they wish, each worker over sixty-five can take one month's leave without pay the first year, two months the second year, and so on. Other companies use various strategies such as shortening the number of days worked each week as retirement approaches. All phased-in retirement programs help workers adjust to retirement and keep them productive longer.

Allow People to Work at Home

It's possible to perform many jobs at home. A smart organization can harness the productivity of many older workers by assigning tasks that they can perform without having to commute every day. Many clerical and white-collar tasks such as preparing and typing reports and documents, routine correspondence, and telephone calls can be done just as easily at home. Why not assign such jobs to capable older workers and let them work in the comfort of their own domiciles?

With high energy costs commuting has become more expensive. And the coming electronic revolution is going to make it possible for more of us to work at home. Personal computers, display monitors, and other information-processing hardware will soon be standard household equipment. Older people who can't or don't want to commute will be able to perform many jobs in the comfort of their own households, given the tools and the proper skills.

Hire Older Workers as New Employees

Early pension and retirement programs are providing a large pool of older workers who have many productive years ahead of them and a wealth of education and experience behind them. And some companies have been hiring retirees and finding them excellent, stable employees. Much of the hiring of older workers has taken place in high-technology industries such as aerospace, manufacturing, and banking, where skills are in short supply.

A number of companies have been hiring their own retirees with great success. In the 1979 retiree newsletter, Sun (Oil) Company announced it would be hiring its own retirees and was swamped with 600 applications for part-time jobs. The "new" hires worked out so well that a data bank was created to match retiree skills with temporary jobs. Other organizations such as Banker's Life and Casualty Co., Morgan Guaranty Trust Company of New York, and Aerospace Corporation have reported excellent successes in hiring their own retirees. Many retirees are hired to fill in during peak periods of activity and summer vacations.

Hiring retirees as consultants is another option that organizations have used with success. They know the business, have years of experience, and may be able to provide training, insight, or solutions to problems that less experienced workers can benefit from. One example is the Early Retirement Consultant Plan of the San Francisco Unified School District. The plan allows teachers over fifty years of age with ten consecutive years of teaching in the state to be hired as consultants and receive their full pensions. The consultants are paid on a daily basis, allowed to work a limited number of days each year, and provide services in areas such as new teacher training, curriculum development, special studies, general administration, and office work. The plan has been enthusiastically received by both retirees and regular employees.

Redesign and Reassign Jobs

Time takes its toll on us all, and some physical deterioration is a natural part of the aging process. Additionally, we often incur various ailments, aches, and pains that inhibit us from performing certain tasks in our jobs. But this doesn't mean we can't still be productive. A wise organization focuses on what people *can do*, not what they can no longer do, and redesigns their jobs in light of their capabilities. For example, a carpenter in one company was still able to handle saws and lathes but unable to bend due to a back injury. This prevented him from doing trim and molding work. To solve the problem, the trim and molding work was assigned to others and the carpenter was given additional assignments he could handle, such as driving a truck and delivering supplies.

Very often, simple changes such as changing the lighting, providing footrests, or repositioning benches, controls, or tools can add years to an employee's career. One of the key issues in the quality-work-life movement is to design jobs to the individual, based on his unique needs.

When a worker's physical condition prevents him from continuing in his job, consider retraining and transferring him to another job. Manual workers who have difficulty handling tools because of tendonitis or arthritis can be moved to clerical or inspection jobs. Others who can't sit or stand for long periods can be retrained for jobs where they can have mobility as needed. Still others can be trained to work on project teams to improve quality, productivity, or sales. With a little effort and imagination, management can give older workers a new lease on life and turn a disabled worker into a valuable human resource.

Tap the Re-entry Market

Another large pool of older human resources is women who have left work to become homemakers and return to the labor force some years later. The skyrocketing cost of rearing a family, coupled with the high divorce rate, is causing more women to seek employment. And many of them are over forty-five.

To my way of thinking, re-entry workers are a real gold mine of human potential. Many of them are highly educated and intelligent; some even have advanced degrees. In addition to their innate abilities and education, they have developed management, organizational, and interpersonal skills in their roles as homemakers. And many of these skills can be transferred very readily to the workplace.

Because they have been away from the work world (or perhaps were never in it), re-entry workers usually require counseling and training, but most of them are eager and willing to learn. Today's seminars, workshops, and college classrooms are frequently filled with eager-to-learn re-entry types. I assure you they are excellent students and fast learners.

A number of support organizations have been formed to

help re-entry workers obtain necessary training and employment opportunities. The American Woman's Economic Development Corporation was established with government funding
to provide entrepreneural training and skills to women wanting
to start or manage their own business. And a number of
displaced-homemaker programs have appeared throughout the
country to assist women forced into the workforce by divorce,
widowhood, abandonment, or the disability of a spouse. The
National Science Foundation has sponsored programs to seek
out and find employment for the hundreds of thousands of
women holding degrees in math and science who are unemployed. These and other programs are providing major services
for re-entry workers and showing excellent results.

HOW TO HARNESS YOUR OWN GRAY POWER

If you aren't already an older worker, the chances are you will
be. Premature death is going to become more the exception than
the rule, and many of us will experience lifespans well into our
eighties and beyond. No matter how old you are, now is the time
to ask yourself "What quality of life do I want for myself after
age sixty and what can I do about it starting today?" You can
begin preparing for your later years now—and the younger you
begin, the better your current and later years will be. Basically
you can do four things:

1. *Prepare financially.* As I recommended in Chapter 2, put
aside at least 10 percent of your income with religious zeal. Take
advantage of every program that will allow you to shelter income
before taxes. Find a way to finance the purchase of property and
buy it. Waiting for the prices to come down in a real-estate crash
is the wishful thinking of a fool. Establish a diversified investment strategy that won't put all of your eggs in one basket. And
don't depend on Social Security!

2. *Keep on learning.* It's been said that we're entering an era
of turbulence characterized by unpredictable changes. If this is

true, the lessons you learned at twenty or thirty will be irrelevant by the time you're forty or beyond.

Being educated is much more than getting the proper academic credentials. It's making a lifetime commitment to learning and keeping current in a turbulent world. The most important thing you gain from formal education isn't a storehouse of knowledge. In the final analysis, the best educated are those who have learned how to learn and keep on learning.

Those who keep on reading, training, and learning never become obsolete, no matter what their age. And there's another bonus. People who keep mentally active are less likely to lose their memory and other faculties as the years go by.

3. *Think in terms of more than one career.* Although it's perfectly all right to spend your entire worklife in one endeavor, if that's your preference, early retirement programs and longer lifespans give you the option of enjoying two or more careers. By the time you reach forty or fifty you may find that you've grown tired of your current livelihood. Take stock and investigate other options. Second and third careers are the wave of the future.

4. *Take care of yourself.* To quote Leon Eldred, "If I'd known I was going to live so long, I'd have taken better care of myself." One study conducted by UCLA surveyed almost 7000 people for living habits, quality of life, and longevity. The study found that the healthiest people followed seven simple habits:

- Never smoke cigarettes
- Get regular physical activity
- Use alcohol moderately or never
- Sleep seven to eight hours each night
- Maintain proper weight
- Eat breakfast
- Avoid eating between meals

Ten years after the first survey, the researchers checked to see how the subjects had fared. They calculated that the life expectancy of a forty-five-year-old man who followed all seven practices was eleven years longer than those who followed three or fewer. In addition to those seven simple practices, you can up your chances for a healthier old age by controlling your blood pressure and avoiding large amounts of emotional stress (more about stress in Chapter 13).

If you're an older worker seeking employment or a second career, take advantage of the numerous organizations that are available to help you. For example, Mature Temps is a nation-wide employment service that specializes in placing older work-ers with client customers. In 1979, Mature Temps placed more than 15,000 people over the age of fifty and reports that they could have placed more. Job Finders of San Mateo, California, is a three-week self-help workshop which teaches people the basics of how to find and get a job. Other services such as Retirement Jobs, Inc., of San Francisco; Second Careers Program of Los Angeles; and the Senior Personnel Employment Council of Westchester (New York) are just a few of many services that can offer assistance in helping older workers find employment. Seek them out and see what they have to offer.

Most important, don't fall for the "I'm too old" trap. Society has brainwashed us into believing that most of life's activities are the sole province of the young. Nonsense! It's your life—take charge of it and do what's meaningful to you regardless of your age. If you want to take up disco dancing at seventy or computer programming at eighty, do it. We all have to age but we don't have to stagnate. That's a choice.

CHAPTER 9

BREAKING OUT OF THE PAPER PRISON

*"Red tape is proliferating
In a hundred thousand ways.
I'm filling out forms and records
Until I am in a daze."*

—Sid Taylor

Paperwork and the proliferation of bureaucratic clutter have gotten totally out of control. How bad is it? It's so bad that managers spend the bulk of their days doing time in a paper prison instead of managing people and resources. It's so bad that registered nurses spend about half of their working hours filling out forms instead of tending to patients. It's so bad that universities receiving federal funds must submit reports whose lengths are better measured in pounds than pages. In fact, if the cost of government paperwork continues to increase at the rate of the past twenty years, it will consume our entire gross national product sometime in the next century. Is that bad enough?

Well, if it isn't, consider that government paperwork is just the tip of the iceberg. Every organization generates its own mountains of memos, internal reports, forms, policies, procedures, and computer printouts that have just about all of us drowning in a sea of clutter.

Paperwork is one of our major productivity killers. It diverts time, energy, and money but usually adds nothing to the value of

171

a product or service. Most paperwork only adds to the cost of doing business and gives nothing in return. And if you raise the cost of doing things without increasting output, you're decreasing productivity.

Paperwork eats up profits too. For example, let's assume you own a small business that averages a 10 percent return on investment. Your paperwork burden increases and forces you to hire a new clerk at $15,000 per year. This means that you must increase your total revenues by $150,000 just to pay the clerk's salary. In addition, you have to pay fringe benefits, and the increased paperwork will also require storage space, file space, and other additions to overhead. On the other hand, $15,000 saved is $15,000 earned and a direct addition to profits. In short, paper is money.

In addition to the financial costs, paperwork has huge psychological costs. Doctors, nurses, teachers, managers and sales reps, and numerous other professionals complain of the endless hours they spend pushing paper instead of performing the tasks they're trained to do. All of which leaves them feeling overworked, frustrated, forced into doing meaningless work, and burned out. If your job comes equipped with a huge amount of paperwork, you know exactly what I mean. Hours spent shuffling paper leave us with the empty feeling that we are spinning our wheels by filling our days with trivia. And those gut-level sensations are usually very accurate. Foster Fowler summed it up well: "In a bureaucracy, accomplishment is inversely proportional to the volume of paper used."

WHY THE PAPER PRISON GROWS

Clearly, the growth of government is one of the largest single contributors to today's paperwork explosion. But a number of other major forces are clogging up the productive arteries of our organizations with paper. Here are a few.

Computers

In 1970, Peter Drucker wrote: "At present the computer is the greatest possible obstacle to management information because everybody has been using it to produce tons of paper. Now, psychology tells us that the one sure way to shut off all perception is to flood the senses with stimuli. That's why the manager with reams of computer output on his desk is hopelessly uninformed." Drucker's observation is truer today than ever.

In the midst of our clamor to improve productivity, it's interesting to see the various computer manufacturers promising to quell our paperwork problems with the latest in state-of-the-art systems. It's also interesting to note that these are the same companies that promised to eliminate clerks with the installation of computerized management-information systems.

If technology was the answer to the paperwork problem, it would have been solved long ago. But the computer has caused more paperwork headaches to date than it ever thought about solving. Companies invest large sums in data processing systems and then feel compelled to justify their existence. And how do they justify it? By keeping the system working around the clock, spitting out stacks of letters, reports, data, facts, figures, and all sorts of information—much of which is unnecessary. And the necessary and useful information is usually hidden somewhere in the reams of printout paper like a needle in a haystack.

Copy Machines

Photocopy machines can be a real asset to organizations (especially if the organization is Xerox, Canon, Savin, IBM, or Sharp). But all too often the use of copiers isn't properly managed and the result is a lot of unnecessary paper. It's so easy to run those two or three extra copies just in case you need them for tomorrow's meeting.

It's hard to imagine how organizations got along before photocopiers, but they did. Carbon copies were messy and more trouble to make. Consequently, not as many copies were made. The problem with photocopies is that we have too many and they are too accessible. As a result, copies of memos, reports, and documents are run and circulated to people who have no need for them.

Creeping Bureaucracy

Small businesses rarely have severe paperwork problems other than those imposed by the government. However, as businesses begin to grow, the volume of paperwork begins to increase. The bureaucratic cycle described in Chapter 4 takes hold and new layers of management add various reports, memos, and documents to the work routine.

Creeping bureaucracy happens so gradually that it's often difficult to detect. A report is added here, a form there, and no one seems to notice. The only problem is that once printouts, forms, or various paper documents are added to the routine, they are rarely dropped. Sooner or later the continuous addition of paperwork takes its cumulative toll. The organization finds itself inflexible, unresponsive, and choking on red tape.

Job Insecurity

Many clerical and administrative jobs exist simply because of the tremendous volumes of paperwork that have been created. And the logical incentive for people who make their living shuffling paper is to create more paperwork. Any attempts to reduce the flow of paperwork could end their livelihood. Who can blame them?

In Chapter 1 I pointed out that an American factory worker has incentives to slow down productivity because he's paid a straight salary, has no guarantee of lifetime employment, and can be thrown out of work by hard times or automation. Much the same is true for the paper-pusher. He usually works on a straight salary, usually has no guarantees of lifetime employment, and discovering ways to reduce paper and improve office productivity could mean the end of his job. Consequently it's in his best interest to create more forms, records, policies, procedures, printouts, or whatever regardless of how much doing so strangles productivity. And if he succeeds in creating enough new paper, it's possible the company will reward him by hiring an assistant to help him.

Personal Insecurity

See Jack work. Work, work, work. His desk is full of paper. Paper, paper, paper. It keeps Jack busy. Busy, busy, busy. And it makes Jack and his boss very happy. Happy, happy, happy. Isn't Jack terrific?

Not necessarily. Activity and productivity aren't the same things. Jack may be terribly unsure of himself so he continuously stays busy to impress the boss and quell his pangs of insecurity. And shuffling paper is a great way to stay busy. It's much like the saying from the French cavalry: "When in doubt, gallop."

As long as there's plenty of paper to shuffle everyone can stay busy and no one has to worry about not having anything to do. To many, paperwork means productivity and they churn out the reams of paper like robots, giving little thought or meaning to its purpose. It makes them feel important, gives them a sense of power and a reason for being.

Poor Management

Too much paperwork is often a symptom of poor management. Whenever goals and objectives are unclear all of us have a tendency to fill a void of purpose with activity. And creating and processing paper can provide us with plenty of busy work.

It's also important to remember that management is the prime shaper of the work climate in any organization. And hostile work climates are almost always paper-intensive. Why? Because whenever workers are put on the defensive their top priority isn't doing the job but protecting themselves from threatening managers who are ready to pounce on them at the slightest transgression. Consequently they become card-carrying members of the CYA (short for "Cover your ass"). And how do they cover themselves? By putting everything in writing and filing all memos and directives.

On the other hand, a supportive work climate that builds a worker's sense of security and self-esteem enables him to concentrate time and effort on being productive and doing a good job.

The more secure people feel about themselves and their jobs, the less likely they are to originate, collect, and shuffle paper.

As you can see, the paperwork problem is usually due to a combination of governmental, technical, and psychological factors that all come together and choke productivity. But not every organization (believe it or not) really has a paperwork problem. How can you tell whether your workplace does? Here are thirteen key signs of too much paper:

- Skyrocketing overhead is squeezing profits.
- Getting anything done is a complicated, lengthy process.
- Things rarely get done on time.
- People have difficulty working together and coordinating efforts.
- New staff positions and levels of management are rapidly increasing.
- Decisions aren't being made and approval takes forever.
- There are rules and forms for everything.
- People have trouble finding necessary information.
- Everyone goes through the motions but no one seems to care.
- Making innovations or changes seems nearly impossible.
- People are confused about their job's priorities.
- The whole organization seems too cumbersome, fragmented, and unmanageable.
- Managers work long hours and take home brief cases stuffed with paper.

None of these symptoms is a guarantee that an organization has too much paper, but if four or more of them describe where you work, the odds are that you're logging time in a paper prison. If so, it's time to stop doing nine-to-five at hard labor and break out.

HOW TO BREAK OUT OF THE PRISON

Is the paperwork problem hopeless? Are we destined to flounder forever in a sea of clutter? Only if we choose to. Paperwork isn't an impossible problem, but—like dieting—an ongoing one. We created all this paper and we can get rid of it if we choose to. Tearing down the paper prison is going to take a concerted effort with government, organizations, and individuals all working together. Here are some things we can do.

1. Work to Reduce Government Paper

Unfortunately, most of us have little direct control over the massive amount of government-imposed paperwork. But this doesn't mean it's hopeless. Companies, hospitals, universities, and others doing time in the government paper prison need to get organized, unite, and lobby for paperwork reforms. At the same time government agencies need to be contacted, told what paperwork is unnecessary, and given suggestions for streamlining and eliminating much of it. Point out to government agencies how reducing the paper flow can save both of you time and money. And, most important, don't treat government paperwork as uncontrollable but rather as a cost that needs to be planned and budgeted for. One large company undertook a $50,000 study to reduce government regulatory costs and as a result saved $10 million. If we want to increase productivity, it's imperative that government paperwork be reduced.

2. Start a War on Paper at Work

Here is a great way to get everyone involved. Almost everyone dislikes paperwork and programs to reduce it can be very successful. For example, at B. F. Goodrich Co. employees were asked to "Help BFG slay the paper dragon" that added $2 million to headquarters expenses in 1980. The Goodrich campaign portrays employees as knights and pits them against paper dragons such as computerized reports, memos, photocopies, fat files, and the like. The campaign was publicized by posters that portrayed a knight armed with scissors (BFG employees) doing battle with a paper dragon. And the message on the poster was very direct: "Do your part to reduce unneeded correspondence. Don't write it. . . . Don't copy it. . . . Don't file it." The main purpose of the program was to enlist the creative ideas of the rank-and-file worker in an attempt to reduce paper. In a very short time BFG's paper costs dropped 17 percent.

A paper-reduction campaign doesn't have to be a companywide affair. You can start one where you work. Ask your boss what he thinks about the idea. Chances are he will want to help any way he can.

3. Create Incentives for Eliminating Paper

One reason we have so much paper is that people are being rewarded for producing it. Instead we need to reward people for eliminating it. Needless to say, the best reward is money. For example, one possibility would be to pay cash amounts of one year's savings for each idea. Thus, if Mary finds a way to reduce the photocopy bill $100 per year, her reward would be $100. And be sure that Mary gets plenty of recognition for her idea, too.

If you launch a program of paper-elimination incentives be sure that everyone understands that it's paper, not people, that you're trying to eliminate. If workers feel that their jobs are in jeopardy, they will probably create more paper.

4. Control the Copy Machine

The basic problem with photocopy machines is that there are too many, they are too conveniently located, too easy to operate, and do such a good job. As a result the temptation is overwhelming to run extra copies of everything from important documents to personal things such as cartoons, recipes, and maps to the weekend picnic. In extreme cases, some people have gone so far as to copy an entire textbook because it's "cheaper" than buying one. Here are some simple ideas that can help reduce the number of excess copies. Perhaps one or more of them can be applied where you work:

- Reduce the number of copy machines. We could probably cut the number of copy machines in this country in half and have no significant impact on business. In fact, the long-run advantages would be positive. If you are a manager, try putting an "out of order" sign on one or more of your machines for a month and see what happens.

- Make the photocopier less accessible. Practically every office has one. Instead of having one in every office, centralize them and put someone with a nasty disposition in charge of controlling their operation. Try to choose a somewhat inconvenient location.
- Replace the office photocopier with a slower, less attractive copier. Photocopy manufacturers are always selling new models that produce more copies of higher quality in less time. And companies that buy or lease them are sure to generate more paper. Slower, poorer-quality copiers are cheaper and less tempting. Rely more heavily on thermofax, ditto, and carbon copies.
- Lock up the photocopier and dispense keys to a selected few.
- Remove the knob from the multiple-copies control on the machine. Every time someone wants to make an additional copy he has to push the start button.
- Allocate each person a part of the photocopy budget and allow him to keep what he doesn't spend as a bonus.

5. Curtail Computer Clutter

No doubt, computers are a technical marvel that will benefit all of us for the rest of our lives. But until we learn to use them judiciously, they will continue to be a gigantic trivia generator that drowns productivity in a sea of information overload.

Data processing people can't provide necessary and relevant information to help you unless you tell them what you do and don't need. And if they don't hear from you, they will continue to bombard your desk with reams of printouts. Here is a simple procedure for removing computer clutter from your job.

- Take each computerized report or document you receive and ask yourself "Does this cause me to take some action?" If the answer is no, throw it away and request that it not be sent to you.
- If the answer is yes, look at every page and every line of the report and repeat the question. Every line and page that doesn't cause you to act is unnecessary. Make note of only the information you need. You'll soon find that a huge printout may contain only a page or two of relevant information.
- Inform the data processing people about your findings and request that they provide you with only the necessary information. Rank the information you want in order of importance and ask if they can provide it in that order. Instead of stacks of paper, you may soon be receiving a few pages of vital information.

6. Question Every Line of Every Document

One of the most successful paper-reduction campaigns began with a question. In 1956, Sir Simon Marks, chairman of Marks and Spencer (a large British clothing store chain), saw a clerk in one of his stores poring over a form. "What are you doing?" he asked. The clerk explained that he was trying to fill out a stock order form but that it was too difficult to understand. "What's the form for? Why do we use it?" Simon asked. "I don't know, sir. It makes no sense to me, but it's the system" was the reply.

Simon promptly abolished the form and launched a campaign to reduce paper in the company. "If in doubt, throw it out" was the battle cry. Every document, every report, every card, and every form was questioned. What's this for? Do we really need it? What forms can be combined? Why is that card necessary? Why? Why? Why? Questioning all the existing paperwork made it apparent that mountains of clutter could be easily done away with and not be missed. Within two years Marks and Spencer abolished 22 million forms weighing 105 tons. Profits, morale, and productivity all increased.

Every organization needs to continuously review, question, and prune the volumes of paper that flow through it. And this is truer today than ever. It's been estimated that most companies could reduce their paperwork by one-third and have absolutely no impact on operations. And paperwork brought under control can reduce operating costs anywhere from 15 to 40 percent. What would a 15 percent savings do for your operation's profit picture?

The next time you pick up a piece of paper, ask yourself questions like these:

- What's it for?
- What's it worth?
- How does it help me do my job?
- Do I need to see this?
- What's the worst that can happen if I throw it away?
- What can be eliminated?
- Is this information available somewhere else?
- How can this document be simplified?
- Is it necessary to file this? (According to *The Odds Almanac*, the odds are less than one in twenty that a filed piece of paper will ever be looked at again.)
- Can this be combined with another document?
- Am I processing this piece of paper more than once?
- What can I do now to get this piece of paper out of my life?

Answers to these questions followed by positive action can knock a large hole in paper prison walls.

7. Develop Good Paperwork Habits
You may not have the clout to eliminate forms, curtail photocopies, or modify computer printouts, but all of us can practice techniques that minimize the paperwork hassle. Here are some of the basics:

- Focus on results. You're paid to get results, not shuffle paper. If picking up a piece of paper and acting on it contributes to your job productivity, go ahead and take care of it. Otherwise set it aside and see what you can do to eliminate it.
- Don't generate it. Every letter, form, memo, or report you create adds another brick to the paper prison walls. Make it your policy to generate as little paper as possible. Instead of typing replies to letters, pick up the telephone and give a reply, or write the answer on the bottom of the incoming letter and send it back. Don't be memomaniac. Face-to-face communication is often better. Instead of handwriting correspondence, dictate it. If you have trouble dictating, try keeping your sentences and paragraphs short.
- Shield yourself from it. When he became president of the family company, Eberhard Faber was, at first, overwhelmed by enormous amounts of paper that were dumped on his desk. But he quickly learned to deal with it and wrote:

I let this avalanche pour over me for a while; but finally, guided by a powerful instinct for survival, I took a deep breath, prayerfully apologized to the puritan God of Hard Work, and instructed my secretary to hide most of it in the closet.[1]

Faber's decision represents the triumph of common sense over trivia. Take a similar approach and don't ask for any paper unless its absolutely essential. Take your name off of buck slips and mailing and subscription lists. If you have a secretary or assistant, prepare a priority list of paperwork you need to see and have him screen it for you.

---

[1] Eberhard Faber, "What Happened When I Gave Up the Good Life and Became President," *Fortune*, December, 1971, p. 178.

- Throw it away. Every time you pick up a piece of paper ask yourself "What's the worst that can happen if I throw this away?" If the answer isn't too bad, throw it away. Make it a practice to go through file cabinets, desk drawers, and storage areas at regular intervals and throw out all outdated and unnecessary paper. It's always tempting to hold on to something "just in case I need it," but the cost of creating enormous amounts of clutter far outweighs the benefits. A good rule of thumb is to throw away anything over one year old (unless the law requires otherwise).

- Try to handle each piece of paper only once. Every time you pick up a piece of paper resolve to throw it away, file it, or move it on its way. Letting stacks of paper accumulate on your desk can only hurt your productivity. If you find yourself handling a piece of paper frequently, put a dot on it every time you pick it up. This will remind you to get it out of the way before it gets the measles.

3

Practical Productivity Techniques

CHAPTER 10

SETTING AND MEASURING PRODUCTIVITY GOALS

*"Nothing is more terrible than activity
without insight."*

—*Thomas Carlyle*

Author Evan Esar wisely noted, "You don't have to plan to fail; all you have to do is fail to plan." And productivity is no exception to this rule. Achieving high productivity is rarely an accident. It's usually the result of solid planning coupled with diligent effort. Until you define what productivity is and how you're going to measure it, your chances of improving it are slim and none. Let's not have this happen to you.

The purpose of this chapter is to show you how to set up a system of goals and measures to improve your productivity at work. Measuring productivity can get terribly complicated. Volumes have been written on the subject and large corporations have created all sorts of complex and intricate procedures to serve their own needs. I promise you two things:

1. I'll keep it simple.
2. If you follow these guidelines, your productivity will increase.

DEFINING PERSONAL PRODUCTIVITY

It makes little sense to start setting and measuring productivity goals until you have a precise definition of what you're seeking. Here is a definition of personal productivity that applies to everyone who works:

$$\text{Personal Productivity} = \frac{\text{What you produce}}{\text{The number of hours it takes you to produce it}}$$

In other words, increasing personal productivity means making better use of time. No doubt there are other resources that you can make better use of in your job, but time is the one resource we all have in common—and the one we use most poorly. Furthermore, as our economy continues to become less manufacturing- and more services-oriented, managing time becomes even more crucial.

In addition to our definition of personal productivity, we need to define and distinguish between two other crucial terms: effectiveness and efficiency. Effectiveness means results. It involves deciding which goals are most important and worth concentrating on. Efficiency, on the other hand, assumes that the goals have already been decided on and proceeds to find the best way of achieving them. In a pure sense, productivity is the same thing as efficiency but in the broadest and most real sense, productivity begins with effectiveness. Efficiency is doing the job right, but effectiveness is doing the right job. Thus, the first step to increasing personal productivity is to set goals (define effectiveness)—the subject of this chapter. In a following chapter I will assume you know what results you're after and give you some ideas for improving efficiency.

WHY GOALS ARE IMPORTANT AND NECESSARY

Whenever I speak about the importance of goals I'm frequently asked something like "Why do I have to have a goal? Why can't I just practice being more efficient and working harder? I know what I'm supposed to do." My answer is that goals are necessary for several reasons.

First, goals fulfill a basic human need. Human beings are natural goal-seeking creatures. Show me a healthy person who feels bored, tired, and unenthusiastic and I'll show you someone without meaningful goals. It's a basic tenet of psychology that most behavior is goal-directed. Everyone needs goals to give his life a sense of meaning and purpose.

Second, goals provide an effective vehicle for channeling your time and efforts. An old axiom from the Koran states "If you don't know where you're going, any road will get you there." A well-thought-out system of goals points the way to getting more done with less time and effort.

Third, the exercise of setting goals forces you to spend time thinking seriously about your job and deciding what the most important aspects are. The tendency is overwhelming for those of us who work in large, bureaucratic structures to fall into the activity trap and lose our basic sense of purpose. And as I pointed out earlier, the activity trap has enormous economic and psychological costs. Focusing on results and setting goals can keep this from happening.

Fourth, it's been shown time and again that productivity improves when people know what their goals are. More often than not, failure to produce doesn't result from a lack of ability or effort but rather a lack of information and direction. A large proportion of our productivity problems today is caused by people who don't know their job's main purpose. Most organizations stand or fall on how clearly employees understand their job's goal and how it relates to the goals of the organization.

Finally, goals are necessary because there is no alternative to take their place. If you know of a way to channel productivity effectively without goals, I'd like to hear from you.

BEGIN WITH THREE CRUCIAL QUESTIONS AND THREE CATEGORIES

Getting started is the most difficult part of goal-setting. Here's an initial exercise to get you moving in the right direction. Take three sheets of paper or three index cards and write each of the following questions on a separate card:

1. What are my organization's goals and how does my job help the company achieve them?
2. How does my job help my boss achieve his goals?
3. What key results am I responsible for achieving?

Now, turn the cards over and answer the questions in order. The purpose of the questions is to clarify in your own mind how your job makes a positive contribution. Everybody's job should make some positive contribution or it isn't productive. And if you aren't paid to be productive, what are you paid for?

If you have trouble coming up with answers for questions 1 or 2, forget about Question 3 (unless you're self-employed). Your job doesn't exist in a vacuum, and before you can accurately identify your job's key results you have to get more information. Show the questions to your boss and see if he can provide you with some help. Your job is like a piece of a puzzle, and before you can identify the key results you need to know how it relates to the larger scheme of things.

Admittedly, these questions are much easier for some to answer than for others. For example, sales reps, typists, and assembly-line workers usually know what results they're seeking. But for the growing numbers of us working in white-collar, information-oriented jobs, these questions can be very difficult. Yet they demand an answer. Don't waste your time trying to set goals until you have accurate answers to all of the questions and thoroughly understand them.

One final word of caution: Be very careful to answer Question 3 in terms of results, not activities. As you answer the question keep these points in mind:

- You aren't paid to be busy. You're paid to get things done.
- You aren't paid for working hard. You're paid for working smart.
- You aren't paid to be efficient. You're paid to be effective.

Don't allow yourself to fall into the activity trap. For example, if you're a sales rep, you aren't paid to call on customers, process orders, and attend meetings. You're paid to move the goods. If you're a custodian, you aren't paid to sweep, mop, and vacuum. You're paid to keep the place clean. If you're a department manager, you aren't paid to write reports, attend meetings, and dictate correspondence. You're paid to see that your department achieves its goals. Focus on the end products of your work.

Once you have accurately answered Question 3, you're ready to begin thinking about setting goals to help you achieve those final results. Take three or more index cards and label each one with the following headings: Routine Goals, Quality Goals, and Innovative Goals. Your next task is to list several goals you would like to achieve in each of these areas.

Routine Goals

Routine goals are the easiest to define and achieve. Everyone's job consists of basic, recurring responsibilities that have to be carried out. Secretaries must type, file, and take dictation. Teachers have to prepare for class, give tests, and assign grades. Department managers have to evaluate employees, prepare budgets, and schedule work activities. These are examples of routine goals. Write down the ones in your job.

It's important to point out that routine goals are the bare minimum everyone should do in his job. If you only meet the maintenance requirements of your job, you aren't helping to increase productivity.

Quality Goals

As pointed out in Chapter 7, improving quality improves productivity. Therefore, another key area worth concentrating on is improving the quality of work. To set quality goals, look for problems that need solving and list possible solutions to the problems. Reducing job reruns, product defects, typing errors, warranty claims, and customer complaints are examples of quality goals.

Innovative Goals

These are the highest-level and usually the most difficult goals to achieve. Setting innovative goals means making a commitment to try new things that will increase your job's productivity. It means breaking with the past, making changes, and venturing into the unknown. Innovative goals often carry the distinct possibility of failure. They also carry the greatest potential for improving productivity.

To set innovative goals, ask yourself "What could I do that I'm not doing now that would make my job more productive?" Can you learn a new skill such as dictation or a foreign language? Can you think of a new product or service that the company can easily produce with existing resources? Can you come up with a way to reduce the mounds of paperwork? The basic idea is to set goals that get you doing more than the routine and improve your value to the organization.

The best goals are the ones that apply to all three categories. For example, purchasing a word processor could be an innovation that improves the quality of clerical workers and reduces the time spent on routine correspondence. So, if you come up with a goal that contributes to more than one category, it's probably one worth pursuing.

When you have a list of goals in all three categories, take the quality and innovative goals and choose two you want to pursue in each category. These are the goals you will concentrate on achieving in addition to carrying out your routine duties. For the time being, forget about the rest of the quality and innovative goals. The key to improving productivity is to concentrate on doing a few things well.

GUIDELINES FOR REFINING YOUR GOALS

You now should have a rough outline of your routine duties and a broad idea of two quality and two innovative goals you would like to achieve. The next step is to refine, shape, and polish these rough ideas into formal goals that will cause you to take action and increase productivity. Here are some major guidelines for formulating your goals that will make them effective.

Set Your Own Goals

There are two good reasons why you should set your own goals. First, you're the one who's closest to the job. Therefore you probably know more about it than anyone else and can choose the best goals.

The second reason is that people who set their own goals are usually more committed to achieving them. This doesn't mean that you shouldn't confer with your colleagues, your boss, or your friends. Indeed, they may be able to give you some ideas or goals you wouldn't have thought of by yourself. However, make a serious effort to originate your own goals. If a goal is set by you and is something you really want to achieve, the chances for success are much greater.

When setting your goals state them as a positive result to be achieved rather than as a displeasure to be avoided. For example, don't aim for zero defects. Aim for 100 percent acceptance. Don't strive to reduce absenteeism. Instead aim for higher attendance. State your goals in positive terms and they'll bring out the best in you. Anyone who has ever played a competitive sport knows there's a big difference between playing to win and playing not to lose.

Put Them in Writing

Writing your goals is important for two reasons. First, it helps you clearly identify what you're trying to accomplish. Most of us have goals but never write them down and as a result they get lost in the shuffle of daily activities. This is far less likely to happen with written goals.

The other reason for writing goals is that it increases your personal commitment to them. You're investing more of yourself in the goal and this one investment with high-payoff potential. If it's an important goal, be sure to write it down.

Your Goals Should Be Challenging but Attainable

Difficult but attainable goals result in the best performance. A good goal causes you to stretch and grow but is well within your grasp. If you set an easy goal, it won't give you much satisfaction and you'll probably lose interest in it. Likewise, setting an impossible goal also results in little or no motivation. Choose goals that will require your wholehearted effort but that you feel you can achieve. If you feel you can achieve it, it's a possible goal and worth pursuing.

Check Your Goals for Compatibility

When you set important goals, they should be compatible from two aspects: (1) with each other and (2) with the organization.

It's easy to fall into the trap of setting major goals where the achievement of one prohibits the attainment of another. For example, resolving to double sales volume and cut the promotion budget are very likely incompatible goals. Or hiring an administrative staff to help reduce overhead costs could also be seen as contradictory and incompatible. Be sure to check your goals and make sure that one doesn't cancel the other.

Also, check to make sure that your goals mesh harmoniously with those of your boss and the organization as a whole. Share your goals with your boss and ask him to comment on them. A good set of goals helps you, helps your boss, and contributes to the organization.

Every Goal Should Have a Specific Performance Indicator

Specific and measurable goals provide the most direction and result in the highest performance. Therefore, every goal you set needs to be measured by one or more yardsticks of performance. Resolving to do your best or work harder isn't enough. You need a specific target to shoot for.

"You can't measure what I do" is a very common statement. Nonsense! Some measurable indicator of performance can and should be established for everyone's job. Admittedly, performance measures often yield imperfect information. But whoever said this was a perfect world? Imperfect information is usually better than no information at all, and performance measures, at least, provide useful feedback. Here are some key guidelines for establishing performance indicators:

1. Use direct measures of output whenever possible. Dollars of sales per month, barrels of oil refined per day, number of lines typed per week, or number of vouchers processed per month are all examples of direct measures.

2. When you don't have direct measures available, indirect measures can be useful. For example, a manager whose goal is to increase morale and the quality of work life has no direct measure. However, he can measure the rates of absenteeism, grievances, and turnover each month and use the measures as yardsticks for judging the progress of a QWL program.

3. Ratios and percentages can provide useful performance indicators. For example, performance ratios for a company recruiter could be:

- $\dfrac{\text{Recruiting costs}}{\text{Number of employees hired}}$

- $\dfrac{\text{Recruiting costs}}{\text{Number of recruits retained over one year}}$

- $\dfrac{\text{Number of employees hired}}{\text{Number of interviews}}$

or any number of other possible ratios. None of these indicators alone provides a total measure of productivity, but each can contribute a piece of valuable information. Cost-benefit ratios can make excellent performance indicators and you may wish to use one or more of them as performance indicators.

4. If you have trouble coming up with direct or indirect measures for a goal, construct a rating scale from 1 to 10 with 1 representing the poorest performance and 10 representing the best. Then you can estimate where on the scale you think you are now and decide where you would like to be.

5. If the rating-scale approach doesn't work, verbally describe the situation as vividly as you can. For example, if your goal is to climb the corporate hierarchy, be specific. How high do you want to climb: What position do you want to hold in five years? Ten years? Twenty years? What types of assignments do you want to carry out? How much money do you want to earn? The more clearly you can specify and measure the results you're after, the greater your performance will be. If you can't quantify it, measure it, rate it, or describe it, forget it as a goal. You don't know what you want.

6. Once you have established performance measures for your goals, choose a number and shoot for it. Or better yet, choose a range of numbers. For example, if you're marketing a new product, a realistic goal might be to sell 100,000 units the first year. But you feel that sales could be as low as 75,000 and as high as 120,000. Thus you have optimistic, realistic, and pessimistic goals of 120,000, 100,000, and 75,000 units respectively. The point is that it's wise to decide at the beginning what your criteria for success will be. And it's also wise to establish a range of success rather than an arbitrary figure.

Every Goal Needs a Target Date

Here's a good rule to impose on yourself: A goal isn't a goal until it has a deadline. Goals without deadlines become pipe dreams that we never seem to get around to achieving. Do you want to reduce turnover to 12 percent? By when? Do you want to double your sales volume? By when? Do you want to open another branch? By when? If it's important enough to be a goal, it's important enough to have a deadline.

Deadlines, like goals, should be reasonable but challenging. They should be far enough away for you to achieve the goal comfortably but close enough to cause you to take action. Here are three easy steps to scheduling a deadline:

1. Determine the deadline target date and mark it on your calendar.

2. Estimate the amount of time it will take to achieve the goal. Be sure to allow time for unexpected delays, mishaps, and

whatever. Murphy's law is always with us.

3. Once you have estimated how much time it will take to reach the goal, work back from the deadline and block off remaining hours to devote to the task. This will also tell you the latest possible date you can expect to start and successfully meet the deadline.

Put Your Goals in Perspective

When setting major goals it's essential to assess their long- and short-range consequences. Remember that short-sighted planning is a major cause of our productivity ills. We tend to make too many choices on the basis of short-run payoffs. And this is bad for individuals and organizations.

When deciding which goals to pursue, ask yourself "How is this going to help me five, ten, or twenty years from now?" and "How is this going to benefit the organization in the long run?" Choose the goals that show the greatest promise to both you and the company. If your company's focus is short-run and you will be penalized for making a good long-run decision, don't do it. I'm not advocating martyrdom. All that I ask is that you try to find win-win goals that will benefit your long-range career and your employer's future as well.

Getting the Most from Your Goals

If you answered the questions and followed the preceding guidelines, you probably have a number of excellent goals that can point the way to better performance. However, as you try to achieve them, it's wise to follow several basic guidelines.

Most important, don't start pursuing your goals until you decide which are the most crucial to the success of your job. The plain fact is that in most jobs there aren't enough hours in a day to do everything, but there are enough hours to do the most important things. Thus your next, absolutely essential task is to set priorities.

How do you set priorities? There are several ways of doing it, but the basic idea is simply one of putting first things first. One way is simply to take your goals and number them. Another way is to break your goals into three categories:

A. Must do
B. Should do
C. Nice to do

Then number the goals in each category according to its importance. Your most important goal is labeled A1, second most important A2, and so on. Whatever priority system you use, just be sure to do it. Some people simply number their goals; others label them Ace, Queen, King, Jack, and still others use the A, B, C system. Choose a system that works for you and stick to it.

Pareto's law or the 80/20 rule explains why setting priorities is so important. In the nineteenth century an Italian economist named Vilfredo Pareto noticed that in a large number of items, a high percentage of the value of the items was usually concentrated in relatively few of the items. For example:

• Eighty percent of the dollar value of an inventory is usually found in 20 percent of the items.
• Eighty percent of sales generally come from 20 percent of your customers.
• Eighty percent of all television viewing is spent watching 20 percent of all programs.
• Eighty percent of your telephone calls come from 20 percent or fewer of your callers.
• Eighty percent of your headaches come from 20 percent or less of your problems (remember the Pareto charts?).

Pareto's law applies to goals as well. Usually you will find that 80 percent of your achievement results from meeting 20 percent or less of your goals. The key is that they must be your most important goals, which is why setting priorities is so important.

Develop an Action Plan for Important Goals
Once you have set a specific, measurable, important goal you're ready to swing into action and start achieving it. Or are

you? You can't *do* a goal. A goal is an end result and you need to formulate an action plan for achieving the goal.

The following is an action-planning exercise. Take several sheets of paper and answer the following questions and statements:

1. State clearly and specifically a goal you would like to achieve and a target date for achieving it.
2. Why do you want to achieve this goal?
3. If you succeed, how will it improve your productivity at work? What will it do for you as an individual?
4. What will you consider a moderate success? A good success? A tremendous success? Be specific.
5. How much do you want to achieve this goal?
6. Is this a long-range goal? If not, how will achieving this goal contribute to the attainment of longer-range goals?
7. What price will you have to pay to achieve this goal? Are you willing to pay it?
8. What are your chances of achieving this goal?
9. What will happen if you aren't successful?
10. List the major activities involved in achieving this goal and assign target dates for completing them.
11. What obstacles stand between you and achieving this goal? How will you overcome them?
12. What can you do today that will start you on the path to achieving this goal?

Periodically Review and Revise Your Goals

Never make the mistake of thinking of your goals as inflexible and carved in stone for the ages. Everything changes. Companies, bosses, customers, governments, economic conditions, and—most important—you are in a continuous process of change. All of which means that the goals you set today may be totally meaningless or unimportant in five years.

This doesn't mean that goals are useless in turbulent times. In fact, just the opposite is true. But failing to review and revise your goals periodically can result in achieving empty goals. Don't let this happen. Sit down every six months and review your goals. Which ones have you achieved? Have you outgrown any of them? Are any of them unattainable? Has your organization moved in a direction that requires that you set new goals? What do you know now that you didn't know when you set your goals? The main point is to question, revise, and set new goals on a regular basis. Good planning gives you a sense of direction but accommodates change and adapts as necessary.

Keep Your Attention Focused on Your Goals

It's so easy to lose sight of your goals in this busy, hurry-up, activity-oriented world. And any goal becomes useless when you lose sight of it. Keeping your goals in focus is an absolute must. How do you do it? Here are several ways:

1. Put up signs or reminders of your major goals and place them where you work. You don't have to advertise them to the world. Write one of your major goals on a small card and tape it inside your desk drawer or on top of your desk.

2. Read your goal's statement at the beginning of each day. Then make a "things-to-do" list and be sure to include activities that will contribute to achieving one or more major goals.

3. Chart your major goals over time. For example, a sales rep may wish to chart the dollars of sales revenue generated each month, or a typist may wish to chart the number of lines typed each week. Charting the performance indicators also can serve as a basis for measuring the progress of recurring goals.

4. Visualize achieving your goals. Try this exercise. Every day set aside ten minutes or more and visualize the achievement of your most important goal. Close your eyes and block yourself from interruptions and distractions. Imagine achieving this goal in as great a detail as possible. If you practice diligently enough you'll find yourself behaving in a manner that's consistent with achieving the goal and increase your chances of success.

For example, when I decided to write my first book, *Working Smart*, I practiced visualizing what it would be like to be a published author. I imagined walking past a bookstore and seeing a book in the window. I imagined receiving letters of congratulations and gratitude from readers, signing books, going on tour, and many other trappings of being published. And all of these things came to pass.

Obviously, achievement involves a whole lot more than visualization, but you have to think success before you can achieve it. And visualizing achieving your goals will, at the very least, keep your attention focused on them.

Establish Rewards for Achieving Your Goals

Achieving a meaningful, challenging goal can be very satisfying, but it usually isn't enough to sustain continuous motivation and commitment. Every goal needs an incentive attached to it.

I have stressed several times earlier that productivity will increase when it's rewarded, and your productivity is no exception to the rule. Every time you set a goal, ask yourself "What's in it for me?" More money? A promotion? Recognition? Self-satisfaction? Human nature demands that you be given meaningful rewards for achieving your goals or you won't pursue them with much vigor.

If you set your goals as part of a companywide program, ask your boss how you will be rewarded for achieving your goals. Also, set up your own personal reward system. Every time you set a meaningful goal, choose a fitting reward to give to yourself when you reach the goal. For example, a sales rep who happens to be an avid golfer could promise himself that deluxe set of clubs he's been admiring if he increases sales by 20 percent this year. Or how about lunch at a favorite restaurant as a fitting reward for completing the budget report on time?

The reward you choose should be meaningful to you and commensurate with the goal—that is, big goals get big rewards and lesser goals should get lesser rewards. Be scrupulously honest with yourself. Don't reward yourself if you didn't achieve the goal and be sure to reward yourself if you do achieve the goal. The right rewards create the right performances, and that's what improving productivity is all about.

CHAPTER 11

MANAGING TIME MEANS MANAGING YOURSELF

*"Millions are idle—even if they have jobs. Some
carve great careers while others simply chisel."*
—*Laurence J. Peter*

Many years ago, Winston Churchill was being introduced as a
guest speaker by a woman who strongly objected to his fondness
for alcohol. At the end of her introduction she needled him by
drawing an imaginary line about three feet from the ceiling and
said, "If all the alcohol consumed by our guest speaker could be
poured into this room, it would fill the room up to here." Churchill ambled up to the podium and sized up the three-foot space
between the imaginary line and the ceiling. Then, after a moment of silent reflection, Sir Winston replied, "So much to do
. . . so little time."

No matter how you look at it, time is your most precious and
unique resource. You can measure it but you can't save it. Few of
us have enough but everybody has all there is. All of us are given
a certain amount of time but we don't know how much until it's
all gone. And when it comes to business, Ben Franklin said it
best: "Time is Money." Yet, despite its value, most of us waste
about half our time and the best of us waste two hours each day.

As noted in Chapter 10, the key to improving your productivity begins with learning to manage time. If you created a set of productivity goals and measures, you've already taken the first big step by deciding how you can become more effective. The next step is to learn specific tools and techniques that will help you reach those goals efficiently. And that's what this chapter is all about.

Time management is a subject near and dear to my heart. My earlier book, *Working Smart*, deals exclusively with time management, and it's my opinion that teaching people to make better use of time holds the greatest potential for improving productivity. Why? Because productivity improvement begins with people improvement, and making people more productive begins with making better use of time.

Whenever I conduct seminars and lectures on time management one question I'm frequently asked is "How do I know these ideas work?" My answer is that they won't unless you conscientiously make the effort to apply them. But there is mounting evidence that learning time management principles can be a very sound investment.

In one study, Professors Martha Rader and Joseph Schabacker of Arizona State University evaluated the effectiveness of time management training over a one-year period. The subjects, 200 managers from thirteen state agencies, were given a two-day training seminar in time management. After nine months seminar participants were surveyed as to how much time they had saved as a result of techniques learned at the seminar. The answers ranged from one to ten hours saved per week by each respondent. Translated into dollars, this amounted to a salary savings of $505,000—which was thirty times the cost of the training program! One year later, comparisons of managers who attended the seminars were made with those who didn't. The results revealed that seminar attendants showed a significantly better use of time than those who hadn't received the training. Clearly, learning to manage time can be an excellent investment for companies and individuals.

Another question I'm frequently asked is "Won't managing time restrict my personal freedom?" My typical answer is "If it did, I wouldn't teach it." Good time management is liberating, not restricting. It means learning to get things done more simply, faster, and with less hassle. All of which leaves you with more time and energy to pursue things other than work, if that's your wish. So let's look at some practical time management techniques that will help you work smarter.

GOOD TIME MANAGEMENT IS FIRST-RATE HABITS MADE SECOND NATURE

The first thing to learn about time management is that it's really self-management. It isn't time that's being managed. It's you. Therefore, in order to master the clock, you must first assume responsibility for your own behavior. In the final analysis, every hour of your life is your own and you will ultimately be the one who decides how to spend it.

Assuming you have a clear set of goals, your next step is to get an objective picture of where your time on the job is spent. Most time is spent in habitual patterns of behavior, and many of these habits are time-savers. Yet many habits waste time and practically all are unknown to us until we make the effort to find out what they are. Thus, your first step to better use of time is to find out where you're wasting time.

Keep a Time Log for One Week

At the outset, let me make it clear that the purpose of this exercise isn't to turn you into a time nut who compulsively fills every minute with activity. I wouldn't wish that on anybody. Everybody wastes time and all of us need to be unproductive some of the time. But in order to be more productive you need to find out where you're spinning your wheels, and this exercise will tell you.

1. Begin by making a list of as many of your job activities as you can think of. They might include such things as meetings, telephone calls, conferring with the boss, visits from subordi-

nates, chatting with colleagues, preparing the budget, reading, routine correspondence, coffee breaks, commuting, and lunch. You may also find it helpful to list mental activities such as worry, guilt, daydreaming, anger, frustration, meditation, and creative thinking since time is often devoted to these activities on the job. When you finish making a list of activities, estimate how much time you think you spend each week on each of those activities and write it down.

2. For the next week, carry this list with you and record how much time you spend on each activity. For example, if it takes you twenty-five minutes to commute to work on Monday, record the amount of time next to commuting. If the boss takes forty-five minutes of your time on Tuesday morning, write it down. Every time you make or place a telephone call, record how long it takes. If you spend twenty minutes Thursday afternoon daydreaming, be honest and write it down. Your time log should be confidential and for your eyes only, unless you wish to share it with someone. And be sure to write down all unanticipated activities that you didn't list and how much time they took.

3. At the end of the week, add up the total amount of time you spent on each activity and compare it with how much time you estimated you would spend. Surprise! Most of us think we know where our time goes, but few of us really do.

4. Now that you have an objective measurement of where your time is going, be very honest with yourself and write down the answers to these questions:

- How did I waste time? What can be done to prevent or reduce wasted time in the future?
- How did I waste other people's time? Whose time did I waste? How can I prevent this from happening?
- What am I doing that's unnecessary? What activities am I performing that can be reduced, combined, or given to someone else to do?
- How did other people waste my time? Can anything be done to reduce or eliminate this in the future? If so, what?

- What did I do that was urgent but unimportant?
- Am I spending most of my time pursuing my goals? If not, why not? If so, how?
- Starting today I'm going to do the following things to make better use of my time. . . .

The time log and answers to the questions will give you a lot of insight into where your time is going and how you can make better use of it. It's also a good idea to repeat the entire exercise every six months to help you uncover new time-wasters before they become ingrained. It's easier the second time around, and you'll probably see an improvement in your use of time if you've made a serious effort at improving.

Once you uncover time-wasting habits, your next task is to eliminate them. And that's easier said than done. Bad habits are hard to kick, but there are a number of things you can do:

- Allow absolutely no exceptions. Once you decide to break a habit, never allow yourself to indulge in it. Otherwise you'll likely lapse into the old pattern of behavior.
- Get the support of others who care. Alcoholics Anonymous, Weight Watchers, Smokers Anonymous, and numerous other support groups are living proof that peer pressure and social support can be very effective in correcting bad habits. Maybe we should have a Paper Shufflers Anonymous.
- Replace a negative habit with a positive one. Choose a new habit and practice it at every opportunity. And speaking of new habits, here are several good time management habits that can help anyone become more productive:

Make a Daily To-Do List

The daily to-do list is the most well-known and practiced time management technique of all. It's sheer simplicity and can be done by everyone. All you do is sit down at the beginning of each day or at the end of the preceding day and make a daily list of things you want to accomplish. Once you make the list, use the A, B, C priorities system (A—Must do; B—Should do;

C—Nice to do). Your objective isn't to finish the list but to get the most important things done. A to-do list is simply a statement of daily goals and priorities that should be used to help you achieve longer-range goals.

If you have ever made a to-do list, I don't have to tell you how valuable it can be. When Charles Schwab was president of Bethlehem Steel he said that learning to make a to-do list was one of the greatest lessons he ever learned; he reportedly paid a consultant $25,000 for the advice.

In addition to making the list, practice doing "worst things first." That is, take the most unpleasant "must do" and do it as the first item of business. This will give you a feeling of accomplishment and make the rest of the day go better.

Capitalize on Your Prime Time

Here's another powerful technique you can use in conjunction with the to-do list: Take the most important thing you have to do each day and do it when you do it best. We all go through subtle changes in our moods and abilities throughout the day. For most of us, memory levels peak at around 11 A.M. and math skills are best in the morning. Business performance levels tend to fall off after lunch, but stress is best handled in the late afternoon.

What constitutes prime time depends on you and the job, but for most of us it falls between 10 A.M. and 2 P.M. However, this is by no means universal.

The simplest and best way to determine your prime time is to take your temperature throughout the course of the day. Assuming you're in good health, your prime time is when your temperature is high normal. Schedule important mental activities and creative work for the time of day when your temperature is highest. And leave the routine tasks such as correspondence, reading, and running errands for the time of day when your temperature is lowest.

Capitalizing on your prime time is extremely important because it means you're giving your best self to your most important tasks. And that's the most anyone can give.

Give Yourself a Quiet Hour

Would you like to accomplish two or three hours of normal work in one hour? If so, the quiet hour is your answer. Each day give yourself an hour of uninterrupted time to work on the most important tasks that only you can do. Don't accept telephone calls, visitors, or any other types of interruption, unless there's an emergency. During this time you can also consider your goals, make your to-do list, and plan how to make the best use of your time.

Many successful executives know the value of quiet hours. They arrive at the office an hour or two before the regular workday begins. Because they aren't subjected to the normal distractions and interruptions they can plan and consider important decisions in a solitary and tranquil environment. All of which keeps them from falling into the activity trap. Also, arriving early usually means they can leave early and beat both the morning and afternoon commuter traffic.

A number of companies have established a quiet hour policy with success. For the first hour of the day, everyone works alone. Telephone calls, meetings, and drop-in visits are ruled out. Everyone works on his most important, solitary tasks and plans the rest of the day. After the hour, it's business as usual. It's an interesting concept that many companies have found useful. Perhaps it can help where you work.

Whether or not your company has a quiet time, be sure to schedule one for yourself. You need time to be alone with your thoughts and decide how to make today move you closer to achieving your goals. Even if you can only spare five or ten minutes, do it. It's an investment of time that will repay you many times over.

Keep a Flexible Schedule

A commonly believed myth is that good time management means scheduling every hour of the day with something to be done. Not so! Tight schedules are one sure route to frustration and fatigue. A tight schedule is built on the assumption that everything is going to go according to plan. And few, if any, days go exactly as planned. Murphy's Law is always with us, and the only way to prevent the unexpected from disrupting your day is to plan for it.

Only schedule time each day for the most important activities—and try your best to complete them. One good rule of thumb is to schedule only half of your day. If you think a task will take an hour to complete, give yourself an hour and fifteen minutes. Or if you're unfamiliar with the job, give yourself an hour and a half.

Make the Most of Committed Time

If you work for a living, the fact is that much of your day is already committed. However, everyone's day has gaps of time that are unproductive unless we plan ahead to make use of them. With a little forethought and effort, previously wasted minutes can become useful, enjoyable, and productive. To get the most out of committed time usually requires tape recorders, reading material, and note pads.

Commuting and travel time are the largest blocks of committed time for most of us. Perhaps you can use commuting time to read, study, or listen to tapes about subjects that interest you. And, if you're moving, think about moving closer to work. Moving only fifteen minutes closer to work gives you 125 hours of extra time in one year.

A sales rep I know uses travel time between customers very well. After calling on a customer, she uses the time in travel to record whom she just visited, what they discussed, and what business was transacted. Six months later, before she goes to call on that same customer, she plays back the tape. Her customers are astounded by her memory. Another sales rep I know studied for his MBA degree during travel time. He recorded the professor's lectures and played them back while traveling between customers.

Waiting for appointments is another time-killer in today's business world. However, with a little extra effort you can capitalize on waiting time too. Bring essential reading material with you and you'll always be able to make use of the smallest bits of time. Or you can update your goals, evaluate your to-do list, or plan next week's meetings. Of course, there's nothing wrong with using the time to relax or meditate. Think of it as a gift of time.

Most of us operate with a time horizon of hours, days, and weeks. It's the lifetimes and minutes that seem to get away from us. With a little planning and imagination we can make the most of both.

Manage Trivia by Batching It

Everyone's job consists of a number of routine, necessary but relatively unimportant tasks that require little thought. Reading computer printouts, routine correspondence, and signing documents are examples of nickel-and-dime tasks that can disrupt your day if you don't take steps to manage them. The best way to manage trivia is to batch it. Hold your routine correspondence and answer it every other day, or once each week if possible. And, if possible, schedule your trivia sessions for non-prime time. Napoleon was a master at managing trivia. He opened his mail once every three weeks! He not only saved time every day but by the time three weeks had passed, many of the problems had been resolved without his help.

CONQUERING INTERNAL TIME-WASTERS

It's easy to place the blame on other people and things for wasting our time. But the plain fact is that, when it comes to wasting time, each of us is our own worst enemy. As Pogo remarked, "We has met the enemy . . . and he is us." Make no mistake about it. Meetings, drop-in visitors, telephone calls, and unplanned crises are external to us and can waste a lot of time (more about this later). But the biggest time thieves are being disorganized, trying to do too much, and procrastination (the biggest one of all).

Are You Well Organized?

Being well organized doesn't mean having everything neatly tucked away in its appointed place and keeping a totally clear desk. However, it does mean knowing the results you're seeking, having the proper tools to do the job, and a work environment that enables you to work comfortably and efficiently. Most of us could profit with a little better organization, but we need to remember that hard-and-fast rules aren't the answer. Your job and your personality are unique, and any organizing you do has to be done to suit both you and the nature of the job.

Before you set out to do any job, ask yourself "Do I have the right tools?" Keep in mind that I'm using the word *tool* in a very broad context to mean anything that you use to achieve your goals. No matter what the nature of your job, it involves tools. For example, if you work in an office, the office itself with its desk, chair, and floor space is a tool. Sources of information such as newspapers, books, and statistical tables are tools. And knowledge, transportation, computers, expertise, and the proper credentials to do a job are also tools. If you stop and think about it, you probably use an enormous number of tools in your job. If you don't have the tools to do a job efficiently, consider hiring someone who does. It will save you a lot of time, frustration, and fatigue. It's an old adage, but true, that a worker is no better than his tools.

Assuming you have the tools to do your job, your next task is to create an efficient and comfortable work environment. Once again, this is a matter of personal taste, but you should organize your environment with four basic factors in mind:

1. Choose a location (if you have the option) that's conducive to performing the task. For example, jobs that require single-minded concentration usually need a quiet, private location. On the other hand, opening a new business usually requires a well-traveled, busy location.

2. Measure how much space you have to work with. You probably have less than you want, but you need to know how much you have so you can make the best use of it.

3. Make a list of the tools you use in your job and rank them in order of how often you use them. Then arrange your tools so that you have the easiest access to the ones you use most frequently.

4. Be sure your work space has comfortable seating, lighting, and ventilation. All of this depends on your individual tastes, but discomfort is only another distraction that can lower your productivity.

Years ago, efficiency experts believed that the secret to productivity was to be compulsively neat and keep a clear desktop. The fact is that people who are well organized know how to put their hands on what they want when they want it, regardless of how the desk looks. As one sage noted, "If a cluttered desk means a cluttered mind, what does an empty desk mean?"

The Overcommitment Trap

Do you feel that time is oppressive? Do you have so many things to do that you feel confused or as if you're fighting a losing battle? Do you work after hours or take work home? If so, you're suffering from overcommitment—an almost universal problem of people who have trouble managing time.

What's the problem? It all really boils down to expecting too much of yourself. You can't be all things to all people and if you try, you'll end up being nobody to everybody. The secret to getting more done is to do less better. This means concentrating your time and energy on the few tasks with the high payoffs and delegating or ignoring the rest.

Overcommitment is frequently the result of the inability to say no. But learning to say no to the many unessential time-robbers is necessary if you want to be productive. In the final analysis, your success won't be based on to whom you say yes or no but on how well you do your job. Competent people are always in demand and competence is usually the result of doing a few things well. If you have trouble saying no here are some guidelines that may help:

1. Say no rapidly before people anticipate that you may say yes. Answers such as "I don't know" or "Let me think about it" only raise false hopes. A delayed no only increases the chances of animosity.

2. Realize you have the right to say no. You don't have to offer a reason every time you turn down someone's request.

3. Offer your refusals politely and pleasantly. There's no need to be defensive—it's your right to say no.

4. Soften your refusal with a counterproposal if you think it's appropriate. "I can't sit in at the meeting this afternoon for you, Chuck, but I'll be happy to answer your phone."

Another solution to the overcommitment trap is effective delegation—assigning to others the tasks you want to get done. There are all sorts of irrational reasons many of us don't delegate as much as we should, such as:

- It doesn't occur to you. The next time you have a job to do, ask yourself "Can someone else do this?" If so, delegate it.
- "If I don't do it, it won't get done." Don't worry, if it's really important, it *will* get done.
- "I don't have time to train someone else." This only means that you'll have to do the job the next time it has to be done.
- "If I give it to him, he'll screw it up." Maybe so, but intelligent mistakes are part of the cost of learning.
- "I like doing it myself." That's great, but is it the best use of your time?

Those are just few of the many excuses people give for not delegating. But effective delegation is the way to leverage your time. Here are a few simple ground rules:

1. Choose the right person or people and the battle is 80 percent won. Be sure they have the training and the tools to do the job.

2. Specifically communicate the results you expect. If the job is an involved one, set priorities and stress what's most important.

3. Be sure that the person has the authority to carry out the task. Otherwise he won't be able to do the job satisfactorily.

4. Let people do it their way. What works best for you may not be best for them.

5. Check the results to see how the job was performed.

6. Be lavish in your praise for a job well done. Remember, good performance needs good rewards.

Do It Now!

Procrastination. It's been called the science of keeping up with yesterday and it's the greatest time and productivity killer of all. In my time management seminars, I ask all procrastinators to raise their hands. Usually about half the audience does, and I reply "Thank you very much. Now we know who's honest." The plain fact is that all of us play the put-off game and delay tackling important jobs from time to time.

Habitual procrastination is another matter. If that describes you, you're putting yourself under a useless burden and wasting your life away. Procrastinators live with the constant anxiety of trying to do everything at the last minute. All of which usually leads to poor results or no results at all. Problems tend to pile up without being resolved and unresolved problems create more problems. Procrastination may be idleness but it certainly isn't leisure. It's a gut-wrenching, fatiguing, frustrating, and anxiety-laden way to go through life. And nobody needs that.

We usually procrastinate for a number of reasons, but the two biggest ones are feeling that a task is overwhelming or unpleasant. Whatever the reason for procrastination, the cure is usually to create momentum. Once you're in motion, the chances are you'll keep going. The following are several ideas you can use to create momentum the next time you're putting off that important job:

1. Look procrastination squarely in the eye. Decide what's important that you're putting off. Write it down. Why are you delaying it? Is it overwhelming? Unpleasant? Time-consuming? Define the problem and you'll probably come up with a strategy for solving it.

2. Don't wait for inspiration or tell yourself that you'll wait until the last minute because you work best under pressure.

Those are nothing more than excuses for delaying, and in the final analysis results count and excuses don't.

3. Take that large, overwhelming task you've been consciously ignoring, break it into as many small steps as you can, and tackle them one at a time. Large successes are usually nothing more than a string of small ones. A book is written a word at a time. Sports championships are won a play at a time. A house is built a brick at a time.

4. Schedule a block of time to work on an unpleasant task you've been putting off and stick to it. For example, block off thirty minutes next week to devote to straightening out your desk or cleaning out your files. Resolve to work nonstop for the duration and quit when the time is up. If the task is one that can't be handled piecemeal (like firing someone or being a bearer of bad news), just do it and let it be done. By delaying you're creating a more unpleasant future for yourself.

5. Do a start-up task. Sometimes doing the smallest task is all you need to get you moving toward achieving a major goal. Are you putting off making an important decision? Take out a sheet of paper and list all the pros on one side of the paper and the cons on the other—now. Are you putting off answering an important letter? Try sharpening your pencil or putting a sheet of paper in the typewriter—now. Have you been putting off calling an important customer to settle a misunderstanding? Look up his number—now.

6. Make your moods work for you. You may not feel like tackling that mammoth report, but do you feel like gathering or reading some background material? Become sensitive to your moods and do things when you're hot to do them.

7. Give yourself a deadline and promise someone. Tell your boss you'll have the report done by Friday or buy him dinner. Things rarely get accomplished without deadlines and making a commitment to other people will give you the motivation to get moving.

8. Reward yourself for meeting deadlines. I have already mentioned this in Chapter 10. Rewards provide the positive incentive to keep you moving toward meeting your goals.

9. Practice doing nothing when you find yourself delaying. Go sit in a chair and do absolutely nothing. No television, no reading, no visiting, no nothing. Pretty soon you'll become terribly bored with the blandness of your own thoughts. When you can't stand it any longer, get up and start on that job you're avoiding—now.

10. Each morning, ask yourself "What's the greatest problem facing me and what am I going to do about it today?" Also, throughout the day ask yourself "What's the best use of my time and energy right now?" Following the answers to these two questions will take a lot of the procrastination burden off your shoulders.

Manage Those Costly Interruptions

A major key to good time management is to carve out large blocks of uninterrupted time. This allows you to concentrate your energies on the few items with the highest payoffs. Unfortunately, large blocks of uninterrupted time are hard to come by in today's work world. If your job is like most, you're constantly hassled by a never-ending stream of meetings, visitors, telephone calls, and various crises. All of which keep you from giving your best attention to the things that count most.

Of course, many of these interruptions are necessary and an essential part of your job. And that's the problem. Because meetings, visitors, telephone calls, and firefighting are seen as legitimate ways to structure time, the tendency is to let them fill up your day. And fill it up they do.

Interruptions can't be eliminated but they can be managed. With a little foresight, self-discipline, and effort on your part you can turn many of these so-called time-wasters into assets that work for, rather than against, you. Here's how.

Make Meetings Worth It

If my career as a university professor taught me anything, it's that a vast lot of taxpayer money is wasted on unnecessary meetings. But universities aren't unique. Every large bureaucracy has its share of useless committees and conferences that need to be avoided like the plague if you want to be productive. Thus, the first step to making meetings more productive is to review critically all existing committees and meetings. Add up the per-hour salary of those attending and ask "Is it worth it?" Eliminate and combine any committees you can. Every committee needs to be regularly reviewed to make sure the benefits are worth the cost. Never call a meeting if there's an alternative. Can the job be done by an individual? Can you use teleconferencing? Assuming you have to call a meeting, here's how to get the most from it:

- Keep the number of attendees as small as possible.
- Make a list of goals that you want to accomplish at the meeting and set priorities.
- Set starting and ending times for the meeting and stick to them. It's best to schedule meetings back-to-back, before lunch, or near the end of the day. Important decisions tend to be reached right before lunch or quitting time.
- Make an agenda and circulate it to those who will be attending well in advance.
- Once the meeting begins, stick to the agenda and tackle the items in order of importance.
- Excuse those who finish making their contribution. Ask to be excused after making your contribution. If you have nothing to contribute, don't go.
- If your meetings seem to drag on, try holding a stand-up meeting. Meetings without chairs can become terribly efficient.
- Have a nonparticipant present to take minutes, which should be duplicated and sent to members as soon as possible.
- After each meeting, evaluate what you accomplished in light of the goals previously set.

Dealing with Drop-ins and Call-ins
For most of us, drop-in visitors and telephone calls are our two greatest interruptors. They're almost always unplanned

and, if you don't take steps to manage them, visitors and telephone calls can really cut your productive time and disrupt your day. Keeping a loose schedule is one way to keep them from upsetting your workday because no matter how hard you try to minimize them, some visitors and callers will always get through. Accept that fact and budget time for it.

To manage visits and telephone calls, begin by finding out who your visitors and callers are. Keep a log for one week. Write down who calls or visits, what they wanted, how much time they took, and whether or not the interruption was necessary. Usually the 80/20 rule will apply—80 or more percent of your time taken up in interruptions comes from 20 percent or fewer of your interruptors. Once you know who your interruptors are, you can devise a strategy for dealing with them. The basic strategy is to shield yourself from the unnecessary visitors and callers without cutting off important communications or seeming rude. The following ideas can help if you're having trouble with drop-in visitors:

1. Close your door for part of your day. It's important to keep communications open and maintain good relationships. But you don't have to be on tap whenever someone wants to see you. Open doors invite those with nothing better to do to drop in and socialize.

2. Remove excess chairs and social amenities from your office. Is your office the place everyone gathers for coffee breaks and socializing? Maybe it's because you're attracting visitors with the extra chairs or the coffee pot or the refrigerator. Get rid of these things if you're being constantly interrupted. If someone complains, volunteer to move the chairs, coffee pot, refrigerator, or whatever to his office.

3. If someone wants to see you, go to his office. This gives you control over the time of the visit. When business is over you can then go back to work in your empty office.

4. If you're a boss who is constantly interrupted by subordinates wanting help with problems, try this: Have them write down the problem, list alternatives, and rank them in order of

preference before seeing you. This will exercise their decision-making abilities and reduce the amount of time they spend with you.

5. If your main interruption is your boss, back off and look at the situation. Perhaps your boss is using you as a sounding board for his ideas, which is a real compliment to you. However, in your informal conversations you can tactfully remind him of the tasks and deadlines you have pending. Very few bosses don't want their subordinates to do a good job. After all, your success is his success.

6. If someone suddenly walks into your office, stand up. If someone knocks on your door, confer in the hall. Your body language will communicate that you're busy. Be tactful but candid with visitors. Most people are very considerate once they understand the pressures you're under.

7. Arrange your desk and chair so that you aren't facing the door. If you make eye contact with the person roaming the halls, he is apt to drop in. By not facing the door you prevent this from happening.

8. Schedule regular visiting hours and encourage visitors to call at those times unless there is an emergency.

9. If you have a secretary or assistant, position his desk where he can screen your unexpected visitors. Provide information that will allow the assistant to handle problems without you.

10. Use coffee breaks, lunch hours, or other committed times to meet with important visitors. This makes multiple use of time, and important information can be exchanged.

According to Jean Skinner, "Anyone who owns a telephone is at the mercy of any damn fool who knows how to dial." It seems ironic that the most frequent interruptor of all is also one of our greatest potential time-savers. Conference calls can save meetings and the transportation time involved. The telephone gets you instant information that letters would take weeks to acquire. The telephone saves trips by substituting a telephone call for a personal visit. Yet most of us waste huge amounts of time on the telephone. One survey revealed that 40 percent of all executives spend more than two hours per day on the phone. What's the problem?

More often than not, telephone problems are caused by a lack of self-discipline. It almost always is more fun to answer an incoming call than it is to work on the job at hand. So we allow our days to be randomly interrupted and take the calls as they come. If you're having problems with the telephone, here are some tips that may help, in addition to keeping a log:

1. Use your telephone to save time. That's what it's there for. Substitute telephone calls for letters, meetings, and personal visits whenever possible and appropriate.

2. Have a secretary, assistant, answering service, or answering machine screen your calls. Secretaries and assistants can usually provide callers information on routine matters, thus eliminating your need to call back.

3. Establish a telephone time each day for placing and receiving calls. Mornings are usually the best for most of us. Encourage your callers to call at that time.

4. Outline information before placing a call. This will clarify the main points in your mind and you'll be less likely to forget to discuss one of your reasons for calling. Once you're on the phone, set the tone of the conversation at the beginning: "The reason I am calling is . . . "

5. Once you've transacted business, bring the conversation to a prompt and polite close. If you have trouble getting rid of a long-winded caller, hang up in the middle of one of your own sentences. It's rude to hang up on a caller, but who ever said it's rude to hang up on yourself? Just quietly push the button in the middle of your own sentence. If he has anything important to add, he will call back, and if not he will probably go bother someone else.

6. Put a small three-minute hourglass by your phone. Every time you place or receive a call, see if you can complete it in three minutes. Don't rush. Obviously some calls will take much longer, and rightly so. Keep a score card and see if you can increase the

percentage of your telephone calls that take less than three minutes. Make a game out of it. Reward yourself every week you reduce your telephone time with a nice treat such as a new pair of shoes, a special dinner, or that blouse you've been admiring.

In addition to these tips for managing meetings, visitors, and telephone calls, let me offer one other piece of advice. If all else fails, hide! They can't interrupt you if they can't find you. Go to a library. Swap offices with someone who also needs solitude. Rent an apartment or hotel room if you need long periods of solitude. For shorter periods, get in your car and drive your way to seclusion. The point is that when you need time free from interruptions there are always options available. Be smart, and take advantage of them.

Don't Waste Your Life Fighting Fires

A common complaint at time management seminars goes something like this: "I come to work all organized with my to-do list and schedule of activities. As soon as I get in the office, I'm hit with a crisis and the whole day is shot to hell. How do I prevent crises from controlling my life?" If that's your problem, there are several things you can do.

First, learn to distinguish between urgency and importance. When Dwight Eisenhower became president he arranged his administration so that only urgent and important matters were called to his attention. Anything that was urgent and unimportant or important and not urgent was delegated. However, he soon discovered that urgency and importance seldom appeared together. The important items were seldom urgent and the urgent items were rarely important. For example, planning and goal-setting has no sense of urgency but is terribly important. On the other hand, being punctual at meetings and answering the telephone or the knock on the door are usually unimportant matters that have a great sense of urgency. Don't let urgent matters keep you from achieving important goals. The next time you encounter a crisis ask yourself "What's the worst that can happen if I don't do anything? How important is this? Will this crisis resolve itself?" You may be able to save yourself from a lot of firefighting, frustration, and fatigue.

Second, try keeping a crisis log for a period of time. Write down the nature of the crisis, when it occurred, who or what was involved, how much time it took, how it was resolved, and (most important) how it could have been prevented. You'll soon discover that many crises are routine and recurring. You can minimize their impact by taking steps to prevent them. Most situations don't become crises without a warning. Look for the warning signals and extinguish the sparks before they escalate into a raging blaze. If you can't prevent a recurring crisis, draw up a plan for resolving it. This will reduce the amount of time you spend dealing with it.

Finally, practice good time management habits and a lot of your crises will disappear automatically. Overcommitment, procrastination, and a lack of well-thought-out goals and priorities invite crisis situations. In a nutshell, the key to managing time is to spend your life making things happen for you rather than letting things happen to you. Remember, what you do today is important because you're exchanging a day of your life for it.

CHAPTER 12

PRODUCING WITH THE RIGHT SIDE OF YOUR BRAIN

*"Just as we can throttle our imagination we can
likewise accelerate it. As in any other art,
individual creativity can be implemented
by certain techniques."*
—*Alex F. Osborn*

When it comes to productivity, imagination and innovation are America's greatest capital resources. Men such as Ben Franklin, Thomas Edison, and Henry Ford knew that. And so does Nick Kelley. Nick Kelley?

Kelley was a broke college sophomore who saw piles of blank paper waiting to be hauled off to the city dump. Nick took the paper, cut and glued the pieces together, turned them into scratch pads, and sold them to businesses. A paper magnate was born. Later he expanded and diversified into legal pads, tea-bag paper, and special papers used to make fingernail-mending tissue and semiconductor devices. In 1980, some ten years after that one good idea, Nick Kelley was a millionaire and provider of jobs for 100 people.

Success in today's business world takes a tremendous amount of knowledge and skill. But the real advantage comes when you add creativity and innovation to the process. Knowing how to generate good, new ideas and turn them into successful realities is the most valuable business skill anyone can have. And the best news is that creativity is a natural human talent that can be systematically developed, applied, and improved. Every organization needs good idea people. This chapter will show you how you can become one.

I know what you're thinking. "Who, me? Creative? You've got to be kidding!" Most of us think of ourselves as uncreative for two main reasons. First, we don't understand what creativity is and how new ideas are generated. There's a tendency in our society to view creativity as some mystical, magical trait that's the sole domain of a gifted few and beyond the reach of the masses. Baloney! Everyone has a large reservoir of untapped creative ability. Some have more than others, but everyone is creative to some degree.

The second reason we feel uncreative is because much of our education ignores or inhibits original thinking. For purposes of illustration, let's divide our mental abilities into four basic functions:

1. Observe and pay attention
2. Memorize and recall
3. Analyze and judge
4. Generate new ideas, foresee and visualize the nonexistent

We spend years in school developing the first three functions while the fourth goes almost totally neglected. We spend countless hours reading books and listening to teachers and professors. We are constantly tested in school on the basis of our ability to memorize facts and figures and regurgitate them on command. As students we're bombarded with numerous assignments that teach us to analyze, evaluate, and critique. But almost never are we given the opportunity to exercise our creative abilities. The system teaches us what to think and how to think but not how to think up. And as a result our creative abilities shrivel rather than flourish due to a lack of exercise. Have you ever noticed how children's imaginations dwindle after they start school?

MAKE UP YOUR MINDS

Let's begin our look at creativity by studying the two halves of the brain. A number of experiments in split-brain research have concluded that each hemisphere of the human brain has its own way of thinking and its own memory. It appears that just as we have two eyes, ears, and hands, we also have two minds. The left brain tends to think in terms of symbols and words while the right brain thinks in terms of sensory images. We use the left brain for logic, judgment, speaking, and mathematical ability, while the right brain is the source of dreaming, feelings, visualization, and intuition. Remembering someone's name is a function of the left-brain memory while remembering his face is a function of the memory in the right brain. Reading a book on how to improve your tennis or golf game is the job of the left brain, but getting "a feel for the game" is carried out in the right brain. Thus your two minds have a partnership in which one side handles the language and logic while the other side does things that are hard to put into words or symbols. Creativity works best when you have a flow between the two halves.

Here are some of the basic differences in left- and right-brain functions:

We use our left brain for:	*We use our right brain for:*
speaking	awareness without description
reading	seeing whole things at once
writing	recognizing similarities
analyzing	understanding analogies and metaphors
idea linking	intuition
abstracting	insight
categorizing	gut-level feeling
logic	synthesizing
reasoning	visualizing
judgment	spatial perception

We use our left brain for:	*We use our right brain for:*
counting and mathematical ability	recognizing patterns
verbal memory	visual memory
using symbols	"feeling" our way
managing time	relating things to the present

Long before there was split-brain research, great thinkers acknowledged the importance of relying on right-brain mental abilities. Aristotle, the founder of formal logic, spoke of the importance of thinking in mental pictures. And Einstein and other innovators in science and mathematics relied heavily on visual thinking before transforming their theories into precise equations.

Similarly, successful business executives rely heavily on the right side of the brain. In one experiment, University of Hawaii B-school professor Robert Doktor wired a number of chief executives to an electroencephalograph to find out which side of the brain they rely on most. The right side was the clear choice. And after years of in-depth study in managerial behavior, Henry Mintzberg of McGill University has concluded that the job of managing is primarily a right-brain skill. Mintzberg describes the chief executive as a holistic, intuitive thinker who revels in a climate of calculated chaos and relies on hunches to cope with problems far too complex for rational analysis.

When the results of split-brain research are considered in light of our education, it becomes clear that we're developing the left side of the brain while the right side is being suppressed and ignored. Education teaches how to be critical, verbal, logical, and analytical. But it rarely teaches us how to rely on hunches, deal with an unstructured problem, visualize the unforeseen, and use the "feelings" side of information.

In terms of split-brain abilities, the computer is nothing more than a gigantic left brain that is, in many ways, far superior to man's. As we progress into the microcomputer age, more left-brain jobs will be delegated to computers that will be able to do them faster and better than we can. The challenge to industry, education, and society will be teaching people how to use the right side of their brain to work in harmonious partnership with the giant electronic left brains we have created.

UNDERSTANDING CREATIVITY

The French physician René Laennec remembered how he signaled to his childhood friends by tapping on a hollow log. From this memory he conceived and eventually invented the stethoscope.

During a trip to Canada, Clarence Birdseye ate some fish that had been naturally frozen and thawed. He borrowed the idea from nature and the frozen-food industry was born.

Ben Franklin got tired of changing from one pair of glasses to another. Why not combine them? The result was the invention of bifocals.

The heart of all new ideas lies in the borrowing, adding, combining, or modifying of old ones. Do it by accident and people call you lucky. Do it by design and they'll call you creative. New ideas are nothing more than a rearrangement of old ones: that's the essence of how to be creative. Understanding that the cornerstone of new ideas lies in the association of old ones gives all of us the ability to create new ideas almost at will.

But knowing where new ideas come from isn't enough. You also need to know how to use your mental muscles to turn out good ideas at a rapid rate. This entails understanding the creative process, learning some simple idea-generating techniques, and creating an environment that encourages rather than discourages the production of new ideas. Let's look at each of those in order.

It's generally agreed that the process of developing good, new ideas goes through a somewhat predictable cycle that will occur over varying periods of time. This process can be divided into five steps:

1. *First insight.* Usually first insight comes as the result of dissatisfaction with things the way they are. The very seeds of creation are sown in this step. You realize that you have a problem you want to solve or a goal you want to achieve, and this is the first moment it occurs to you.

2. *Preparation.* Once you have a germinal idea conceived, your next step is to immerse yourself with information and explore all the possible avenues to solving the problem or developing the idea. Read up on the subject. Take notes. Talk to others. Collect information and learn as much as you can. In order to think up new ideas, you must first familiarize yourself with the ideas of others. This forms a springboard for launching your own imagination.

3. *Incubation.* This is the easy part. Once you're deluged with information, forget about the problem and let your right brain take over. Let your thoughts go underground and put your subconscious to work. Take a walk. Take a nap. Forget about it for a week. Work on another project. Sleep on it. Most important insights and decisions are made at the subconscious level. Don't get impatient and try to bypass this stage. The next stage of the creative process can't occur until the subconscious can do its work. As author Edna Ferber once remarked, "A story must simmer in its own juices for months or years before it's ready to serve."

4. *Illumination.* This is that exciting and joyous moment when everything falls into place and a new idea suddenly pops into your mind. Creative insights are likely to occur at the least-expected times such as while taking a bath, driving, or awakening in the middle of the night. And there's usually a great deal of intuition attached to them.

5. *Verification.* Illumination is great stuff but terribly unreliable, and most new ideas aren't good ideas. The raw material of creative achievement has to be examined, tested, and refined. Intellect and judgment are now brought into play and the value of all the brilliant insights is confirmed or denied. Back off and look at your ideas objectively. Ask someone else to evaluate

them. Usually you can revise your idea and come up with an even better one.

Did you notice how the creative process relies on both sides of the brain? Incubation and illumination are right-brain functions while preparation and verification are clearly functions of the left brain. Creative problem-solving requires relying on intuition, hunch, and gut-level feeling, but they're no substitute for research and sound judgment. Successful creativity generally results from a harmonious blending of research, intuition, and judgment.

GROUP CREATIVITY TECHNIQUES

Linus Pauling remarked "The best way to have a good idea is to have lots of ideas." And the best way to get lots of ideas is to get lots of people involved. The use of group creativity techniques is one of the key reasons that quality circles have met with so much success. Ideas are generated in such enormous quantities that the odds of having at least a few good ones is almost a certainty. Teaming up to create new ideas also improves morale and communication—and can be a lot of fun as well.

Over the years a number of effective techniques have been developed that enable groups to generate lots of ideas in a little time. But all techniques share one common rule: *Never try to think up and judge your ideas at the same time.* It's like trying to step on the brakes and the accelerator of your car simultaneously. This rule also applies when you're generating ideas alone. Think up first and judge the ideas later. Criticism kills creativity. With that thought in mind, here are the ground rules for three popular group ideation techniques:

Crawford Slip Writing

Named after Professor C. C. Crawford, who invented the concept, slip writing is the simplest, but a most powerful, idea-generating technique. At a meeting each person is given a 3-by-5-inch note pad and the leader presents a problem to the group in how-to form, such as "How can we reduce the departmental photocopy bill?" The leader then asks all present to write as many answers to the question as they can think of, with each answer written on a separate slip of paper. Before beginning, the leader stresses that judgment and criticism of ideas should be withheld. After the participants finish writing their ideas, the slips of paper are collected, categorized, and evaluated.

Slip writing is very effective for several reasons. First, ideas are submitted anonymously, ensuring that even the shyest person can submit an idea without fear of ridicule. Second, the anonymity factor assures that ideas will be judged on their merits rather than by who their creator happens to be. But most important, the slips of paper can be shuffled and considered in various combinations, which usually results in even better ideas.

Brainstorming

Brainstorming is the most popular of the group creativity techniques. A brainstorming session is simply a creative meeting the single purpose of which is to produce a checklist of ideas which can be evaluated *later*. The greatest value of brainstorming is that it provides more ideas than a conventional meeting and in less time.

Ideally, a brainstorming session has twelve members and lasts about thirty minutes. The leader begins the session by stating the problem and laying down four basic rules:

1. *Judgment and criticism are forbidden.* The purpose of the session is to think up ideas. Judgment comes later.

2. *"Freewheeling" is welcomed.* The wilder the idea, the better.

3. *Go for quantity.* The greater the number of ideas, the greater the odds of finding a useful idea.

4. *Seek to combine and improve ideas as they are mentioned.* Members should try to improve and build on each other's ideas as well as think up their own.

Once the session begins, members uninhibitedly blurt out any ideas that come to mind and the ideas are recorded.

The leader should strive to create a freewheeling, relaxed atmosphere during the session. The type of spirit that could be found at a party or picnic is the atmosphere you're looking for. The object is to get people to loosen up.

Brainstorming is highly effective in producing lots of ideas for several reasons. First, it has the power of idea association. Whenever someone states a new idea he stirs his own imagination as well as everyone else's. Second, research testing the free association of adults reveals that people produce from 65 to 93 percent more ideas in a group activity than when thinking alone. Finally, brainstorming can also motivate people by having them compete to think up ideas. Psychologists have shown that mental output can be increased by 50 percent or more when stirred by competition.

The Nominal Group Technique

As mentioned earlier, all new ideas are the rearrangement, modification, and combination of old ones. The Nominal Group Technique (NGT) is a prime example. NGT combines many of the features of slip writing with brainstorming and the result is a new way to stimulate the production of ideas. Before the meeting, the NGT facilitator issues a clear statement of the problem to be considered. The meeting itself is organized into four parts:

1. *Silent Generation.* During this first part of the meeting each member silently and independently writes as many solutions to the problem as he can think of.

2. *Sequential Brainstorming.* During this second phase, everyone is asked to contribute ideas out loud. However, members aren't allowed to blurt out ideas spontaneously as in conventional brainstorming. Instead, each member is polled in sequence, on a round-table basis, and asked to contribute an idea that is recorded and numbered. During this period, the facilitator encourages members to contribute a maximum number of ideas and build on the ideas of others.

3. *Discussion.* Each idea is now discussed for purposes of understanding the idea, not judging it. This gives the members

an opportunity to communicate and share the reasoning behind their ideas.

4. *Selection, Priorization, and Evaluation.* Each member independently selects the five to ten best ideas or suggestions, ranks them, and assigns them a value. For example, if members were asked to choose the five best ideas, the best idea would be weighted a 5 and the fifth best idea would be given a value of 1. Individual scores are then collected and tabulated to see which ideas have the greatest consensus.

When using creative group problem-solving techniques, keep the following guidelines in mind:

- The problem should be specific, simple, and well-defined. The more complex and nebulous the problem, the harder it is for the group to focus its efforts on a single target. For example, a problem such as "How can X corporation reduce its paperwork?" is too broad for a brainstorming or NGT session. But "How can X corporation reduce the photocopy bill in the purchasing department?" is a specific, well-defined problem that lends itself to group problem-solving.
- Choose a problem having a large number of possible answers. Problems with a limited number of options (like whether to buy or lease) aren't suitable for creative group techniques.
- Once a problem has been chosen, circulate a memo to participants explaining the problem and how the meeting will be conducted. Give several examples of new, freewheeling ideas. This will prepare people so they will know that this isn't a conventional meeeting.
- Once the meeting starts, restate the basic rules. It's a good idea to write them on a flip chart or a chalkboard or have them written on a placard. This can be displayed as a visual aid throughout the meeting.
- As the meeting progresses, keep the atmosphere informal and free of perfectionism. Encourage ideas that are sparked by previous ideas. The goal is to get a chain reac-

tion going where participants are creatively feeding off of each other.

OTHER TECHNIQUES FOR GENERATING IDEAS

In addition to group techniques, thinkers and problem-solvers have come up with all sorts of ways to get their creative juices flowing. The following are some of the more popular and interesting ones.

Use Checklists

With the checklist technique, all you do is get a list of topics or words and consider them in light of the subject you're trying to think creatively about. For example, here's a checklist of creative questions formulated by the late Alex Osborn. Perhaps you or your group will find it useful:

Could we . . .

1. Modify?
   - _____ what to add
   - _____ more time, greater frequency
   - _____ stronger, higher, longer, thicker
   - _____ duplicate, multiply, exaggerate

2. Minimize?
   - _____ what to subtract
   - _____ smaller, condense
   - _____ omit, streamline, split up
   - _____ lower, shorten, lighten

3. Substitute?
   - _____ other process, ingredient, material
   - _____ other place, other approach or form of approach

4. Rearrange?
   - _____ interchange components
   - _____ other sequence, schedule, pattern, layout
   - _____ other person

5. Reverse?

_____ transpose positive and negative

_____ try opposite, turn backward or upside down

_____ reverse roles

6. Combine?

_____ uses, purposes, ideas, approaches

7. Put to other uses?

_____ new ways to use

_____ other uses if modified

_____ what else is like this?

You don't have to have a checklist already made up to take advantage of the technique. For example, leafing through the Yellow Pages can give an alert entrepreneur ideas for new products, customers, and services. Or thumbing through the daily newspaper or magazines may provide you with just the idea you need to launch a new advertising campaign. Checklists don't usually get you a satisfactory solution to the problem, but they're useful for making a start.

Force Relationships

Mickey Mouse watches and combination electric can openers/knife sharpeners are examples of forced relationships. The idea is to take two or more unrelated ideas and combine them to see if a third useful idea can be created. In my neighborhood, someone recently opened a combination pizza parlor/electronic game arcade. Every time I drive by, there's a long line of children eagerly waiting to get in and spend their money. That's one example of a forced relationship that's making somebody rich.

The best way to force relationships is to build yourself an idea bank. For example, if your job is to write advertising copy, begin collecting good advertisements, clippings, ideas, and designs and put them in a box. When you have a new ad to write, shake up the box and pull out two or more at random. Can any of these ideas be applied to your new ad? If not, shake the box and pull out two more. If you keep doing this, you'll eventually come up with a useful idea.

Are you looking for new products or services to offer? Write down each product or service you currently offer on a separate slip of paper, then put the slips in a bag and shake it. Now pull out two and see if you have an idea for a new product. You may only get one good idea for every 500 tries, but remember that one good idea can be worth an enormous sum of money.

List and Question Attributes

Attribute listing is a special application of checklists. You begin by listing all the characteristics of whatever you happen to be working on. Then each attribute is questioned by applying a checklist of questions such as the one presented earlier.

For example, if you want to design a better screwdriver, begin by listing its common attributes: (1) round, (2) steel shaft, (3) handle, (4) wedge-shaped tip, (5) manually operated, and (6) torque provided by twisting action.

Now question each attribute separately. Could the round shaft be made hexagonal so that a wrench could be used to turn it? What if we remove the handle and design the shaft to fit an electric drill? Now we have a power tool. What if we make interchangeable shafts for different-size screws? The basic process is to look at each component and ask "Why does this have to be this way?" and "How can we do it better?" It's a great way to take the blinders off our thought processes. As Woodrow Wilson noted, "Originality is simply a fresh pair of eyes."

Use Analogies and Metaphors

Another key to creative problem-solving is to make new things seem familiar and familiar things seem new. One way to achieve this is through the use of analogies. It's no accident that many of the parts of a camera parallel the human eye. Alexander Graham Bell conceived the telephone by modeling it after the human ear. And when George Thomas was looking for a better way to apply underarm deodorant, he used a ballpoint pen as his model and invented the roll-on deodorant applicator. All three of these products were conceived using analogies.

Analogies also aid us in the preparation stages of the creative process. When you're trying to learn unfamiliar concepts, they make new things familiar. For example, the analogy of water flowing through pipes for a water tower is a useful tool for understanding the basic electrical concepts of current, resistance, and voltage.

The next time you're trying to solve a problem, ask yourself "What can I model this after?" or "What's this like?" You may come up with just the answer you're looking for.

Think Visually
Our left-brain-oriented society teaches us to think in terms of symbols, such as words or numbers. However, creative people often develop the knack of blocking out all verbal thoughts and forming images in their mind's eye. For example, Einstein conceived his theory of relativity by visualizing the possibility that a person falling from a roof was both in motion and at rest at the same time.

Visual thinking is much more fluid than verbal thinking, and many new ideas can be induced this way. The next time you're searching for a new idea, close your eyes and form visual images of the problem or the desired result in your mind. Block out all verbal thoughts by repeating a simple word over and over in your mind until it becomes meaningless. Any visual ideas can be verbally expressed, drawn, or written down later.

Don't Let Those Ideas Slip Away
Ideas are slippery things. They appear and dart away in an instant. They frequently disguise themselves as crises, misfortunes, and accidents. And often the best ones won't appear without conscious effort on our part. The point is that you can't act on your ideas until you make the effort to capture them. Here are four things you can do to harvest a large supply:

1. Always be prepared to record your thoughts. There's no way to tell when a great idea is likely to pop into your mind. If you can't record it, you'll run the risk of losing it. Always carry writing materials or a microcasette recorder with you.

2. Create an idea bank. Have a file folder, desk drawer, shoebox, or other container for storing ideas related to a particular problem or subject. Store your own ideas as well as clippings, cartoons, articles, quotes, or anything else related to the topic. You'll soon have a large supply of ideas that can be combined, rearranged, reversed, and so on to produce more ideas.

3. Capitalize on the unexpected. Many great ideas are discovered by accident. After years of trying to make rubber more useful, Charles Goodyear dropped some crude rubber on a hot stove and discovered the beginnings of vulcanized rubber. Similarly, Dr. Alexander Fleming stumbled on the discovery of penicillin when he examined a mold-contaminated culture through a microscope. Companies often stumble on ways to turn waste materials into profitable byproducts. The basic idea is to keep your eyes and your mind open for accidental discoveries. There's no substitute for luck, but luck happens to people who know what they want.

4. Schedule an idea time. Like most worthwhile things in life, creativity involves hard work; if you wait to be inspired, you may wait forever. If you're trying to generate ideas, reserve an amount of time and devote that time to generating ideas. They may come slowly at first, but just be persistent. Eventually the ideas will start to flow and you'll be there to catch them.

Create the Ideal Idea Climate
Like a delicate flower, the spirit of creativity and innovation has to be nurtured in a proper climate. All the techniques in the world are useless unless people want to be creative. In the final analysis, it's the drive to produce new ideas that matters most.

The following are seven key ingredients to a sound creative climate:

- A heavy emphasis on results with little emphasis on structure. Creative organizations (and people) know what they want but give people the latitude to do it their way.
- The incentive to produce ideas. New ideas are encouraged, solicited, evaluated, tried, and (most important) rewarded.
- The right to be wrong. Trying new things is a risky business, and many new ideas fail. A climate that harshly penalizes or criticizes honest failure destroys creativity.
- The pressure to produce ideas. Like everything else, the production of new ideas and things works best in a reasonable but challenging time frame. Without deadlines, nothing happens. And competition helps too.
- Opportunities for association and solitude. People need interaction to feed off each other creatively. But many of the best ideas come forth in moments of quiet solitude. In the final analysis, every new idea is the product of a single brain.
- An informal, open work environment. Little emphasis is placed on dress, appearance, rank, and formal status. The focus is on getting jobs done.
- Plenty of support and encouragement. Positive feedback and recognition are tremendous creativity boosters.

My discussion of each point was brief because most of these ideas have appeared earlier. Keep these points in mind when trying to encourage creativity in yourself and others. How many of them are present where you work?

Now, the $64,000,000 question.

HOW DO YOU KNOW WHEN YOU'VE GOT A GOOD IDEA?

You don't. And neither does anyone else. Investing your time and effort to turn an idea into a reality is always a risky business. There's no way to innovate and avoid risk, but you can take steps to reduce it and stack the cards in your favor.

First, after you've had that flash of brilliance, let your idea cool off. You need to get away and reduce your emotional attachment to it. As time goes by you'll be able to evaluate it more clearly.

Second, solicit the help of other people who can be objective. Friends and relatives are usually too biased to be of much help. But a colleague or expert may fill the bill. Keep in mind, though, that experts make mistakes too. And most of them are extremely good at knowing why something can't be done.

Third, establish a set of criteria for judging your ideas. Here are six useful questions you can use to evaluate an idea:

1. *Will it work?* Does it get the results you want? Most ideas won't pass this first crucial test. Don't give up yet. Maybe you can improve it and come up with something better. It took Thomas Edison 6000 tries before he came up with working filament for the electric light.

2. *Is it better than what already exists?* If your idea isn't any better than the status quo, there's no incentive to change. No point in reinventing the wheel.

3. *Is it people-compatible?* If people have to change or alter their behavior drastically to use it, forget it. Its chances for success are nil.

4. *Is the timing right?* Timing is everything in business, and a lot of it is pure guesswork. In judging the timing of an idea start with the present. Would it be practical now? How long will it take to implement it? What's the future probably going to be like then? Are there any trends developing that would make your idea more or less valuable? Remember, there's no such thing as the right idea at the wrong time.

5. *Is it worth it?* Many new useful, workable ideas cost more than the benefits they deliver.

6. *Is it simple?* The best ideas are usually simple.

If your idea scores high on each of those criteria, it's probably worth pursuing. In addition, here are two more useful checklists for judging ideas:

The Value Engineering Principle

1. What is it?
2. What does it do?
3. What does it cost?
4. What else will do the job?
5. What does that cost?

The U.S. Navy Checklist

1. Will it increase production—or improve quality?
2. Is it a more efficient utilization of manpower?
3. Does it improve methods of operation, maintenance, or construction?
4. Is it an improvement over the present tools and machinery?
5. Does it improve safety?
6. Does it prevent waste or conserve materials?
7. Does it eliminate unnecessary work?
8. Does it reduce costs?
9. Does it improve present methods?
10. Will it improve working conditions?

Evaluating a hunch is something else. In 1960, Ray Kroc bought a small hamburger enterprise called McDonalds for $2.7 million. His lawyer called it "a bad deal" but, according to Kroc, "I felt in my funny bone it was a sure thing." Kroc's "bad deal" grosses billions of dollars every year.

Very often a hunch is a collection of facts stored at the subconscious level. Whenever you have a strong gut-level feeling about an idea, ask yourself "Is it possible that I've managed to gather information about this without consciously realizing it?" If so, pay close attention to it. But a word of caution: Confusing hunches with wishful thinking is courting disaster. Don't confuse what you feel with what you want.

Creativity is one of the most valuable skills all of us can learn to help increase productivity. All of us can be creatively productive if we understand the process and use the right techniques. Question the status quo and challenge assumptions. Look for patterns and similarities in different ideas and events. Seek ways to make new things seem familiar and familiar things seem new. Try making connections between unrelated concepts and things. Pay attention to hunches and capitalize on the unexpected. And, once you've got a good idea, don't be afraid to take a chance and make something happen. The real payoff is in innovation. Inventor Charles Kettering said it best: "There exist limitless opportunities in every industry. Where there is an open mind, there will always be a frontier."

CHAPTER 13

HOW TO BE HAPPILY PRODUCTIVE

"Success or failure in business is caused more by
mental attitudes than by mental capacities."
—*Walter Dill Scott*

A popular poster reads "When the rush is over, I'm going to have a nervous breakdown. I've worked for it, I've earned it, and nobody is going to deprive me of it." Does that sound like you? If it does, don't feel like The Lone Ranger. You have plenty of company.

Feeling overworked, frustrated, and anxious about work is something we all occasionally experience. But prolonged negative feelings create excessive stress—and stress is one of our biggest productivity- and people-killers. It's related to absenteeism, high turnover, alcoholism, drug addiction, ulcers, strokes, heart attacks, suicides, nervous breakdowns, and numerous other immobilizing or fatal illnesses. To quote the Work in America study, *Occupational Stress and Productivity*, "The financial cost of decreased productivity due to stress is so enormous as to be incalculable." It's becoming very clear that managing job-related stress is a major key to increasing productivity and the quality of life in general.

242

Notice that I said *managing* stress, not eliminating it. You can't totally eliminate stress and you wouldn't want to if you could. We experience stress from the good things in life as well as the bad. And all of us need a certain amount to keep us creative, challenged, and fulfilled. For example, pursuing lofty goals and meeting deadlines is stressful. Feeling nervous before taking a test, speaking before a group, or interviewing for an important job is stressful. Taking on a new job with more responsibility in a strange city is stressful. But as long as the level of stress is moderate, it keeps us sharp and active and motivates us to do our best. The relationship between stress and performance is positive up to a point. But after some optimum level, stress starts to take its toll and becomes more of a crippler than a motivator.

In recent years there's been a lot of research in the area of managing stress; some useful insights and stress-management tools are emerging. The purpose of this chapter is to provide you with some of those ideas and tools. Later we will look at some other interesting findings about highly productive people and how you can become one.

UNDERSTANDING AND MANAGING STRESS

Technically speaking, stress is your attempt to adapt to perceived changes in your environment. And that definition carries some heavy implications. First, stress is not what happens to you. It's your physical and mental reaction to what you perceive. In other words, most of the negative emotions and physical symptoms of stress are caused by thinking. This means that one key to reducing stress is to examine, evaluate, and adjust your thoughts. Do you think of your feelings as uncontrollable sensations that govern your thoughts and behavior? Just the opposite is true. Feelings are an emotional reaction to your thoughts and aren't determined by what happens to you but what you *think* about what happens to you. You can't have an emotional reaction to a happening until you think about it.

Think Your Way out of the Gloom

Change your thinking and you change your feelings. That's the basic message of cognitive therapy,[1] a new approach to treating stress and psychological disorders. In a pilot study at the University of Pennsylvania School of Medicine, cognitive therapy has been very effective in treating severely depressed patients. Yet the system is simple and straightforward and can be applied on a self-help basis when you find yourself in the doldrums. The theory of cognitive therapy is based on three very commonsense principles:

1. Your moods are created by your thoughts. You feel the way you do right now because of what you're thinking.
2. When you feel down and depressed it's because your mind is dominated by negative thinking.
3. Negative thoughts are almost always grossly distorted.

Therefore, when you're feeling down, one key to feeling better is to identify distorted negative thoughts, write them down, and realize how ridiculous and irrational they are. Cognitive therapist David Burns has assembled a list of ten of the most common types of erroneous, negative thinking and suggests "When you are feeling upset, this list may make you aware of how you are fooling yourself." The following is a paraphrased summary of Dr. Burns' list:

1. *The either-or trap.* You see everything in only two categories. You're either a winner or a loser, a success or a failure, lazy or ambitious, and so on. As a result you set yourself up for an endless series of put-downs.

2. *Overgeneralizing.* You expect total misfortune to follow because of one or more bad experiences. Someone else gets the big job you applied for and you say to yourself "That will teach me to be ambitious. I'm never going to apply for another job again."

---

[1] For a comprehensive treatment of cognitive therapy see David D. Burns, M.D., *Feeling Good: The New Mood Therapy* (New York: William Morrow & Co., 1980).

3. *Positive filtering.* You look for the negative aspects of a situation and dwell on them while ignoring the positives. Pretty soon you're convinced that everything is negative.

4. *Automatic discounting.* Compliments are brushed aside and criticisms dwelt on. If your boss or a colleague compliments your work, "He's just being nice," but constructive criticism is taken to mean "I'm a loser."

5. *Jumping to conclusions.* You automatically assume others look down on you without checking or you peer into the future and see only disaster.

6. *Magnification and minimization.* Situations are viewed out of proportion. You magnify your perception of your weaknesses and underestimate your strengths.

7. *Reasoning emotionally.* This is the guilt trap: "Because I feel bad, I must have done something bad."

8. *The shoulds.* I should do this or I must do that. Rather than motivating you to act, should and must statements only make you feel guilty.

9. *Labeling.* Confusing your worth with what you do is another trap. Instead of saying "I made a mistake," you label yourself a failure. But neither you nor anyone else can be equated with any one thing you do.

10. *Personalization.* You feel personally responsible for the actions, feelings, and wellbeing of others and set yourself up for a massive ongoing sense of guilt. In the final analysis, everyone is individually responsible for his own behavior, not you.

The next time you're feeling low:

- Write down your negative thoughts.
- Read over the list of ten distortions and note the ones that are clouding your thinking.
- Replace the negative thoughts with positive, rational, objective ones.

Cognitive therapy sounds too simple and too good to be true, but it's having a very high success rate, and I can personally attest to the fact that it picks me up whenever I feel down. It's an effective, commonsense way to become the master of your moods and reduce your level of stress. If you think right, you'll feel right.

Don't Overload Yourself with Changes

Excessive stress has been labeled the disease of the twentieth century. Why? Because stress is activated by your attempts to adapt to changes. And coping with change and uncertainty is one of the greatest problems of modern living.

One of the most useful stress-management tools is the life-change index developed by Thomas Holmes and Richard Rahe of the University of Washington School of Medicine. After interviewing 5000 people over a twenty-year period, Dr. Holmes and Dr. Rahe found that serious physical and emotional illnesses frequently follow an overdose of major life changes. Furthermore, they found that they could assign numerical values to certain changes, add them up, use them up, and use them as predictors of impending illnesses. The self-evaluation exercise on the next page is one result of their research.

If your score is less than 150, your chances of incurring a serious illness in the next two years is less than one in three. A score between 150 and 300 gives you a 50 percent chance. But, according to Holmes and Rahe, a score over 300 gives you over an 80 percent chance of having a major health breakdown.

The point is not to avoid major changes in your life but to look ahead, plan, and space them over reasonable periods of time. Usually you can't plan for the most traumatic ones such as the death of a loved one or a major injury. But everyone has some control over many of life's changes such as taking a new job, marriage, buying a new home, having children, and retirement. The more you can implement major life changes on a smoothly planned basis, the more successful and less stressful they're likely to be.

Heed the Warning Signals of Excess Stress

Inasmuch as we are all different, we all react differently to excessive stress. However, there are a number of warning signals

Compute Your Life-Change Risk
Which of These Changes Have You Experienced in the Past Year?
Add Up the Point Values of Each Event.

Event	Life-Change Units	Event	Life-Change Units
Death of a spouse	100	Son or daughter leaving home	29
Marital separation	65	Trouble with in-laws	29
Death of a close family member	63	Outstanding personal achievement	28
Personal injury or illness	53	Wife beginning or stopping work	28
Marriage	50	Revision of personal habits	24
Loss of job	47		
Marital reconciliation	45	Trouble with business superior	23
Retirement	45	Change in work hours or conditions	20
Change in health of a family member	44	Change in residence	20
Wife's pregnancy	40	Change in schools	20
Sex difficulties	39	Change in recreation	19
Gain of a new family member	39	Change in social activities	18
Change in financial status	38	Taking out a small mortgage on your home	17
Death of a close friend	37	Change in sleeping habits	16
Change to a different kind of work	36	Change in number of family get-togethers	15
Increase or decrease in arguments with spouse	35	Change in eating habits	15
Taking out a big mortgage on home	31	Vacation	13
Foreclosure of mortgage or loan	30	Minor violations of law	11
Change in work responsibilities	30		

that may indicate too much tension. Be alert for these signs in yourself and others:

- Overreacting to small irritations and volatile changes in moods
- Developing nervous habits
- Rushing through meals
- Laughing less and feeling that life is no fun any more
- Distrusting others without reason
- Feeling trapped and inadequate
- Increases in drinking, smoking, or use of drugs
- Insomnia or sleeping excessively
- Nightmares
- Working late or more obsessively than usual
- Difficulty making decisions
- A loss of perspective and the inability to think, write, or speak clearly
- Excessive worrying about the future or regrets about the past
- Loss of memory
- Brooding anger
- Increased frequency of errors or accidents
- Difficulty getting along with other people
- Frequent thoughts of or references to suicide

One general symptom of too much stress is any reversal or large change in usual behavior. Examples might be the social butterfly becoming a recluse, the independent person suddenly having to always be with others, or the efficient worker who suddenly becomes irresponsible and careless.

In addition to the psychological symptoms, the following physical symptoms can indicate too much stress:

- Allergies
- Feeling chronically tired without good reason
- Headaches
- Backaches
- High blood pressure
- Indigestion

- Hives
- Nausea
- Cold hands or feet
- Constipation
- Aching neck and
  shoulder muscles

- Diarrhea
- Menstrual problems
- Chronic colds or the flu
- Loss of appetite
- Sexual problems

From time to time all of us are troubled by one or more of these symptoms, and they're usually no cause for concern. However, if one or more symptoms keeps you from feeling and acting like your normal self for a period of time, get help from a physician or competent professional counselor. All of these symptoms can be caused by problems other than stress.

Exercise Those Tensions Away

The desk and the swivel chair may well be our greatest occupational hazards. Most jobs in skyscrapers and automated factories subject us to a lot of pressure and little or no chance to release it. Noise, conflicts, deadlines, commuter traffic, and the general pressures to produce create physical tensions that must be released if you're going to avoid excess stress. And one good way to release them is with regular exercise.

We really don't know whether regular exercise increases productivity. But we do know that keeping physically fit is good business from the dollars-and-cents viewpoint. Consider these facts:

- Industry loses approximately 132 million work days and $25 billion each year from premature deaths.
- Another $3 billion is lost due to sickness.
- Still another $5 billion is lost due to disabling injuries.
- The National Safety Council reports that American industry pays $225 billion each year in workmen's compensation.
- Heart disease alone costs industry an estimated 52 million

workdays of lost production. Most medical experts agree
that exercise can help prevent or reduce heart problems.
- Backaches (which frequently result from neglected muscles) account for $1 billion lost output each year.

With statistics like these, it's no wonder that companies in
large numbers have been jumping on the physical-fitness bandwagon. And it's no fad. Company fitness and exercise programs
are here to stay, if for no other reason than that they have a
favorable impact on the bottom line. Fitness programs cut absenteeism and raise morale, and participants report improved self-
images.

Whether or not your company has such a program, make an
effort to work your stresses off. You don't have to participate in
an elaborate program to get more exercise. Do isometrics in your
office. Get off the bus or park your car five or six blocks from
work and walk to the office. Get in the habit of taking long walks
with your spouse to unwind from the daily grind. Take up
aerobic dancing, bicycling, swimming, jogging, or a new sport
with a friend, relative, or your spouse. The greater the stresses
of your job, the more you need physical exercise. With a little
imagination and effort you can put more physical activity into
your daily living. And you'll feel a whole lot better.

Take Time out to Relax

The idea of taking a relaxation break is so simple that
people underestimate its value. Yet research carried out by
Ruanne Peters and Herbert Benson of the Harvard Medical
School reveals that learning and practicing the proper relaxation
technique can lower blood pressure and increase job efficiency.

In the study that yielded these results, subjects were taught
the following relaxation technique and asked to practice it twice
a day for fifteen minutes. Perhaps it will work for you:

1. Sit quietly and comfortably.
2. Close your eyes.

3. Gradually loosen your muscles, inch by inch from your toe to the top of your head.

4. Breathe through your nose and become aware of your own breathing. As you exhale say the word *one* silently to yourself. Breathe easily and naturally.

5. Continue for 10 to 20 minutes. You may open your eyes to check the time, but don't use an alarm. When you finish, sit quietly for several minutes, first with your eyes closed and later with your eyes open. Don't stand up for a few minutes.

6. Don't worry about achieving a deep level of relaxation. Maintain a passive attitude and let relaxation occur at its own pace. When distracting thoughts occur, try to ignore them and return to repeating *one*. You'll get better with practice. Don't practice within two hours after any meal as digestive processes may interfere with relaxation.

Needless to say, this is only one of many relaxation techniques that can be used to counter stress. Perhaps another technique such as yoga, meditation, prayer, or deep breathing will work better for you. The main thing to look for is something that you choose to do, is enjoyable, makes sense to you, and enables you to put your mind in neutral for ten to twenty minutes.

Additional Strategies for Low-Stress Working

Adjusting your thinking, managing change, taking relaxation breaks, and regular exercise can go a long way to reducing the stresses that sap your productive energy. But there are a number of other things you can do to prevent excessive job stress from entering your life. Here are seven more tips for making your life on the job more enjoyable, fulfilling, and productive:

1. Put the present in perspective. We all have a natural tendency to exaggerate the importance of what's going on in our

lives right now. Back off and look at the present from a lifetime perspective. Your ultimate success or failure doesn't depend on what you do in any single hour, day, month, or year. Your career is a marathon, not a sprint. Do your best in the present and concentrate on the task at hand. But don't fool yourself into believing it's a do-or-die situation. If you do, you'll only weigh yourself down with more stress.

2. Learn to laugh at life in general and yourself in particular. Samuel Butler remarked "All of the animals, excepting man, know that the principal business of life is to enjoy it." Taking your life or work too seriously can be hazardous to your health and it almost always keeps you from doing your best. Furthermore, if you practice the act of laughing at yourself, you'll never cease to be amused. Most of us are on this planet for only about 25,000 days, and a well-developed sense of humor can only make the trip more pleasant. Resolve to put more laughter in your life. It's the ultimate therapy for negative, stress-producing emotion.

3. Practice slowing down. Continually pushing yourself to work at a frenzied pace is stressful and usually results in poor-quality work. Relax, slow down, and move calmly but steadily toward achieving your goals. If an important deadline is pressing you, try to negotiate for an extension. Most bosses or customers prefer quality work later instead of slipshod work now. The next time you have an important project, resolve to start earlier and take your time. Both you and your work will be better off.

4. Build quality relationships at work. The stresses and strains of the work world are such that no one can go it alone for extended periods of time. We all need the support, friendship, and understanding of people who care. And a good relationship with your boss or colleagues can greatly lighten your burdens. Seek out and surround yourself with positive people who will encourage and support your efforts. And do your best to provide the same support for them. Avoid critics, cynics, and nega-

tive personalities. And if your boss is one, consider getting another job. Life's too short to spend your working hours in the company of a troll.

5. Practice good time-management techniques. Much of today's stress boils down to the pressures of the clock. Setting goals and priorities, effectively delegating, blocking interruptions, and the other techniques discussed in Chapter 11 are all helpful in reducing stress as well as enabling you to get more done.

6. Balance your work with play. Making a habit out of long hours isn't only bad for you. It's bad for business, too. You need time to get away from your job so you can return to it with a fresh perspective. Otherwise you run the risk of falling into a rut, losing your creative edge, and burning out.

Get yourself some hobbies or pastimes that allow you to escape from work physically and mentally. And be sure to choose pastimes that meet needs not met on the job. For example, if you're a writer who works alone, choose an activity that gives you contact with people. If you're a nurse or counselor who spends time caring for others, do something that allows you to be selfish. Make something for yourself or learn a skill you've always wanted to master. If you work all day as a team member, choose a solitary hobby that will enable you to have time for yourself. And one word of caution about hobbies: If you choose one that's similar to your work (like the executive who becomes president of the country club) you run the risk of tiring yourself even more.

7. Shield yourself from excess noise. Does the noise where you work keep you from concentrating and getting things done? If so take steps to reduce it. Studies reveal that loud, meaningless, and unpredictable noises can be damaging to productivity, behavior, and mental health. Close your door. Request a move to a quieter location or see if you can get your office soundproofed. Talk it over with your boss or colleagues and see what can be done to reduce noise at work. Noise pollution is becoming an

increasingly larger problem in today's work world of clattering typewriters, rumbling subways, and honking horns. But there's usually something you can do.

For example, while writing this book I've been subjected to the shrill barking of a neighbor's dog. And believe me, this dog has a piercing and frequent bark. I solved the problem by purchasing a set of ear-stoppers at the local drugstore and a white-noise generator. The white noise masks the bark and the ear-stoppers reduce the level of noise I hear. Consequently I'm now oblivious of practically all random noises and able to get hours of uninterrupted concentration.

8. Don't try to be so perfect. Are you always striving to be number one? Do you measure your self-worth in terms of what you produce and achieve? Are you forever setting unreachable goals? If so, you're a likely victim of your own drive for perfection. And perfectionism is self-defeating and counterproductive. Not only do perfectionists tend to achieve less; they also set themselves up for a life of troubled relationships and severe mood disorders.

This doesn't mean you should strive to do mediocre work. Setting high goals and the pursuit of excellence are two of life's greatest rewards. But habitually striving for perfection is a blueprint for high-stress living. Resolve to do your best and call it a success. And if it doesn't work out, to hell with it! Pick yourself up and go try something else. Remember, winners lose more than losers lose. And that's because winners never stop trying.

HOW TO BE A PEAK PERFORMER

What makes for a top producer? Is it the workaholic who leaves the office at ten each evening and brags about never taking a vacation? Definitely not. Workaholics are rarely top performers because they're hooked on work rather than results. Consequently they get a poor return on their investment of time and effort. And they tend to be difficult to work with because they resent all those "lazy" people who don't work as hard as they do.

Workaholics do contribute but usually aren't very creative because they tend to lead one-dimensional lives. It's common for them to be driven by a fear of failure, and many use hard work to escape from feelings of worthlessness or poor relationships at home. Most are classic victims of the activity trap, and, to make bad matters worse, many organizatons reward workaholics for their nose-to-the-grindstone behavior. Needless to say, workaholism isn't the answer to America's productivity problems.

The peak performer is an altogether different breed. He works hard and has a strong commitment to work but focuses on results. He also knows how to manage stress, relax, communicate, delegate, surround himself with competent people, and lead a balanced life.

Would you like to be a peak performer and realize your highest potential? It isn't as impossible as you might think. Research studies on peak performers reveal that they approach life and work differently from most of us. But the skills and habits they practice are ones that all of us can adopt and profit from. Here are six keys to peak performance that you can use to get better results in anything you try:

1. Turn off Your Internal Critic

For purposes of explanation, let's divide the personality into two parts, the critic and the doer. All of us have that little voice inside our head that berates us about past mistakes and worries us about future ones. And the unfortunate result is that the critic breaks our concentration and causes us to focus away from what we are trying to achieve. Instead of telling us what to do, the internal critic tells us what went wrong and what not to do. "Why did you do that, stupid?" "You're never going to be any good." "Man, you're a real loser."

Peak performers have learned that when the internal critic is silenced, a second self that automatically gets the job done takes over. Thus, one key to peak performance is to shut off your internal critic and let your built-in capacity for success go to work. Turning off the critic is tough, but there are several things you can do to help silence it or, at least, turn the volume down.

First, trust yourself and don't question your potential. Self-trust is the first lesson of success and self-doubt is almost always self-fulfilling. Dwell on your past successes and realize that failure is an abstract concept that doesn't really exist. Failure is only someone's opinion that a given act wasn't satisfactorily performed. And as for potential, no one—including you—knows what you're capable of. Most of us grossly underestimate our abilities. And that's the biggest performance limiter of all.

Second, focus on results and concentrate on what you're doing right now. When eighty-year-old conductor Arturo Toscanini was asked to name his most important achievement, he replied "Whatever I happen to be doing at the moment is the biggest thing in my life." Being able to focus your efforts on a desired result is essential for peak performance. And by concentrating on the here and now, your mind is filled with what *is* happening rather than regretting what has happened or worrying about what might happen. The internal critic only deals with yesterdays and tomorrows. So, as long as you concentrate on the present, it has nothing to say.

Finally, when you're performing a task, don't worry about how you're doing—just do it. Peak performers have learned that the less you worry about end results the better they're likely to be.

2. Set Increasingly Larger Goals

Psychologist David Viscott wrote: "There is nothing quite as exciting or as wonderful as choosing a difficult goal, working hard and succeeding. It's not the success that's so important but the process of growth, of becoming more than one set out to be and in the bargain discovering a better part of yourself." That quote describes the motivation of a peak performer.

The peak performer in business, sports, or entertainment is internally driven. Although he is usually a good team player, company quotas and keeping up with the Joneses don't turn him on. Instead, he sets his own goals and pursues them for the sheer satisfaction that comes from achieving something that's meaningful and worthwhile to him. And once he reaches a lofty goal, you can count on him to set and achieve an even greater one in the future.

The peak performer realizes that with each major achievement comes increased capacity to achieve. And he uses his newly created capacities to carry him to greater heights.

The peak-performer's approach to goals is simple in concept and one we can all profit from:

- Set an attainable goal you can get excited about that causes you to stretch.
- Don't compete with anyone but yourself.
- Once you achieve the goal, try and top yourself by achieving an even bigger one.
- Don't equate your worth with what you accomplish.

3. Don't Get *Too* Comfortable

Do you feel that you've done everything there is to do in your job? Has your job become a very soft, comfortable, predictable routine? If so, your chances for peak performance are slim or none.

To quote an unknown philosopher, "Discontent is the penalty we pay for being race horses instead of cows." Show me a person who is totally satisfied with his work, and I'll show you someone who isn't going to achieve much. Peak performers realize this and as a result don't allow themselves to be lulled into a work situation where they feel too much at home. Meaningful achievement is always preceded by a healthy dissatisfaction with the status quo and the challenge to do new and better things.

Does this mean you should abandon your job security, fringe benefits, and retirement package to be a high producer? Not usually. We all need a certain amount of comfort and security to function effectively; how much you need depends on your own personality. The point is that there should always be a new product, service, or a new challenge of some kind to keep you interested and performing at your best.

4. Be a Problem Solver, not a Blame-Placer

Placing the blame and castigating yourself and others when things go wrong is a totally counterproductive pastime. If you doubt me, try this exercise: Take a sheet of paper and list several problems or situations troubling you at work. Next to each problem write the names of everyone who's to blame for it. Now, what have you done or discovered that's going to improve the situation? Nothing. Blame-placing is just one form of living in the past. And nothing can change the past. All you can do is learn from it.

Peak performers focus on solving problems. Instead of asking "Who did it?" they ask questions like:

- What's the heart of the problem?
- How can it be corrected?
- What can we learn?
- How can we keep this from happening again?
- Does this problem give us any unexpected opportunities?
- What good can come from this?

Every problem or crisis is, at the very least, a learning experience and can often present a creative opportunity. High producers realize this and capitalize on it.

5. Consider the Worst and Take a Chance

The rewards in this world belong to those who know how to take calculated risks—and take them. No guts, no glory. No risks, no rewards. Yes, Virginia, you can be too careful, and risk-avoidance is one sure path to mediocrity.

High performers aren't foolhardy daredevils, but they aren't afraid to take large risks. Their basic approach to risk-taking is simple. Before taking a chance, they ask themselves "What's the worst thing that can come from this, and if it happens can I live with it?" If the answer is yes, they take a chance, let the chips fall where they may, and don't second-guess themselves. Most of us don't do this. Instead of thinking through the consequences beforehand, we hope for the best and agonize over whether we made the right decision.

The next time you're faced with deciding whether or not to take a risk:

- Write down the worst possible outcomes and estimate the odds of them happening.
- Write an alternate plan for what you'll do if the worst happens.
- If the worst is survivable, the rewards worthwhile, and the odds good, go for it and don't look back.

This isn't to say you're going to win them all—you won't. But you won't lose them all, either. And by acquiring the habit of taking risks you're increasing your chances for a productive and fulfilling life.

6. Visualize and Mentally Rehearse the Future
Long before there was research on peak performers, clergyman and author Harry Emerson Fosdick gave this advice: "Hold a picture of yourself long and steadily enough in your mind's eye and you will be drawn toward it. Picture yourself vividly as defeated and that alone will make victory impossible. Picture yourself vividly as winning and that alone will contribute immeasurably to success. Great living starts with a picture, held in your imagination of what you would like to do or be."

Many peak performers are masters of the art of purposeful daydreaming. They prepare themselves for success by mentally rehearsing important upcoming events and visualizing a successful conclusion. Visualization techniques have been popular for years in sports and they can be successfully applied to all aspects of life, including work.

The next time you're facing an important upcoming event, prepare yourself for success with some purposeful imagination.

For example, if you're faced with making an important presentation, mentally rehearse doing a terrific job in as vivid detail as possible. Try to imagine every facet and feeling you experience as you capture the imagination of your audience. What does the room look like? Visualize your audience. What parts of your presentation are going over best? How are you getting and holding their attention? What key point will you leave them with to convince them at the end? How does it feel to know you successfully got your points across?

Obviously, there's a whole lot more to making a successful presentation than visualizing it. You also have to be organized, arm yourself with the facts, and do a lot of hard thinking and preparation beforehand. But a top performer prepares his agenda and his psyche because both are crucial to success.

In this chapter, I've given you the best tools I know for managing stress with the goal of increasing your productivity and happiness. But in the final analysis, it all boils down to this: Being happily productive is the result of a series of choices that only you can make. For example, you can choose to:

- Think in a rational, positive manner or a negative, distorted one.
- Overload yourself with changes or take charge of your life and manage it.
- Heed the symptoms of excess stress and act on them or do nothing and hope for the best.
- Take steps to relieve stress-created tensions through exercise, hobbies, and relaxation or do nothing and continue to feel like a pressure cooker.
- Adopt the techniques of a peak performer or forget about them because change is just too tough.

Your life is an endless series of choices that ultimately determine what you achieve and how you feel. Perhaps an unknown philosopher summed it up best: "A person's life is like a piece of metal—it can be forged into a tool to aid him or a weapon to destroy him."

CHAPTER 14

EVERYBODY HAS A PIECE OF THE PUZZLE

"No one in this country wants to be a loser. They want to work hard. They want to win, and they want to be united in a single purpose. We've got to get excited—get back our pride. . . . It takes a long time to get consensus in this country, but when it comes, the power that is released is awesome."
—William Weisz

In this book, we have looked at productivity problems and solutions from an individual, organizational, national, and international perspective. Which brings us to the main issue: What's it going to take to solve the productivity puzzle, expand the shrinking American pie, and get all of us living better? The answer to that question can be summed up in one word: Plenty!

Meeting the productivity challenge is going to take nothing less than a healthy dose of commitment, consensus, change, patience, and persistence on the part of us all. It isn't going to be easy, but the challenge is exciting and the rewards will be more than worth the effort.

In this final chapter, I've put together a brief summary of recommendations for getting us back on the path to working smarter and increasing our standard of living. Like the book, this chapter is organized like a funnel. We will look first at the broadest recommendations and complete the summary with specific things that you can do.

First and foremost, we have to realize that from now on we are competing in a world economy where we no longer reign supreme. In the decades following World War II, we had no real competition because West Germany, Japan, France, and other countries were rebuilding themselves from the rubble. But those days are over and from here on out it's going to be a whole new ballgame requiring a different strategy. It's to our benefit that these nations are economically strong and growing. But if we hope to keep up with them, it's going to take some major changes.

WHAT THE GOVERNMENT MUST DO

How did the competition catch up? The answer is rather simple. While we were concerned with redistributing the American pie, Japan and other countries concentrated on building a bigger pie. They saved, sacrificed, invested, and worked in a coordinated effort—and if we hope to compete with them in the future, that's exactly what we must do. We have no choice.

If we hope to increase productivity, it's imperative that we have a national commitment to do so. And government can set the pace by doing a number of things. Here are a few:

1. Support the growth of industry. We need more leaders in Washington who have the guts to stand up and say that the creation of wealth is more important than redistributing what we have. It may not have always been that way and it may not always be that way. But as long as the pie is shrinking, expanding the pie should be our top priority. Like Japan, America needs to build on its strengths and the government can help by targeting and encouraging the growth of such key industries as computers, robots, domestic energy, steel, machinery, and automobiles. The creation of a government organization similar to Japan's MITI would be a positive step in that direction.

2. Encourage capital formation. Without funds for investment, productivity growth is impossible. More tax and spending cuts are needed to encourage savings, investment, and the incentive to work.

Most important, steps have to be taken to encourage the formation of long-term capital. We need patient money, and this means that laws must be changed to make our banks more competitive with other fund-raising institutions. One possibility is to create a system of investment banking. Our current savings rate of under 5 percent is totally inadequate to produce the necessary capital, and without adequate capital investment in research, new tools, and new equipment is impossible.

3. Stop being the keeper of the universe. The U.S. government is simply overcommitted. Too many of us suffer from the "If Uncle doesn't help me, I won't make it" mentality. This isn't true just for welfare recipients, but also for big businesses with fat defense contracts, foreign competitors who enjoy our protection, and numerous federally funded sacred cows in the public and private sectors. Too many of us rely on the government as a great big crutch. And crutches can make cripples out of people.

The sheer size and weight of the government is choking the productive sector of the economy and destroying the incentive to work. The government bureaucracy needs to be seriously reduced—and in some areas totally abolished. The only way that will ever happen is to put a ceiling on the federal budget and stick to it.

All areas of the federal bureaucracy must share in the belt-tightening, including the defense department. Let our foreign competitors start carrying more of their own defense burdens. They're big boys now and can afford it. The expense of wasteful government regulations must be lifted off the backs of business. And all of us better start relying less on the government and more on ourselves. We did it before there was big government and we can do it again.

4. Encourage foreign trade. The fact that we are now competing in a world economy of equals makes it imperative that we focus our attention on selling U.S. goods and services abroad. In the past, Washington has given little attention to aiding U.S. exports. Laws and regulations to encourage export sales must be

created. Special tax breaks on income received from international sales can provide a healthy incentive for businesses. Government influence can be used to ease trade barriers on the sale of U.S. goods abroad. Special incentives can be created for banks and lending institutions that finance U.S. business exports. The Commerce Department can expand its efforts to provide U.S. businesses with the market data, information, and know-how necessary for profitable international trade. These are just a few things government can do to add a few foreign apples to the American pie.

5. Place a high priority on innovation and technology. Technology and innovation are the backbone of American productivity and our competitive edge in the world market. Our lead is eroding, however, and to get it back we need to place a heavy, long-range emphasis on basic research. The government can help by providing healthy tax credits and write-offs to business investments in research and development. Governmental funding needs to be targeted to support specific research in areas such as microelectronics, computers, bioengineering, robots, and other fields that show a healthy promise of profitability at home and abroad. Scholarships, loans, and grants should be provided to universities to support education and research in high-technology areas. And incentives must be created to encourage more research and engineering in nondefense areas. A large percentage of our best research minds are doing defense-related work while our competitors' researchers are doing profit-oriented work.

MANAGEMENT HOLDS THE BIGGEST PIECE OF THE PUZZLE

While government must set the pace and provide the right climate, the responsibility for increasing productivity falls squarely on the shoulders of American management. In the final analysis, management calls the shots and decides how well we use our human, technical, and financial resources to get things done. As I see it, the success or failure of American management to meet the productivity challenge depends on how successfully it achieves the following goals:

1. Top management must have longer time horizons. Long-range planning is the main job of top management. But it's very common for executives to receive as much as 40 percent of their total compensation based on short-term financial performance. This has to be changed. Owners, boards of directors, and others responsible for the long-term success of companies must see to it that top executives have incentives linked to the long run as well as the short haul. Deferred compensation plans can be created with payoffs ten or fifteen years later based on long-term results. Internal accounting systems can be changed to encourage long-range investments in people and resources. Strategic factors crucial to long-term company growth must be identified and linked to managerial performance. If there's one lesson management can learn from the past twenty years, it's that the price of short-sighted decisions is long-range stagnation.

2. A greater commitment to employees and the development of human resources must be made. As Arthur Imperatore remarked, "People are not just bodies. If you hire bodies, the soul is left home when they come to work." It's management's job to create a trusting, positive climate that makes people want to produce, grow, and develop as workers and as total human beings. And in this area, American managers can learn a lot from their Japanese counterparts. We need to manage more by results and less by activity. New work incentives must be created, and rewards need to be more clearly linked to performance. Special programs for improving the quality of work life and harnessing the talents of older workers need to become integral parts of the American work scene. And it's crucial that our corporations move toward a policy of providing lifetime employment coupled with lifetime training for all employees. While Japanese factories have very low turnover, America's turnover rate in manufacturing is nearly 50 percent per year. We can't have almost half our workers change jobs every year and hope to remain competitive.

Both management and unions have to realize that the days

of conflict and confrontation are over and they're going to have to work together to meet the challenges of foreign competition. Unions need to lobby less for pay and fringe benefits and more for job security and profit sharing based on performance. Such a strategy will be good for companies, good for workers, and good for productivity.

Finally, management must realize that the labor force has changed drastically in the past thirty years and that many of the traditional incentives to work are outdated. The new breed of worker wants much more than just a day's work for a day's pay. He expects the job to satisfy a wide range of needs and that's not easy for most bosses to provide. But, in the final analysis, the successful manager is the one who shows people how to satisfy their needs through working and makes it possible for them to do so.

3. Take advantage of new technology. The industrial world is entering into the era of solid-state brains and steel-collar brawn. In the coming years computers and robots will revolutionize our skyscrapers and factories. Some of the more routine, monotonous, and dangerous jobs have been automated for years. But now sophisticated computers are being used to design new products and "seeing" and "feeling" robots have been created that can do more than weld, solder, and drill. They can also check their own work, inspect finished products, and sift out defective parts. Even better yet, the new robots are retrainable. Whenever a product is changed, instead of buying expensive new machinery, you simply reprogram the robot. With Japan leading the world in the production of robots, it's becoming clear that American firms will have to invest heavily in the development and application of new technology if we hope to stay competitive.

The greatest mistake management can make is to use new technology to throw people out of work. When someone's job is eliminated, retrain and reassign him. Computers and robots are one of the main reasons that management must move toward a policy of providing lifetime training and lifetime employment for all workers. Most blue-collar and many of today's white-collar jobs will be automated by the end of the century. Everyone whose job is eliminated should be given an opportunity to learn a new, productive skill and share in the profits of automation. Otherwise we will continue to work at cross purposes—one cause of our productivity problems.

4. Prune the white-collar bureaucracy. If you could wave a magic wand and make government bureaucracy disappear, American industry would still have a massive red-tape problem. The simple fact is that most American bureaucracy is alive and thriving in the puzzle palaces of private corporations. Like an overweight prize fighter, our top-heavy corporations must trim down if they're going to avoid being kayoed. The Japanese auto industry has one inspector/manager for every 200 workers. The U.S. auto industry has twenty.

Shrinking the bureaucracy and cutting red tape is a never-ending battle that rests on three key principles: (1) Focus on results, (2) Keep it simple, and (3) Eliminate anything that's unnecessary. Goals and priorities must be set for all jobs at all levels and updated frequently. Every job, level of management, policy, committee, and document must be questioned regularly and prove that it delivers more than it costs or be eliminated. We need to stop rewarding employees for creating red tape and start rewarding them for finding ways to reduce it. Any activity, document, or procedure that doesn't help the company achieve its goals is unnecessary. When it's unnecessary to do it, it becomes necessary not to do it. Don't automate it—eliminate it! Then consider automating the necessary activities.

5. Management must make a serious, long-term commitment to quality. Much has been written about Japan's successful transition from junk merchant to high quality producer. But the key to Japan's success is that the impetus to improve quality started with a commitment at the tops of companies and filtered down. Everyone from the president on down learned and practiced the techniques of quality control and spent time each week learning how to do his job better. And that's what we must be

willing to do. We can't build first-rate companies by producing second-rate goods and services. A commitment to quality isn't simply inspecting goods, putting up slogans, or organizing workers into circles. More than anything else, quality is an attitude. And that attitude starts at the top.

6. Improve the selection and training of managers. No doubt, business schools have turned out some first-rate executives in the past twenty years. But there's little, if any, evidence that their excellence can be attributed to what they learned at the B-school. Without question, B-school training can and will be improved. But companies can't sit around and wait for universities to change.

When searching for managerial talent, don't rely on credentials or transcripts alone. Look for someone with a bias toward action and an ability to think logically and creatively and to grasp the big picture. Look for someone who knows how to turn plans into results and doesn't get sidetracked by details. Don't be fooled into believing that the flashiest person makes the best leader. The John Waynes, Teddy Roosevelts, and General Pattons were different leaders for a different time. The effective leader of the future will be a team-building risk-taker who gets the best from everyone by integrating various points of view and helping people to build on their strengths. And future management training needs to be more practical, hands-on, and oriented toward developing these skills.

YOUR PIECE OF THE PUZZLE

I hope this book has given you a greater understanding of our productivity problems and just how serious they are. Even more important, I want you to know that solving the productivity puzzle and raising your standard of living aren't outside your control. There are lots of things you can do to meet the productivity challenge and make it work for you. In closing, I want to summarize fifteen key things that all of us can do to benefit ourselves, our families, and our nation. None of them require lofty executive or government positions. But all of them do require that we start taking personal responsibility for our own wellbeing and that of those who depend on us.

1. Stop expecting the government to be your caretaker and work to reduce the size of it. Every time you receive a government check or service you're supporting the existence of an inefficient bureaucracy that drains the productive sector of the economy. Make plans to provide for your own retirement because Social Security may not be around when you're over sixty-five. Support those in power who do, in fact, reduce the size of government and replace those who don't. If you're thinking about leaving a government position, look first in the private sector. It's terribly difficult to get Americans excited about work when they give almost half of what they earn to an institution that's lowering their standard of living.

2. Get in the habit of saving. Don't let Madison Avenue brainwash you into being a compulsive consumer. Resolve to take at least 10 percent off the top of your paycheck and invest it in savings or securities that will stay ahead of inflation. You'll not only do yourself a big favor but you will also be helping increase the level of capital formation that's necessary to get our economy moving again.

3. Conserve energy. Although we are making real progress in energy conservation, we still import 40 percent of our oil. Let's drive smaller cars, turn down the thermostat and insulate our buildings and homes better. That way we can keep more wealth at home and use it to create capital. And saving energy means more money in the bank for you too.

4. Keep on learning and stay flexible. Second careers, turbulent changes, and an information-producing economy are going to make it imperative that you keep current in your job or profession. Get in the habit of spending time each week learning more about your job and how to do it better. Stay abreast of changes and trends. As our economy becomes less manufacturing- and more information-oriented lots of new jobs will be created and lots of old ones will be destroyed. Keep your eyes open and don't be afraid to learn new techniques and skills. That

way you'll reduce the odds of being out of a job in a changing economy.

5. See that your children learn basic skills. Success in the information economy will require a thorough foundation in basic skills. Unfortunately, sending your children to school is no guarantee that they will learn to read, write, speak, or calculate with any degree of competence. Public education has become a big bureaucracy and any improvements will be slow at best. By the time any meaningful changes are made, your children will probably be grown and it will be too late.

If your children aren't getting the basics at school, they can learn them at home. You don't have to force them. Provide incentives for learning and reward them. Give them games like Monopoly or Parcheesi that cause them to practice arithmetic. Give them interesting books to read and reward them for writing reports on their reading.

One of today's best educational investments is a home computer. The prices are plummeting rapidly and all sorts of programs are available that teach basic skills, foreign languages, typing, programming, and practically anything else you want them to learn. If you have children, I highly recommend a home computer. And if you buy one, set a good example and learn with them. Despite what you may think, home computers are very easy to operate and you can use them for keeping your financial records, playing games, and a great many other things.

6. Set productivity goals for yourself at work. Don't get caught in the activity trap. Decide on the results you want and go after them. Set routine, quality, and innovative goals and check them for compatibility. Spend the bulk of your time pursuing only the most important ones and select goals that harmoniously mesh with your boss' and your company's goals. Attach deadlines and incentives to your goals to keep you motivated and challenged. With a set of meaningful challenging goals, work can become much more productive, profitable, and satisfying.

7. Practice good time-management techniques. Personal productivity improvement begins with making better use of your

time. Remember that good time management is first-rate habits made second nature. Give yourself some quiet time each day and make the daily to-do list a regular habit. Schedule your important tasks for prime time and do trivial tasks in batches. Keep a flexible schedule, avoid overcommitting yourself, and work to keep procrastination out of your life. And be sure to take positive steps to shield yourself from interruptions. Knowing how to use time is the most basic and important personal productivity skill you can learn.

8. Work smarter with your boss. Find out as much as you can about your boss' goals, priorities, and work style and compare them with your own. Build on the strengths of your relationship, and take steps to work around the weaknesses and accommodate individual differences. Keep the boss informed, be loyal, don't promise what you can't deliver, and respect his time. Most bosses are very much overworked, but with a little thought and effort you can make both of you more productive.

9. Be a motivator at work. Praise good work and effort whenever you see it. Give those who are discouraged a positive lift by pointing out the good things they do. Think up ways to keep people motivated and excited about work and pass them along to the boss. Organize activities to boost morale and teamwork. And, most important, set an example for others with your own enthusiasm and efforts. Everybody who wants to can be a motivator and help make others more productive.

10. Help dismantle the paper prison. Don't ask for it. Don't generate it. Shield yourself from it. Throw it away. Your job is to get results, not shuffle paper. Talk it up at the office. Hold a contest for ideas to reduce paperwork. We have too many hands shuffling too many papers and strangling productivity. Every time you pick up a piece of paper resolve to throw it away, file it, or act on it and get it out of the way.

11. Give yourself the creative edge. Everyone has creative ability, and by applying the right techniques you can harness this vast, untapped resource of productivity potential. Look for ways to make new things seem familiar and familiar things seem new.

Try forcing relationships between unrelated concepts and things. Ask questions and challenge assumptions. Use individual and group creativity techniques to elicit new ideas from yourself and others. And work to create a climate that fosters innovation rather than stifle it. Better results begin with better ideas.

12. Don't let the pressure build up. Excessive stress is bad for you and your work. Be alert for symptoms of excess stress and take steps to eliminate it. Examine and adjust your thinking when you're feeling low. Most negative thinking is grossly distorted and unrealistic. Plan major life changes and space them over a reasonable period of time. Remember that the more stressful your job is, the greater your need to exercise those tensions away. Take regular relaxation breaks, keep your sense of humor handy, and balance your work with play. Stress, workaholism, and burnout aren't the right answers to our productivity problems.

13. Be a peak performer. Once you set a major goal, don't worry about how you're doing. Just concentrate on doing your best. Every time you achieve a major goal, set a bigger one and go after it. Be a problem-solver instead of a blame-placer and get in the habit of taking calculated risks. Practice mentally rehearsing future key events and visualizing your future the way you want it to be. These techniques work well for super producers and they can work for you too.

14. Do your part to raise America's productivity consciousness. Too few of us realize that our very survival as a nation is linked to the future of American productivity. If you're a teacher, talk with your students about the importance of American productivity and the shrinking standard of living. If you're a union leader, push for pay and benefits related to job performance and security. If you're an executive, make productivity improvement a top priority where you work. If you're a rank-and-file employee, talk up the subject with your boss or colleagues. As C. Jackson Grayson, Director of The American Productivity Center, so aptly put it, "In the end the whole purpose is not productivity; the whole purpose is freedom. The whole pur-

pose of this thing is to allow people to have individual personal freedom."

15. Be patient. As I've pointed out throughout this book, there are no quick fixes and magic cures for our productivity ills. We have been digging ourselves into this hole for almost twenty years and it's going to take years to dig our way out. American business is in trouble and only by all of us in management, labor, government, and education working together will we turn this thing around. I can't believe that any American executive, laborer, teacher, government official, or anyone else wants to live poorer and see our country assume the role of a second-rate, has-been power. Yet the trend is clearly there if we don't do something to reverse it.

In the final analysis, when it comes to productivity, everybody has a piece of the puzzle. We're all a part of the problem and we can all be part of the solution. If enough of us contribute, we can beat this thing.

Let's do it.

INDEX